The Daily
DYNAMIC
ENCOUNTER
DEVOTIONAL

GOD'S DEPENDABLE
WORD

VOLUME 1

The Daily DYNAMIC ENCOUNTER
DEVOTIONAL
GOD'S DEPENDABLE WORD

VOLUME 1

THE DAILY DYNAMIC ENCOUNTER DEVOTIONAL(VOLUME 1)
© CMFIAC

ISBN: 978-1-945055-33-1

PIRACY IS THEFT

Published by
Conquest
COMMUNICATIONS LTD.

13 Sonola Street, Ebute-Metta (West), Lagos.
P. O. Box 4826, Surulere Lagos.
Email: conquestcom@gmail.com
Tel: +234-8033-226-429

Unless otherwise indicated, all Scripture quotations are taken from the New *King James Version* of the Bible.

All rights reserved under International Copyright Law. The author guarantees all contents of this work are original and do not infringe upon the legal rights of any other person or work. No part of this book may be reproduced without the written consent of the Publisher, with the exception of brief excerpts in magazines, articles, reviews.

Design + Print
asbotgraphics

Editorial Team

1. **Chairman**: Professor Joseph Tanyi Mbafor
2. **Editor-in-Chief and Vice Chairman**: Dr. CKC Ezeudemba
3. **Associate Editor and Coordinator**: Mbange Calvin Etongo
4. **Content Contributors**: Dr. Elimbi Celestine Nakeli, Dr. Fidel Ntie-Kang, Pastor James Ekor-Tar
5. **Translations**: Josee Meli, Alice Mbafor, Taju Bertine, Prisca Zebaze, Annie Ngnoung, Annie-Rose Ngniniapa, Adele Ngalame, Julie Pewewo
6. **Proof Readers**: Dr. Barbara Tiedeu, Charlotte Mekoulou, Gloria Chukwujekwe
7. **Public Relations**: Jean-Marc Afesi Mbafor, Bekondo Enya Bekondo
8. **Infotech**: Jean Fabrice Kabasha, Anthony Akpan

RETREATS FOR SPIRITUAL PROGRESS
IN THE MORNING

1. Thanksgiving for the night. Thanksgiving for a new day. Thanksgiving for the good works pre-planned by the Lord for that day.
2. Consecration to the Lord. Receiving the infilling with the Holy Spirit.
3. Asking for daily bread. Asking for other basic needs: transportation, and so on.
4. Placing your body, life, job, finances, feelings, mind and will under the blood of Jesus. Placing all you love and all that is theirs under the blood of Jesus for protection from the attacks of Satan.
5. Praying for your job and all that is happening there and will happen there that day.
6. Further praying for your job.
7. Praying for the right attitude to all you will meet that day.
8. Ask to be led to the person you will witness to that day.
9. Ask that the person to whom you will witness to that day be saved.
10. Pray for all the appointments you have during the day.
11. Pray for your family members.
12. Pray for your friend, friends and all you love
13. Pray about your physical appearance: what you will wear and how you will wear it.
14. Pray about your attitude to time for the day: how to use it; how to redeem it and how to prepare to account for it at the Judgment Seat of the Lord.
15. Ask the Lord to prepare your heart for all the unexpected events and all the unexpected people who will come your way that day.

Praise the Lord

RETREATS FOR SPIRITUAL PROGRESS
AT NOON

1. Confess any sin committed since morning. Receive the infilling with the Holy Spirit.
2. Thank God for all that has happened since morning. Mention specific items and thank Him for answered prayers.
3. Pray for your assembly.
4. Pray for your spiritual leader.
5. Pray for five people who have not yet believed.
6. Pray for the next five people on your list who have not yet believed in the Lord.
7. Pray for five believers.
8. Pray for five backsliders.
9. Pray for two organizations (ministers) serving the Lord's interest in your country or any part of the world.
10. Pray for the ministry that you are a part of physically or financially.
11. Continue to pray for the ministry that you are a part of.
12. Continue to pray for the ministry that you are a part of.
13. Pray for an unevangelized area or country.
14. Pray for the leaders (political) of your nation.
15. Thank the Lord for the privilege of praying. Thank the Lord for this prayer session. Sing a song unto the Lord.

RETREATS FOR SPIRITUAL PROGRESS
IN THE EVENING

1. Confession of all sins committed in thought, word and deed since the afternoon. Repentance and a forsaking of sin and the sinful way. Receive the infilling with the Holy Spirit.
2. Pray for your prayer life.
3. Pray for any outstanding needs in the direction of your spiritual growth and progress. This could include problems in fasting.
4. More praying for any outstanding needs in the realm of your spiritual progress and growth. This could include problems in ministry.
5. Further praying for any outstanding needs in the realm of your spiritual progress and growth. This could include problems in the realm of Christian character.
6. Pray for personal ministry to the Lord.
7. Pray for personal ministry to the Body of Christ.
8. Pray for personal ministry to the world.
9. Pray for guidance about the expansion of personal ministry.
10. Pray for co-labourers.
11. Further prayer for co-labourers.
12. Pray for the ministry of your friend and/or loved one.
13. Pray for the enemies of your ministry.
14. Pray for growth in spiritual experience.
15. Thanksgiving for all that has happened. Write down the key things to be remembered.

RETREATS FOR SPIRITUAL PROGRESS
AT NIGHT

1. The confession of all sin committed since the last time of prayer. Thanksgiving to the Lord for all that was accomplished during the day and especially since one last prayed.
2. Pray for signs to follow personal ministry.
3. Pray for signs to follow the ministry of another
4. Pray for the expansion of personal ministry.
5. Pray for the healing of some believers.
6. Pray for the healing for some unbelievers.
7. Pray for any financial needs.
8. Pray for any material project you are involved in.
9. Pray for Bible translating and producing organizations.
10. Pray for the advance of the gospel in a particular Muslim country.
11. Pray for the advance of the gospel in a Hindu country.
12. Pray for the advance of the gospel in China.
13. Pray for the advance of the gospel in an unreached tribe like the Pygmies.
14. Praise for the blessings you have received in Christ.
15. Praise and thanksgiving for the accomplishments of the day. Commitment of self and all those whom you love to the Lord for protection throughout the night

PREFACE

The need to remain on fire for God is all the more critical as we head into the last days. The icy hands of Satan, sin and the pleasures of this life is freezing the love of many. The Lord will come for a church and believers whose lamps are burning and are on fire for God. The Bible says **"Let your waists be girded and your lamps burning and you yourselves be like men who wait for their master, when he returns from the wedding, that when he comes and knocks they may open to him immediately" (Luke 12:35).** To be like men who wait for the return of their master; we have to gird our waists and our lamps have to be burning. The uprightness or the virginity of the believer will be assumed; the difference maker will be spiritual temperature. Do I have oil in my lamp? Am I burning for God? Do I have an endless, intense longing and burning desire for God? The answer to these simple but far-reaching questions will determine whether we end up as the wise or foolish virgins. God cannot afford those with a cold desire for Him. A. W. Tozer says, **"If you find worship boring, then you are not ready to heaven"**. Our call to be priests is a call to keep a constant spiritual temperature: keep the fire burning. The Bible says, **"And the <u>fire on the altar shall be kept burning on</u> it; it shall not be put out and the <u>priest shall burn wood on it every morning</u>…." (Leviticus 6:12).** The minimum requirement of the Lord for us as priests is that the altar of our hearts should burn perpetually with fire. This requires personal spiritual responsibility, discipline and routine; the priest had to put wood every morning. The believer must therefore not rely helplessly on impartation from others like the foolish virgins (**And the foolish said to the wise, give us some of your oil, for our lamps are going out**) or rely only on impartation from spiritual leadership. There must be personal spiritual cultivation. A normal spiritual condition is a combination of impartation from leadership and cultivation from the believer. The Bible says, **"For this reason I remind you to <u>fan into flame</u> the gift of God which is in you through the <u>laying on of my hands</u>"** (2 Timothy 1:6).

Paul imparted by the laying on of hands and he is asking Timothy to cultivate by fanning into flames that deposit. Great men who were on fire perpetually knew how to fan into flames the spiritual deposit in them. Professor Zacharias T. Fomum used to say that he is a spiritual log, and that he will burn and burn and burn. That he kept in his office toilet a book of Oswald Chambers to read and meditate while in the toilet and that he had read about fifteen books just by using judiciously his time whenever he went in to use the convenience. He remained on fire perpetually.

John Wesley always had a book open on his horse while he rode. These men stayed on fire. They adopted formal and flexible ways to keep their lamps burning.

The Daily Dynamic Encounter devotional is therefore not a replacement of the believer's formal devotional life but a spiritual fan and a flexible addition and complement to that life. We see it as portable spiritual content that can be used anywhere and anytime: in airport lounges, in the plane, in restaurants and many other places to keep the believer spiritually refreshed and burning always. We send it out with prayer, that the Lord will use it to set his children on fire for Him perpetually. Amen.

Professor Joseph Tanyi Mbafor
President of CMFI-AC World Wide

DAY 1 OPENING GREAT DOORS

 *"After these things I looked and behold, a door standing open in heaven"* (Revelation 4:1)

Doors stand open in an atmosphere of praise. Revelation chapter four, reveals life in the throne of God. It is an atmosphere of praise. Gates and doors are linked to praise in the Scriptures. The word of God says**," …But you shall call your walls Salvation and your gates Praise" (Isaiah 60:18).** In Scripture gates represent openings or access points and doors **(Proverbs 8:3).** Praise was always performed at the gates. The Bible says, **"That I may tell of all your praise in the gates of the daughter of Zion" (Psalm 9:14).** Why was praise always performed at the gates? Praise is the key that opens the gates or doors and give us access as seen in the Psalms**, "Enter into his gates with thanksgiving and into his courts with praise…" (Psalm 100:4)**. Step into this new year, with a heart full of praise and as you praise him great doors will open in your life in Jesus Name.

Prayer

 Lord, I pray that I will confront every gate and door with a heart full of praise. Amen

Bible Reading Plan:
Genesis 1, John 1 and Romans 1

DAY 2 KEY TO ANSWERED PRAYERS

 *"Be anxious for nothing, but in everything, by prayer and supplication with thanksgiving, let your requests be made known to God. And the peace of God, which surpasses all understanding, will guard your hearts and minds through Christ Jesus"* (Philippians 4:6-7).

In the Book of Revelation, we see worship to God by the living creatures and the twenty-four elders. They had harps (for praise) and golden bowls full of incense which are the prayers of the saints **(Revelation 5:8).** This reveals the heavenly pattern and model for effective prayer. Paul the apostle also calls us to follow this model of making our prayers with thanksgiving. There are a lot of prayers that are not answered because we have a tendency to leave out thanksgiving. Our thanksgiving honors God and is an expression of faith that God has already heard us and has done it already. The result is peace that surpasses all understanding.

Prayer

 Lord, I pray that I will follow Your pattern of prayer with thanksgiving

Bible Reading Plan:
Genesis 2, John 2 and Romans 2

DAY 3: DANIEL: A MODEL IN PRAYER AND THANKSGIVING

 *"He knelt down on his knees, three times that day and prayed and gave thanks before His God as his <u>custom was since early days</u>"* (Daniel 6:10).

Daniel followed this model of prayer with thanksgiving. It was his custom; a way of life. Daniel was not using giving of thanks and prayer as method on how to get out of difficult situations; it was his custom from early days. He had learnt earlier that we don't come before God only to ask but to also appreciate Him. Every great life can be traced to a routine; Daniel knelt down to pray three times a day. The results in the life of Daniel speak for themselves: the victory in the lion's den, fiery furnace and his prophetic insight and visions.

Prayer

 Lord, I pray for a life given to praise and thanksgiving

Bible Reading Plan:
Genesis 3, John 3, Romans 3

DAY 4: VICTORY IN IMPOSSIBLE SITUATIONS

 *"Whoever offers praise glorifies Me; and to him who orders his conduct aright I will show the salvation of God"* (Psalm 50:23).

You may be going through a very difficult time and you are in great need of the salvation or the deliverance of the Lord. However difficult and impossible your situation may be, dear child of God, we want to assure you that praise and thanksgiving has the power to grant you the needed breakthrough. Consider Jonah, who was swallowed by a fish. Jonah's situation was an impossible one. But through sacrificial thanksgiving, the God who ordered the fish to swallow Jonah, also spoke to the fish to vomit Jonah. The Bible says, **"Then Jonah prayed to the LORD his God from the fish's belly. And he said…But I will sacrifice to You with thanksgiving; I will pay what I have vowed. Salvation is of the Lord. So the LORD spoke to the fish and it vomited Jonah onto dry land" (Jonah 2:1-10).**

Maybe like Jonah, you are also in a tight situation. Offer that costly praise and you will see the release of the Lord.

Prayer

 Lord, in my painful days and moments I will offer You the sacrifice of praise

Bible Reading Plan:
Genesis 4, John 4 and Romans 4

DAY 5 PRAISE IN SPIRITUAL WARFARE: WHEN THERE ARE ENEMIES ALL AROUND

"And when he had consulted with the people, he appointed those who should sing to the LORD and who should praise the beauty of holiness, as they went out before the army and were saying: praise the LORD for His mercy endures forever. Now when they began to sing and to praise, the LORD set ambushes against the people of Ammon, Moab, and Mount Seir, who had come against Judah and they were defeated. For the people of Ammon and Moab stood up against the inhabitants of Mount Seir to utterly kill and destroy them. And when they had made an end of the inhabitants of Seir, they helped to destroy one another" (2 Chronicles 20:21-23).

The people of Judah were encompassed by a great multitude that had come against them for battle. But king Jehoshaphat and the people appointed singers and those who will praise. In course of praise, the great multitude started fighting against themselves and they were self-destruct. Praise divides Satan's kingdom against itself. May be you are in the face of multitude of enemies round about; give yourself to praise.

Prayer

Lord, in the face of multitude of enemies all around me, I will praise You

Bible Reading Plan:
Genesis 5, John 5 and Romans 5

DAY 6: THE DANGER OF COMPLAINING

 *"Do all things without complaining..."* (Philippians 2:14)

If we should do all things without complaining, what then are we to be doing in the place of complaining? The Bible says, "In **everything give thanks**" **(1 Thessalonians 5:18).** When we complain we do not only attract the devil, we are teaming up with him to slander God. We open ourselves up to satanic attacks in the process. No wonder serpents were unleashed on the Israelites who were complaining against God in the wilderness and many died **(Numbers 21:5-6).** Paul the apostle warns us not to murmur or complain as the Israelites did in the wilderness. The Scriptures say, "**Nor murmur, as some of them also murmured and were destroyed by the destroyer. Now all these things happened to them as examples and they are written for our admonition, on whom the ends of the ages have come**" **(I Corinthians 10:10-11).** Complaining is sin. It is speaking against God and attracts His Judgment **(Jude 1:14-16).**

Prayer

 Lord, open my eyes to see the sinfulness of complaining and deliver me from the sin of complaining. Amen

Bible Reading Plan:
Genesis 6, John 6 and Romans 6

DAY 7: SECRET OF SUPERNATURAL INCREASE

"Let the peoples praise You, O God; Let all the peoples praise You, then the earth shall yield her increase...." (Psalm 67:5-6).

Our God is a God of increase and His purpose for us is that we multiply. Thanksgiving is key to causing the earth to yield the increase destined for us by God. The Lord Jesus Christ understood the power of gratitude to yield increase and cause multiplication. With few loaves of bread, multitudes were fed with leftovers. His attitude of gratitude attracted the blessing of God and the little in His hands turned into abundance **(Mark 8:2-9).** It is interesting to note that the Lord was in the wilderness when the miracle of multiplication took place and he could feed the multitude. There are no dry places for those who are grateful. Gratitude ushers in the showers of blessing. Ingratitude ushers in a drought.

Prayer

Lord, teach me to be grateful even with little. I will not despise anything but will make all a subject of thanksgiving. Amen

Bible Reading Plan:
Genesis 7, John 7 and Romans 7

DAY 8: YESTERDAY'S VICTORY, TODAY'S ENCOURAGEMENT

"Be of good cheer Paul; for as you have testified for Me in Jerusalem, so you must also bear witness at Rome" (Acts 23:11)

Every victory is a foundation for the next one. Paul didn't find it easy to minister in Jerusalem. He was not accepted initially by the pillars there but God made a way and he could still testify there and now he is believing God to also go testify in Rome. And God is using his breakthrough in Jerusalem to drum up his faith. I did it for You in Jerusalem, I will also do it for you in Rome. A great Christian once said, **"What I see today in my life teaches me to trust God for what am yet to see".** He that enabled David kill the lion and the bear also enabled him to kill Goliath. He that enabled you to be where you are now will also enable to be where you ought to be.

Prayer

Lord, I thank You for what You have done in my life so far. I trust You to also see me through in the challenges that are before me now

Bible Reading Plan:
Genesis 8, John 8 and Romans 8

DAY 9: HONORING GOD: AN EQUIVALENT MEASURE

 *"Far be it from Me; for those who honor Me I will honor, and those who despise Me shall be lightly esteemed"* (1 Samuel 2:30b).

To be honored by God we also have to honor Him. Eli the High Priest in Israel at the time, had sons who dishonored God. They took the things of God lightly and treated God's people with disdain. To put it simply, they were profane. Our generation faces this danger today. In an era of surplus religion, people are losing reverence for God, the Church and the things of God. The Lord, is watching each person's attitude towards Him. He sends an angel to measure those who are in the temple. Are we going to be found wanting? Am I treating the things of God with seriousness or lightheartedness? Honor or dishonor is at stake. Choose the path of honor.

Prayer

 Lord, I pray that I will treat all that concerns You with all seriousness

Bible Reading plan:
Genesis 9, John 9 and Romans 9

DAY 10: HOW WE LOSE THINGS

 *"Is not this great Babylon, that I have built for a royal dwelling by my mighty power for the honor of my majesty?"* (Daniel 4:30).

When we start taking credit for anything God has enabled us to do, we are formally signing its death sentence. The king of Babylon, is an example. Instead of praising and showing gratitude to God for making him ruler of a kingdom with global reach, he was boasting and taking credit for having built Babylon. As soon as he would not honor God but himself, a voice from heaven spoke saying, **"King Nebuchadnezzar, to you it is spoken: the kingdom has departed from you!" (Daniel 4:31).** When we take pride in what we have accomplished, it is worldliness and that puts us in enmity with God. Am I taking credit for what I am today instead of showing gratitude to Him who helped me all the way? Can you afford the cost of this pathway which is the possible loss of what you are boasting about?

Prayer

 Lord, I refuse to fall into the trap of taking personal credit for what You have done in my life.

Bible Reading Plan:
Genesis 10, John 10, Romans 10

DAY 11 REGAINING WHAT WAS LOST

 *"At the same time, my reason retuned to me and for the glory of my kingdom, my honor and splendor returned to me"* (Daniel 4:36)

Our God is merciful. As soon as King Nebuchadnezzar recognizes that his fall was caused by his ingratitude, he repents and flows in wonderful praise and appreciation to the King of kings and his honor and kingdom was restored **(Daniel 4:34-37).** May be you have suffered some loss and that loss would have been caused by your ingratitude. You had a job and you grew wings; you didn't have time for God anymore. Your job status made you start looking down on other brethren of a lower estate: a job you probably fasted and prayed to God for. Now the job or position is gone. Will you repent like Nebuchadnezzar? God wants to restore you.

Prayer

 Lord, I pray that You show me mercy for my ingratitude. Lord, I ask for Your restoration

Bible Reading Plan:
Genesis 11, John 11, Romans 11

DAY 12: GRATITUDE: AN INSPIRATION OF THE HOLY SPIRIT

"In that hour, <u>Jesus rejoiced in the Spirit and said, I praise You Father</u>, Lord of heaven and earth, that You have hidden these things from the wise and prudent and revealed them to babes. Even so, Father, for so it seemed good in Your sight" (Luke 10:21).

The Holy Spirit is the Spirit of glory **(1 Peter 4:14)**. The mission of the Holy Spirit is to glorify Christ as seen in the word; **"He will glorify Me, for He will take what is Mine and declare it to you" (John 16:14).** When we are grateful, we are glorifying God. The Holy Spirit inspires gratitude to God as shown in the life of Jesus Christ. The Lord, rejoiced in the Spirit and praise flowed to God the Father. When we are filled with the Spirit of God, praise will flow through us. When gratitude dies, then there is a wrong in our relationship with the Holy Spirit. Complaints are an indication of spiritual leakage. We are to thank God in all things and that happens only when we are rightly related to the Holy Spirit.

Prayer

Lord, I pray for deep and full fellowship with the Holy Spirit

Bible Reading Plan:
Genesis 12, John 12, Romans 12

DAY 13: QUENCH NOT THE SPIRIT

"In everything give thanks: for it is the will God in Christ for you. Do not quench the Spirit" (1 Thessalonians 5:18-19).

We are to thank God in everything. When the Holy Spirit is at work in us, there is a desire to glorify God in praise and thanksgiving irrespective of the situation. It is easy to thank the Lord when things are going on well. But in difficult situations, it is easy to yield to the flesh and settle for grumbling, bitterness and complaining. This will put out the Spirit's fire in us and limit the operation and work of the Holy Spirit in us. Ingratitude expressed through complaining, murmuring or grumbling quenches or puts out the fire of the Spirit and thus limit His operation and working in our lives. Am I quenching the Spirit by my complaining? If I am not giving God thanks in all things, then I am quenching the Holy Spirit. Am I guilty?

Prayer

Lord, I pray that I will not quench Your Spirit by failing to give thanks in everything.

Bible Reading Plan:
Genesis 13, John 13 and Romans 13

DAY 14 SPIRITUAL FIRE EXTINGUISHERS

 *"Do not extinguish the Spirit"*
(1 Thessalonians 5:19 Berean Study Bible)

In the book **The Ministry of Praise and Thanksgiving**, Professor Zacharias Tanee Forum wrote the following words on extinguishing the Holy Spirit: **"In a difficult or nasty situation, the believer can choose to praise the Lord in the situation or he can choose to complain, murmur or grumble. Complaining believers are spiritual fire extinguishers. They put out the Spirit's fire. Murmuring believers are spiritual fire extinguishers. They put out the Spirit's fire. Grumbling believers are spiritual fire extinguishers. They put out the Spirit's fire".**

I am a spiritual fire extinguisher? Check your attitude in a difficult situation.

Prayer

 Lord, I refuse to be a spiritual fire extinguisher.

Bible Reading Plan:
Genesis 14, John 14, Romans 14

DAY 15: REMAINING FILLED

"And do not be drunk with wine, in which is dissipation; but be filled with the Spirit, speaking to one another in psalms and hymns and spiritual songs, singing and making melody in your heart to the Lord, giving thanks always for all things to God the Father in the name of our Lord Jesus Christ, submitting to one another in the fear of God" (Ephesians 5:18-21).

Our dealing with the Holy Spirit is once and always. Once, when we are baptized into the Holy Spirit, and always in our labours to remain filled with the Holy Spirit. The baptism into the Holy Spirit is an impartation; it is an act of God. But remaining filled with the Holy Spirit is cultivation. It is an act of man. It requires spiritual discipline and certain spiritual pre-occupations that Paul outlines in our text above. We will remain filled when we speak to one another in psalms and spiritual songs instead of gossip, giving thanks always instead of complaining and submitting to one another instead of fights and quarrels.

Prayer

Lord, I pray that I will be pre-occupied with the spiritual things that will enable me remain filled.

Bible Reading Plan:
Genesis 15, John 15, Romans 15

DAY 16 CELEBRATE AND APPRECIATE MILESTONES

 *"And God saw the light, that it was good"* (Genesis 1:4)

A fundamental part of God's character even right from the beginning of creation reveals that He is full of appreciation and gratitude. In Genesis chapter one, the expression, **"And God saw that it was good"** appears seven times. The creation process took six days and plus one day which was a day of rest (seven days in all). It's no surprise that we also have the expression, **"And God saw that it was good"** or similar expression seven times in Genesis chapter one (Genesis 1:4,10,12, 18,21,25,31). God appreciated each step of the creation process.

Dear saint, celebrate and appreciate each new milestone in your life. It releases grace for the next level.

Prayer

 Lord, I commit myself to celebrate each milestone of progress in my life, however small

Bible Reading Plan:
Genesis 16, John 16, Romans 16

DAY 17: THUS FAR HAS THE LORD HELPED US

 *"Then Samuel took a stone and placed it between Mizpah and Shen, and called its name Ebenezer, saying, "Thus far has the LORD helped us"* (1 Samuel 7:12).

Samuel also celebrated how far the Lord had helped Israel. There are victories in life that require this act from Samuel. The Philistines had suddenly attacked the Israelites while Samuel the prophet was offering up the burnt offering. The Lord thundered from heaven and the Philistines were put to flight without a fight. This could only be God. Can you also like Samuel celebrate Him for the victories you won without a fight? The job you got without even applying, or many who came to your aid without you asking for help. All these was the help of the Lord. Like the prophet, celebrate these acts of God. Thus far has He brought you. Amen

Prayer

 Lord, like the prophet, I acknowledge that, thus far You have helped me

Bible Reading Plan:
Genesis 17, John 17, 1 Corinthians 1

DAY 18 THE POWER OF ONE THING

 *"One thing I have desired of the Lord, that will I seek: that I may dwell in the house of the Lord.... To behold the beauty of the LORD and inquire in His temple"* (Psalm 27:4)

It is said that losers have tons of variety. Great men are men of one thing. John Wesley used to say, **"I am a man of one book"**. The apostle Paul said, "**one thing I do**". The Lord Jesus said, "**But one thing is needed**" **(Luke 10:42).**

There are many who want to be everywhere doing everything. This explains why they lack outstanding results. David knew the power of one thing to control other things: He gave himself to dwell in the presence of Him who holds all things by the power of His word. He was later known as the man after God's own heart. Will I choose that one thing that controls all things: the pursuit of God and His presence? The choice is before us today.

Prayer

 Lord, I make one thing my desire; the pursuit of You and Your presence.

Bible Reading Plan:
Genesis 18, John 18, 1 Corinthians 2

DAY 19: CULTIVATING A GRATEFUL HEART

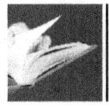 *"Blessed are those who <u>dwell in Your house</u>: they will still be praising You"* (Psalm 84:4).

The practice of the presence of God in a private and corporate sense helps us maintain our attitude of gratitude irrespective of what we go through. Praise dies when we leave God's atmosphere. Praise persists when we live in His atmosphere. It is not situations that diminish the attitude of praise and gratitude; it is our spiritual cultivation and atmosphere. There are many who will not attend even one meeting with God's people; how will such be joyful and full of praise? The early disciples continued daily in one accord in the temple… praising God **(Acts 2:46-47).**

Let's not kill our joy and praise by spiritual intermittence; may we be dwellers in the house of God.

Prayer

 Lord, I pray that I will be a dweller in Your presence.

Bible Reading Plan:
Genesis 19, John 19, 1 Corinthians 3

DAY 20: PERPETUAL VICTORY

 *No man shall be able to stand before you all the days of your life; as I was with Moses, so I will be with you. I will not leave you nor forsake you.* (Joshua 1:5)

God's guarantee for perpetual victory for Joshua was His presence; as I was with Moses so I shall be with you. Joshua was a tabernacle man; he never left the tabernacle. Oswald Chambers says**, "It is the presence of God that is the secret of victory always".** In His presence mountains melt like wax. Joshua killed most of the giants in the Promised Land. Later another tabernacle man, David slew another giant, Goliath. May we embrace the tabernacle life.

Prayer

 Lord, I make Your presence a priority. Turn me into a God chaser. Amen.

Bible Reading Plan:
Genesis 20, John 20, 1 Corinthians 4

DAY 21 GRATITUDE: THE FRUIT OF GROUNDED FAITH

 *"But he was strengthened in faith, giving glory to God"* (Romans 4:20)

To praise and thank the Lord particularly in nasty situations requires a lot of faith. Real faith will give glory to God. A lot of the ingratitude in form of complaining and grumbling is as a result of lack of faith. The Bible says, **"Then they believed His words; They sang His praise" (Psalm 106:12).** But as soon as the Israelites didn't believe anymore, the began to murmur; **"They despised the pleasant land: They did not believe His word, but murmured in their tents..." (Psalm 106:24-25).** Murmuring and complaining flow from unbelief and are expressions of ingratitude. When we believe God and His promises we will still give glory to God irrespective of what happens.

Prayer

 Lord, I pray for faith that will give You glory in whatever situation I am in.

Bible Reading Plan:
Genesis 21, John 21, 1 Corinthians 5

DAY 22: FAITH MORE PRECIOUS THAN GOLD

"In this you greatly rejoice, though now for a little while, if need be, you have been grieved by various trials, that the genuineness of your faith being much more precious than gold that perishes, though it is tested by fire, may be found to praise, honor and glory at the revelation of Jesus Christ, whom having not seen you love. Though now you do not see Him, yet believing, you rejoice with joy inexpressible and full of glory" (1 Peter 1:6-8).

Our faith in God is more precious than gold. There is a story of a billionaire whose wife died. He had taken her to all the best hospitals in the world and the wife still died. This billionaire cursed money. While money has its place, there are things it cannot buy. By faith, healing is the children's bread. By faith, a dead man can be raised to life but no amount of money can raise a dead man to life. Our faith is more precious than gold. George Mueller received millions in his days in dollars by simply praying in faith without asking any man for aid.

Prayer

Lord, open my eyes to see the worth of my faith; help me guard it jealously.

Bible Reading Plan:
Genesis 22, Matthew 1, 1 Corinthians 6

DAY 23 — HEAVINESS: A SATANIC OPPRESSION

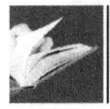 *"The garment of praise for the spirit of heaviness"* (Isaiah 61:3d).

While a lot of pressures in this life are legitimate and weigh us down naturally, in most cases the heaviness is entirely the work of demons. There is a spirit behind heaviness. In the Psalms, we see that mourning is due to Satanic oppression. The Bible says, **"Why do I go mourning because of the oppression of the enemy" (Psalm 43:2b).** Satanic oppression will produce mourning aimed at silencing the believer but the psalmist says as the Lord turns that mourning into dancing, we will not be silent but praise the Lord and forever be grateful to Him **(Psalm 30:11-12).**

Prayer

 Lord, turn every mourning in my life into dancing and singing. I rebuke every satanic oppression in the name of Jesus. Amen

Bible Reading Plan:
Genesis 23, Matthew 2, 1 Corinthians 7

DAY 24 CONQUERING HEAVINESS:
THE TESTIMONY OF DEREK PRINCE

Derek Prince, in the book **Spiritual Warfare** relates his own personal experience with the depression and the spirit of heaviness: "In my own experience, I had a tremendous personal struggle with depression for many years. It was like a dark gray cloud or mist that settled down over me, shut me in, shut me off, and made it difficult for me to communicate with others. It gave me a sense of hopelessness and, although in many ways I am a gifted and qualified servant of the Lord, I got the impression, "Others can, but you can't. You'll never make it. You're going to have to give up." I struggled with this depression for a good many years. I did everything I could. I prayed, I fasted, I sought God, I read the Bible. Then one-day God gave me a revelation that solved my problem. I was reading Isaiah 61:3, To appoint unto them that mourn in Zion, to give unto them beauty for ashes, the oil of joy for mourning, the garment of praise for the spirit of heaviness.... (KJV). When I read that phrase, "the spirit of heaviness," something leaped within me. I said, "That's my problem! That's what I need to be delivered from." I read other passages of Scripture on deliverance, I prayed a simple prayer of faith, and God supernaturally delivered me from that spirit of heaviness". Amen.

Prayer

 Rise up and rebuke the spirit of heaviness in your own life in the name of Jesus. Amen

Bible Reading Plan:
Genesis 24, Matthew 3, 1 Corinthians 8

DAY 25 STAY CONNECTED

 *"A threefold cord is not quickly broken"* (Ecclesiastes 4:12)

The Bible says we should not forsake the assembling of one another (Hebrews 10:24-25). In the book, **Developing Spiritual Roots**, Dr. Christian Ezeudemba and Mbange Calvin lay out why connecting with other believers is very important: **"However mighty we maybe spiritually, if we don't stay in fellowship with others, we will be downcast and pressured beyond our capacity to bear. Elijah was great but was lone ranging. This great man who had dealt with all the prophets of Baal did not only run away from the threats of Jezebel but asked for death (1 Kings 19:1-10). Left his servant and went alone into the wilderness, saying, "I am alone left...." (1 kings 19:10). But God reminds him that, he is not alone but was out of fellowship with others. God says you are thinking you are alone but "Yet I have reserved seven thousand in Israel, all whose knees have not bowed to Baal and every mouth that has not kissed him" (1 Kings 19:18). Stay in fellowship and be strengthened by others. Amen"**.

Prayer

 Lord, I choose to stay connected with other believers.

Bible Reading Plan:
Genesis 25, Matthew 4, 1 Corinthians 9

DAY 26: BE A JONATHAN

 *"Then Jonathan, Saul's son arose and went to David in the woods and strengthened his hand in God"* (1 Samuel 23:16)

Things got so bad that David was now living in the forests in order to hide from Saul. Thank God for Jonathan who strengthened him during this period. David didn't call Jonathan to come and strengthen him. Jonathan knew what David was going through and went out of his way to strengthen him in the Lord. We need men like Jonathan who will go out of their way, to strengthen those who are going through tribulation and difficult times. This week, be a Jonathan or a Barnabas in the life of a saint who is going through hard times. We need many of such men and women in the church today. The pressure in the world is great.

Prayer

 Lord, I pray I will be a Jonathan to my fellow brothers and sisters. Amen

Bible Reading Plan:
Genesis 26, Matthew 5, 1 Corinthians 10

DAY 27 — EMOTIONAL MASTERY: LET NOT YOUR HEART BE TROUBLED

 *"Let not your heart be troubled"* (John 14:1).

John Piper says this age is characterized by emotional fragility. There are few who are capable of sustained emotional stability and containment. Just anything that happens around is capable of throwing them off balance. The Bible says, **"In your patience possess your souls" (Luke 21:19),** **"Be still and know that am God" (Psalm 46:10),** **"Whoever has no rule over his spirit is like a city without walls" (Proverbs 25:28)** and **"Take heed lest your heart be weighed down" (Luke 21:34).** It is our responsibility to make sure our hearts are not troubled. We are called to guard our hearts with all diligence. This is the place of our will in overriding our feelings. The Lord has said in the face of these sorrows and tribulations we should be of good cheer. Don't let your heart be troubled. The Lord, has overcome the world. Amen

Prayer

 Lord, I refuse to let my heart be troubled; I will be of good cheer.

Bible Reading Plan:
Genesis 27, Matthew 6, 1 Corinthians 11

DAY 28  THIS TOO SHALL PASS

 *"It shall come to pass"* (Isaiah 65:24)

One thing we should always have in mind is that situations always come and go. Those who said no condition is permanent are so true today like when they first said so. You may be going through the darkest days of your life; but please know that the longest night will still break into day. Don't allow your temporal hardship to push you into destiny jeopardizing situations. It always pays to wait and hang in there than to give in to the cheap offers of Satan that only give brief reprieve but put us into permanent danger.

God will see us through if we choose to persevere, stand strong and like Shakespeare say, **"This too shall pass"**. Amen

Prayer

 Lord, let me never forget that situations will always come and go. Deliver me from making life-time errors because I want to ease off short-term pressures.

Bible Reading Plan:
Genesis 28, Matthew 7 and 8, 1 Corinthians 12

DAY 29: TRIUMPH IN THE MIDST OF PRESSURE

 *"We are hard pressed on every side, yet not crushed; we are perplexed but not in despair"* (2 Corinthians 4:8)

The Christian life is not about advantageous circumstances; it is advantageous character through the life that is in us. We are overcomers, we are not pampered children. We go through all sorts of pressures in this world but we are not crushed or in despair. Those who are wired for convenient Christianity will not survive. Paul the apostle with all the anointing was still hard pressed on every side but was not crushed; the life of God in him was greater than the pressure exerted by his external environment. Greater is He that is in us than he that is in the world. If the pressures of this life crush us, then we are living a subnormal Christian experience; we are supposed to be more than conquerors and not victims. Victims don't make great pilgrims.

Prayers

 Lord, I pray that my life will experience triumph even in the face of pressure.

Bible Reading Plan:
Genesis 29, Matthew 9, 1 Corinthians 13

DAY 30 THE OPPORTUNITY IN ADVERSITY

 *"For all things work together for the good of them that love the Lord and are called according to His good purpose"* (Romans 8:28).

In Luke 21 from verse 8, the Lord outlines the pressures and the trials that will come upon the world and His disciples in the last days. The joy is that in verse 13 of the chapter, the Lord says that all these will **turn out for you us an occasion for testimony (Luke 21:8-13).** Ezekiel was among the captives by the River of Babylon and while others hung their harps and cried he saw open heavens **(Ezekiel 1:1, Psalm 137:1-2)** and today we have the book of Ezekiel without which we will not understand most of the prophecies concerning the end times. Same for the Apostle John. He was held in the Island of Patmos as a prisoner but saw visions and today we have the Book of Revelation **(Revelation 1:9-19).**

Prayer

 Lord, let me see spiritual opportunities even in hard places

Bible Reading Plan:
Genesis 30, Matthew 10, 1 Corinthians 14

DAY 31: THE OPPORTUNITY IN ADVERSITY II

 *"For all things work together for the good of them that love the Lord and are called according to His good purpose"* (Romans 8:28).

In the book, **Obstacle is the Way: Turning Trials into Triumphs** by Ryan Holiday, it is revealed that most of the big business names in America today started during depressions or economic crises (like General Motors, Proctor and Gamble, Revlon, United Airlines, UPS, Hewlett Packard (HP computers), FedEx, Walt Disney Company, Standard Oil of Rockefeller and many others). According to Joyce Meyer, **In Attitudes of the Mind, "Attitude is the difference between an obstacle and an opportunity. John Bunyan wrote Pilgrim's Progress while in prison. Jeanne Guyon's books have profoundly affected me, and she wrote many of them while in prison. Sir Walter Raleigh wrote The History of the World during a thirteen-year imprisonment. Luther translated the Bible while confined in the Wartburg Castle. Beethoven wrote his greatest symphony while almost totally deaf and burdened with sorrow. Joseph's good attitude took him from the pit to the palace. If a man is truly great, his greatness always emerges during crisis".** There is always an opportunity in every crisis.

Prayer

 Lord, help me see opportunity in any crisis I find myself.

Bible Reading Plan:
Genesis 31, Matthew 11, 1 Corinthians 15

DAY 32 THE OPPORTUNITY IN ADVERSITY III

 *"For all things work together for the good of them that love the Lord and are called according to His good purpose"* (Romans 8:28).

Isaac Newton the great scientist did his greatest scientific discoveries during the Great London Plague of the 17th century. As a 23-year-old student in Cambridge then, and schools shut down due to the plague, he retreated to his family farm of Wools Thorpe Manor where he isolated himself and engaged in groundbreaking discoveries that marked his years of wonders. A plague year became a year of wonders for Isaac Newton. He converted the situation to an opportunity. Amen. May we all develop the ability to see the good in even the worst of situations.

Prayer

 Lord, open my eyes to see opportunities disguised in form of challenges and trials.

Bible Reading Plan:
Genesis 32, Matthew 12, 1 Corinthians 16

DAY 33 IN THE SAME 'MIND-LENGTH' WITH GOD

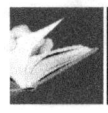 *"Let this mind be in you which was also in Christ Jesus"* (Philippians 2:5)

It is very important to be in the same mind with God. When Moses brought out the children of Israel from Egypt, God had decided not to lead the children of Israel through the land of the Philistines though it was a much nearer and shorter path. God's mind was that, **"Lest perhaps the people change their minds when they see war and return to Egypt. So God led the people around by the way of the wilderness of the Red Sea" (Exodus 13:17-18).** That was God's mind. But as the Israelites saw the Egyptians closing in on them along the God-chosen path, they misread God's intentions. The Bible says, **"Then they said to Moses, because there are no graves in Egypt, have you taken us away to die in the wilderness?" (Exodus 14: 11).** God's decision was intended to seal their spiritual destiny and forever guarantee their freedom. But according to them, Moses brought them to the wilderness to kill them. Their thoughts were far removed from the thoughts of God. Most of them did not enter the Promised Land.

Prayer

 Lord, I pray that my thoughts will line up with Yours so that I don't miss Your best.

Bible Reading Plan:
Genesis 33, Matthew 13 and 2 Corinthians 1

DAY 34 PRODUCTIVE AND CREATIVE DISCIPLE

"At Joppa there was a certain disciple named Tabitha, which is translated Dorcas. This woman was full of charitable deeds which she did......And all the widows stood by him weeping showing the tunics and garments which Dorcas had made......"
(Acts 9:36-39)

Everything was written for our learning. The story of Dorcas has a message for us. The question is why would God create a space in the annals of the greatest spiritual visitation in history for the life of a woman who made tunics, garments and was helping widows. We are told she was a disciple, who was in the creative business and into charity. This is also the work of the Holy Spirit. As we focus on praying, fasting and ministry of the word, let's not forget the creative and the charity dimensions. Many were led to the Lord through the story of Dorcas **(Acts 9:42).**

Prayer

Lord, I pray that I will also see and embrace the creative and the charity side of the gospel.

Bible Reading Plan:
Genesis 34, Matthew 14, 2 Corinthians 2

DAY 35: GOD'S THOUGHTS ARE GOOD

 *"For I know the thoughts that I think toward you says the Lord, thoughts of peace and not of evil, to give you a future and a hope"* (Jeremiah 29:11).

God always means well. This should be settled in our hearts. The problem we have is reconciling His process with His destination. God's process always contradicts his destination; for example, heaven is a wonderful place but the road is narrow and full of tribulation. Joseph is promised rulership but the process to the throne is horrible. God means well even though the process is hard. Once this is settled in our hearts, seemingly impossible, dangerous and difficult situations will not drive us to complaining and bitterness; we will hold on, knowing that good is the end game.

Prayer

 Lord, I believe that Your thoughts towards me are good and are always good.

Bible Reading Plan:
Genesis 35, Matthew 15, 2 Corinthians 3

DAY 36 STIRRING MANY

"And your zeal has stirred up the majority" (2 Corinthians 9:2)

John Wesley asked God for ten men who hated nothing but sin and loved nothing but God and he would changed the world.

We cannot light a fire in others that does not exist in us. People around us are copies of our ruling disposition. If we are on fire, those around us will catch fire. People catch what we have. If we have a contagious disease, people around us will catch it. The question never to forget is, what am I stirring in others?

Prayer

May we be on fire. Lord, set my heart burning. Let me burn for You; a fire that never goes out. Amen

Bible Reading Plan:
Genesis 36, Matthew 16, 2 Corinthians 4

DAY 37 — GOD'S THINKING DIMENSION: THE HOLY SPIRIT WORKING IN US

"For My thoughts are not your thoughts nor are your ways My ways, says the Lord. For as the heavens are higher than the earth, so are My ways higher than your ways and My thoughts higher than your thoughts" (Isaiah 55:8-9).

When we see or perceive what God has in store for us we cannot settle for the misery option. More often than not, we do not see **(1 Corinthians 2:9).** However, our thoughts can align with the thoughts of God through the Holy Spirit and even the deep things of God can be revealed to us and thus have access to God's dimension. The Bible says, **"But it is written: Eye has not seen, nor ear heard nor entered into the heart of man the things God has prepared for those who love Him. But God has revealed them to us through His Spirit. For the Spirit searches all things, yes, the deep things of God" (1 Corinthians 2:9-10).** Knowing and perceiving the things of God, even the deep things is our right as Spirit-filled children of God.

Prayer

Lord, I pray for a deeper walk with Your Spirit; to access the deep things of the Spirit

Bible Reading Plan:
Genesis 37, Matthew 17, 2 Corinthians 5

DAY 38: ACCESSING GOD'S DIMENSION: RENEWAL OF THE MIND

"And do not be conformed to the pattern of this world but be transformed by the renewing of your mind, that you may prove what is that good and acceptable and perfect will of the LORD" (Romans 12:2).

While a close walk with the Spirit is key to perceiving the deep things of God, renewal of mind is another key in helping the believer to be in the same mind-length with God. As we renew our minds through the word of God and the Holy Spirit, we will be able to prove or know or perceive God's mind and will in any given situation. Peter's mind was not renewed; if God did not insist he would not have gone to Cornelius' house and that would have delayed God's move to reach the Gentiles. Our minds need renewal.

Prayer

Lord, renew my mind so that I will be able to perceive Your will in every situation. Amen.

Bible Reading Plan:
Genesis 38, Matthew 18, 2 Corinthians 6

DAY 39 BUILDING SPIRITUAL MEMORIALS

 *"He has made His wonderful work to be remembered: The LORD is gracious and full of compassion"* (Psalm 111:4).

A short spiritual memory is dangerous. God always cautioned the Israelites not to forget His goodness and wonders to them. God wants us to be in remembrance of His wonders and works and this way the sense of God's greatness is registered in our hearts **(Psalm 77:10-14).** In order to avoid this danger of forgetting how wonderful God has been to us, we have to deliberately build memorials or milestones to help us constantly bear in mind the goodness and wonders of God. It has to do with deliberately recording and counting our blessings. When Joshua crossed the Jordan God asked him to take twelve stones and build a memorial for the next generations **(Joshua 4:1-9).** Today, that will mean keeping a record of God's goodness in my life.

Prayer

 Lord, I commit myself to build memorials; records of Your acts of goodness in my life

Bible Reading Plan:
Genesis 39, Matthew 19, 2 Corinthians 7

DAY 40 BUILDING MEMORIALS: REHEARSALS FOR VICTORY IN BATTLE

"Moreover, David said, "the LORD who delivered me from the paw of the lion and from the paw of the bear, He will still deliver me from the hand of this Philistine..." (1 Samuel 17:37)

Why would a young David step out to confront Goliath? David valued his history of victories with God. Every victory with God counts and should be counted and recorded by us. It contributes to our bravery, faith and courage in the face of new challenges. Rehearsing and reading through these records of God's wonders can be a great weapon for us in the face of trial and crisis. According to David, what God has done for us in the past is a source of faith and confidence in the face of giants. Let's not take our past spiritual victories lightly. We need them in new battles.

Prayer

Lord, I pray that I will not take lightly the past victories in my life; I need them for new battles.

Bible Reading Plan:
Genesis 40, Matthew 20, 2 Corinthians 8

DAY 41 HOPE: THE HELMET OF SALVATION

 *"But let us who are of the day, be sober, putting on the breastplate of faith and love; and for a helmet, the hope of salvation"* (1 Thessalonians 5:8 KJV)

The hope of salvation is our helmet. The helmet is worn on the head. It protects the bearer from head injuries. In the spiritual life, hope protects our mind from the onslaught of satanic thoughts and suggestions. According to Derek Prince, **"Hope is a quiet, steady expectation of good based on the promises of God's Word. In a sense, it is continuing optimism. That is the protection of the mind. Hope is an optimistic attitude that always chooses to see the best and will not give way to depression, doubt, and self-pity"**. God expects us to show continuous confidence based on the promises of God; this defeats Satan's doubts and thoughts of discouragement when we are waiting for the manifestation of God's word. Hope is a weapon of warfare of the mind. Dear saint, be hopeful always. God is the God of Hope. Amen

Prayer

 Lord, I put on my helmet: the hope of salvation. I choose to stay hopeful

Bible Reading Plan:
Genesis 41, Matthew 21, 2 Corinthians 9

DAY 42: IGNITING HOPE: THE FOCUS OF THE MIND

 *"This I recall to mind, therefore I have hope"* (Lamentations 3:21)

What we choose to focus on determines whether we are hopeful or not. This calls for mental discipline. The prophet Jeremiah had been focusing on his frustrations and all the wrong things in his environment and he was downcast; meaning depressed. But when the prophet chose to focus the mind on the love, compassions and faithfulness of God, hope sprang. Hallelujah. Because of that change in focus one of the most inspiring thoughts about our God was born; His compassions fail not, great is your faithfulness **(Lamentations 3:22-23).** Our focus should therefore be on God and His goodness, love and faithfulness.

Prayer

 Lord, forgive my wrong focus; I pray that my mind will focus on the things that inspire hope; your love, compassion and faithfulness.

Bible Reading Plan:
Genesis 42, Matthew 22, 2 Corinthians 10

DAY 43 IGNITING HOPE: INVESTMENTS IN THE WORD

 *"For whatever things were written before, were written for our learning, that we through the patience and comfort of the Scriptures might have hope"* (Romans 15:4).

Why was the Bible written? This is an important question. Why a thing exists communicates it importance and value. Paul tells us that it was written for our learning so that through the comfort from the Scriptures, we might have hope. The Bible is a book of hope. To develop a loose attachment to the Scriptures, is to plan for hopelessness. In the Bible we meet hopeful stories and cases that God turned around and this inspires hope in our heart for change in our own situation. In the word, we meet the great and precious promises of God, which are Yea and Amen. D.L Moody says, **"The future is as bright as the promises of God"**. The promises in the word will inspire hope in us. Stay in the word and stay away from hopelessness.

Prayer

 Lord, I pray that my heart will be soaked in and with the Scriptures

Bible Reading Plan:
Genesis 43, Matthew 23, 2 Corinthians 11

DAY 44 IGNITING HOPE: THE INSPIRATION OF THE HOLY SPIRIT

 *"Now may <u>the God of hope</u> fill you with all joy and peace in believing, that you may abound in <u>hope by the power of the Holy Spirit</u>"* (Romans 15:13).

God is the God of hope. Hope is an attribute of God. It is an attribute of the God-head. Christ is also an embodiment of hope; Christ in us, the hope of glory. How does this hope which is an attribute of God and Christ abound in us? Hope abounds in us through the power of the Holy Spirit. The Holy Spirit imparts a supernatural ability to hope in the face of very discouraging situations. A believer who is joyful and peaceful, will also be hopeful; all are fruits of the same Spirit. Hopelessness is an indication of a poor relationship with the Holy Spirit; we have to labour to stay filled and walk in the power of the Holy Spirit. This will enable us to be hopeful always.

Prayer

 Lord, I pray that I will labour to stay filled with Your Spirit; let me abound in hope.

Bible Reading Plan:
Genesis 44, Matthew 24, 2 Corinthians 12

DAY 45 HOPE: INSPIRING FAITH

 *"Faith is the substance of things hoped for"* (Hebrews 11:1).

Faith makes substance what is hoped for. Hope lays a foundation for faith. Where there is no hope there can be no faith. Hope, in the divine scheme of things precedes faith. The Bible says, **"Since we heard of your faith in Christ Jesus and of your love for all the saints, because of the hope which is laid up for you in heaven, of which you heard before in the word of truth of the gospel" (Colossians 1:4-5).** The faith and love of the brethren in Colossae was because of their hope which is laid up in heaven. Thus hope is the foundation of faith and love. Where hope wanes, faith weakens too. We have to keep hope alive. Abraham kept hope alive. He hoped against hope, and that made him the father of faith. His fatherhood in faith was rooted in his conquering hope. The word says, **"Who contrary to hope, in hope believed" (Romans 4:18).** Father of faith, born out of father of hope. May we all keep hope alive.

Prayer

 Lord, let my hope be strong and alive; let my faith be inspired as a result.

Bible Reading Plan:
Genesis 45, Matthew 25, 2 Corinthians 13

DAY 46  HOPE: A DOOR

 *"I will give her, her vineyards from there, and the Valley of Achor as a door of hope"* (Hosea 2:15).

Valley of Achor means trouble (Joshua 7:25-26). Israel lost a battle against Ai, because Achan took the dedicated things. It was an embarrassing incident in Israel. But God says, it will be a door of hope. Hope is a door; seeing possibilities even in the midst of trouble. A great man once said, **"There are no hopeless situations, there are only hopeless men"**. Hope is the eye of possibilities even in the worst of situations. When hope is lost, no situation can be rescued. Hope inspires possibilities in a messy situation. A story is told of an architect who had ordered glass for the walls of a modern building he was supervising. The glass broke into pieces. What was he going to do? Was it case closed? What does he tell his clients? Hope was not lost; in the midst of this seemingly bad situation, he saw the possibility for a new design: turn all the glass into pieces and insert them in a mosaic in the walls of the building. A new design emerged from what would have been a miserable situation.

Prayer

 Lord, I pray for an eye for possibilities even in the face of trouble.

Bible Reading Plan:
Genesis 46, Galatians 1

DAY 47 UNLEASHING GOD'S GLORY

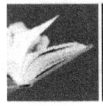 *"But You are holy, who inhabits the praises of Israel"* (Psalm 22:3).

Many believers and even spiritual communities yearn for the manifest presence of God and the manifestation of the Holy Spirit. Like us humans, God will only visit and dwell in an environment where He is appreciated and celebrated. In the Scriptures, God's glory refers to God's very essence, being, nature and character. Thus to tamper with the glory is to tamper with God Himself. In the story of the ten lepers, we see that the one man who returned to give thanks to Jesus glorified God **(Luke 17:15-18).** As a community of believers create an atmosphere of praise and appreciation of God and His goodness, so does His glory descend among His people. God is limited in expression and operation in an environment where He is not appreciated. Jesus didn't do much in his home town in Nazareth. He was not highly appreciated there **(Mark 6:1-5).** However, in Galilee He was highly appreciated. The Bible records that He was glorified by all when He taught in Galilee. In fact, that's where His ministry began **(Luke 4:14-15).**

Prayer

 Lord, let my life be a place where Your glory will manifest; a life that radiates gratitude.

Bible Reading Plan:
Genesis 47, Matthew 26, Galatians 2

DAY 48 UNLEASHING GOD'S GLORY II

 *"But You are holy, who inhabits the praises of Israel"* (Psalm 22:3).

God will not descend in fullness where He is not appreciated. He will always descend with His fullness and power in an atmosphere of gratitude and appreciation. The Bible says, **"Indeed it came to pass, when the trumpeters and singers were one, to make one sound to be heard in praising and thanking the LORD and when they lifted up their voice with trumpets and cymbals and instruments of music and praised God saying: for He is good, for His mercy endures forever, that the house of the LORD was filled with a cloud so that the priests could not continue ministering because of the cloud; for the glory of the LORD filled the house of God" (2 Chronicles 5:13-14).** There was one voice of gratitude and appreciation of God and His goodness: His cloud and glory therefore filled the house of God.

Prayer

 Lord, let me minister in the fullness of Your glory. Let my life be a place of gratitude and appreciation of Your goodness.

Bible Reading Plan:
Genesis 48, Matthew 27, Galatians 3

DAY 49: A NEW SONG TO THE LORD

 *"Oh sing to the LORD a new song! Sing to the LORD all the earth"* (Psalm 96:1).

When God has done wonderful things for us, we cannot but sing and make music to His name. It is good to make music to the Lord. In the very throne of God, the four living creatures and the twenty-four elders sang a new song in worship to the Lamb that was seated upon the throne. New songs are the heartbeat of the throne life **(Revelation 5:8-9).**

If there is one command that is least heeded today, is that of singing to the LORD a new song. Could it be that we are not touching the throne today because of our laziness and old songs? Will I sing Him a new song? Where are the new compositions?

Prayer

 May the Lord have mercy us. Lord, may we arise with compositions of new songs in praise to You. Amen

Bible Reading Plan:
Genesis 49, Matthew 28, Galatians 4

DAY 50: GRATITUDE TO MEN: THE PATTERN OF DAVID

"And they helped David against the bands of raiders, for they were all mighty men, and were captains in the army"
(1 Chronicles 12:21)

David was greatly helped. He is an example of a man who did not forget those who had been good to him. From the time he was anointed king and killed Goliath, things turned for the worst for him. In those rough days of David's life, Jonathan, Saul's son, stood with David at the risk of his own relationship with his father the king. Jonathan stood with and helped David **(1 Samuel 19:1-2, 23:14-18).** When he became king, he went out of his way to look out for any descendant of Jonathan (Mephibosheth) so that he can show kindness to him **(2 Samuel 9:1).** David was on the run most of the time because king Saul was after his life. He and his men received a lot of help from communities while he and his men roamed or roved. David didn't forget these communities. He listed them individually and distributed material gifts to them **(1 Samuel 30:26-31).** Many would have forgotten these people and communities. David did not.

Prayer

Lord, may I not forget those who stood with me in my dark days. Amen.

Bible Reading Plan:
Genesis 50, Mark 1, Galatians 5

DAY 51 GRATITUDE IN ODD PLACES

 *"From the blood of the slain, from the fat of the mighty, the bow of Jonathan did not turn back and the sword of Saul did not return empty"* (2 Samuel 1:22)

David knew God. He was really a man after God's heart. In spite of all he went through in the hands of Saul, he still found a reason to appreciate him.

Saul, the very man who was after the life of David was his king. But David never spoke against Saul. Even when he tore Saul's garment, he repented of it. David never forgot Saul's goodness to him. He was recruited into the palace by Saul. It is Saul who allowed him to fight Goliath. David didn't forget that. He focused on that rather than the evil in Saul's life. When Saul died, David composed a lamentation full of good words and appreciation for Saul: **"The beauty of Israel is slain on your high places. How have the mighty fallen" (2 Samuel 1:19, 22, 23,24).** In a thousand faults, a grateful heart will find one reason to show gratitude.

Prayer

 Lord, for a heart that will in a thousand faults, find one reason to be appreciative

Bible Reading Plan:
Exodus 1, Mark 2, Galatians 6

DAY 52: MEDITATING ON HIS WORKS

 *"I will meditate on all Your work, and I will talk of Your deeds"* (Psalm 77:12).

God calls us to think about His works. We should not only remember but also meditate on his works. Remember the song, "When I think of the goodness of Jesus and all He has done for me, my very soul will shout hallelujah, praise God for saving me". Our praise and thanksgiving is cold because our thinking is shallow. May we like the psalmist say, **"We have thought, O God on Your lovingkindness, in the midst of Your temple" (Psalm 48:9).** R. Herbert in the book **Living Thanks**, presents the benefits of thinking on God's blessings as follows: **"The more we think about a gift, the more we usually come to appreciate it. Sometimes we see added dimensions to the blessing that we would not have otherwise noticed. And it can often really heighten our appreciation for the people and things around us to spend even a small amount of time thinking about what life would be like without those blessings."**

Prayer

 Lord, I pray that I will think and meditate on Your works in my life

Bible Reading Plan:
Exodus 2, Mark 3, Ephesians 1

DAY 53 THINK ON THESE THINGS: DEVELOPING THE RIGHT FIXATION

 *".... Think on these things"* (Philippians 4:8)

> To higher, nobler things, my mind is bent
> - **Nelle Reagan (Mother of Ronald Reagan, former US President)**

It is important what we think about. Our fixation is crucial in our spiritual life. Even our peace is conditioned on the fixation of our mind. The Bible says, **"You will keep him perfect peace, whose mind is stayed on You, because he trusts in You" (Isaiah 26:3).**

We remember Peter walking on water and for as long as he looked towards the Lord, he stayed on top of the water. But when he started looking at the waves and he began to sink. Our gaze and fixation is key in determining whether we stay afloat or drown in the seas of life. There are many today, who are sinking in their souls (depressed and downcast) because they have taken their eyes off the Lord and they are fixated on their challenges and circumstances.

Prayer

 Lord, help me develop discipline for the right fixation

Bible Reading Plan:
Exodus 3, Mark 4, Ephesians 2

DAY 54 — THINK ON THESE THINGS: DEVELOPING THE RIGHT FIXATION II

 *".... Think on these things"* (Philippians 4:8)

Our Lord Jesus could be deep asleep in the boat even in the midst of a storm. He was unmoved while his disciples were in deep care and worry. How was that possible? His mind was fixed on the Lord who can calm every storm.

The Bible says, **"For David says concerning Him: I foresaw the LORD always before my face, for He is at my right hand, that I may not be shaken"** (Acts 2:25). This same Scripture is quoted from Psalm 16:8, **"I have set the Lord always before me; because He is at my right I shall not be shaken"**.

The key to an unshakeable and unmoved life is to set the Lord always before us. It has to be always. The moment we shift our focus, and start looking at our circumstances, we lose our peace and calm.

Prayer

 Father, grant me the fixation on You that results in internal calm in the midst of a storm.

Bible Reading Plan:
Exodus 4, Mark 5, Ephesians 3

DAY 55 MORAL GRATITUDE

"Therefore, I urge you, brothers, in view of God's mercy, to offer your bodies as living sacrifices, holy and pleasing to God-this is your spiritual act of worship" (Romans 12:1 NIV).

Sin is moral ingratitude. The apostle Paul presents moral gratitude so well in the Book of Romans; **".... not knowing that the goodness of God leads you to repentance?" (Romans 2:4).** Those who despise the goodness of God, will show no proportionate change of heart and attitude towards God. Repentance is a gratitude indicator. Attitude towards God and the things of God is a gratitude indicator. The Bible says, "**The children of Ephraim being armed and carrying bows, turned back in the day of battle. They did not keep the covenant of God; <u>they refused to walk in his law and forgot his works and his wonders that he had shown them</u>**" (Psalm 78:9-11). These men did not put their hands in the plow, they refused to walk in God's law or keep His covenant. The reason was: they forgot the works and wonders that God had shown them. Holiness is an act of worship.

Prayer

Lord, I pray that my life will be a reflection of moral gratitude. Let no sin abide in me. Amen

Bible Reading Plan:
Exodus 5, Mark 6, Ephesians 4

DAY 56: COMPARISON: A SPIRITUAL SLIPPERY SLOPE

 *"Truly God is good to Israel, to such as are pure in heart. But as for me, my feet had almost stumbled: my steps had nearly slipped, for I was envious of the boastful, when I saw the prosperity of the wicked"* (Psalm 73:1-2).

Once our eyes shift towards what others have that we do not have, immediately we tend to despise the things that God has done for us. Asaph was a man with an enviable profile in praise and thanksgiving to God. Asaph even wrote some of the Psalms. Asaph upheld the fact that God is good until he started looking at the prosperity of the wicked. From that point, ingratitude set in. He got to the point of even saying, **"Surely I have cleansed my heart in vain and washed my hands in innocence" (Psalm 73:13).** Glory to God Asaph stepped into the presence of God and his madness was cured. The Bible says, **"Until I went into the sanctuary of God, then I understood their end" (Psalm 73:17).** The sanctuary gives true perspective.

Prayer

 Lord, let me not look at others with their lands and gold. May my eyes be on You alone.

Bible Reading Plan:
Exodus 6, Mark 7, Ephesians 5

DAY 57 YOUR TIME WILL COME

"Time and chance happen to all" (Ecclesiastes 9:11d).

Our time will come for the best that God has for us. There is no need to envy those who are seemingly doing better. Those we are envying now once had their time of suffering and a time came when God remembered them and lifted them out of the ash heap.

Obama retired as president at age fifty-five, Trump entered that same office at age seventy. The Edomites progressed faster than the Israelites; they had seven kings before Israel even had one **(Genesis 36:31-39),** but today Edom is just part of a country called Jordan, poorer than Israel today. Your time will surely come. Just stay faithful to Him.

Prayer

Lord, help me stay grateful where I am right now, envying no one for I know that in due time You will lift me up. Amen.

Bible Reading Plan:
Exodus 7, Mark 8, Ephesians 6

DAY 58: SHAPED BY TRIALS

 *"My brethren count it all joy when you fall into various trials, knowing that the testing of your faith produces patience. But let patience have its perfect work, that you may be perfect and complete lacking nothing"* (James 1:2-4).

In shaping our character and conforming us to the image of His Dear Son, God uses our pressures and trials. Once we understand that our trials form part of God's training program for us, our attitude will change and we will gracefully and prayerfully go through our trials taking seriously the lessons we learn in the process. While we see troubles and pain, the Lord sees a process of completion and perfection at work in us. Tribulations form part of God's sequence for our perfection and formation of character **(Romans 5:3-5)**. What we need to do is to cooperate with the Lord and one of the ways is in the attitude we put up: Paul says we should glory in tribulations. Charles Spurgeon noted that, **"The Lord gets His best soldiers in the highlands of affliction"**. Dear saint, yield to God's shaping process through the trials you face.

Prayer

 May we count it all joy when we face all kinds of trials knowing that the Lord is using them to form in us the character of His Son Jesus. Amen

Bible Reading Plan:
Exodus 8, Mark 9, Philippians 1

DAY 59 NO PLACE FOR BOASTING

 *"For by grace you have been saved through faith and not of yourselves; it is the gift of God, not of works, lest anyone should boast"* (Ephesians 2:8-9).

In life we even hear of men who say they are self-made men. Meaning they did all for themselves by themselves. They therefore owe no one any sense of gratitude. They are debt-free, gratitude wise. God understands that this complex of entitlement is very much alive in man and chose to make our salvation by grace so that no one will boast but will give glory to God. Boasting is excluded so that what should flow from us is gratitude for such a salvation without our works but by faith. The Bible says, **"Where is boasting then? It is excluded. By what law? Of works? No, but by the law of faith" (Romans 3:27).** Since boasting which is self-praise is excluded, we are to flow instead in praise, gratitude and thanksgiving to God for such a great gift of salvation.

Prayer

 Lord, thank You for salvation by faith and not of works lest I should boast. I give You praise. Amen

Bible Reading Plan:
Exodus 9, Mark 10, Philippians 2

DAY 60 NO PLACE FOR BOASTING II

 *"For who makes you differ from another? And what do you have that you did not receive? Now if you did indeed receive it, why do you boast as if you had not received it?"* (1 Corinthians 4:7).

There is no gift or talent in us that was not given to us by God. There is therefore no place or reason to boast. We did not work for our gifts. God gave us freely so that we can use them for the benefit of God and man. We therefore should not despise others or boast. Imagine a handsome or beautiful person boasting and looking down on those who are not as handsome or beautiful. We did nothing to earn the handsomeness or beauty. May we be humble and grateful to God for what He has done for us rather than boast.

Prayer

 May God lead us all to deeper levels of humility and gratitude. May the Lord forgive us for times when we have despised and looked down on others.

Bible Reading Plan:
Exodus 10, Mark 11, Philippians 3

DAY 61 THERE IS HOPE

"We have trespassed against our God, and have taken pagan wives from the peoples of the land; yet now there is hope in Israel in spite of this" (Ezra 10:2b).

Israel had sinned greatly. They had disobeyed God. It was a morally hopeless situation. But the word says, in spite of this there is hope. There is the hope of forgiveness and repentance. God is willing to forgive and restore. May be you have sinned greatly and you feel so worthless before God and man. There is hope for you. God is a transformer of lives. He can take the worst of criminals and transform them into amazing saints. Rahab the prostitute is an example. She was a prostitute but today she is in the genealogy of the Lord. He also changed Paul from a persecutor to an apostle. All we need to do is acknowledge our sin and repent.

Prayer

Lord, I ask for Your mercy. In my sin I come to Your mercy seat; forgive and cleanse. Amen

Bible Reading Plan:
Exodus 11, Mark 12, Philippians 4

DAY 62 A LINE OF DEMARCATION

 *"And you will again see the distinction between the righteous and the wicked, between those who serve God and those who do not"* (Malachi 3:18 NIV).

The Bible says, **"The Lord knows those who are His" (2 Timothy 2:19)**. He wants to make a clear distinction between the saint and sinner, between the righteous and the wicked, between the believer and unbeliever. He understands and sees that the world has squeezed itself into the church. He knows that His house is a mixture of fake and genuine and He is committed to bring about a very clear distinction. He wants to make a distinction between God pleasers and men pleasers, those who serve God and those who serve themselves, those who love the truth and those who hate it, those who are sincere and those who pretend, those who hold to godly standards and those who compromise, those who are devoted, wholeheartedly to Him and those who are divided at heart. The question is on which side will you be even as the Lord makes this distinction? It's never too late to realign your life in accordance with the divine will.

Prayer

 Lord, help me to always be on the right side of righteousness, service, commitment, and integrity

Bible Reading Plan:
Exodus 12, Mark 13, Colossians 1

DAY 63 FULLY COMMITTED

 *"For the eyes of the LORD range throughout the earth to strengthen those whose hearts are fully committed to Him"* (2 Chronicles 16:9 NIV)

The Lord expects all those who profess His Name to know a wholehearted commitment to obey the Lord. A wholehearted commitment to honesty, truth and integrity! A wholehearted commitment to live under the complete influence of the Holy Spirit! A wholehearted commitment to the power of the Holy Spirit! A wholehearted commitment to present one's best and all to Him! A wholehearted commitment to holiness and righteousness! A wholehearted commitment to total separation from the world! A wholehearted commitment to the will of God! A wholehearted laying down of one's rights and privileges on the altar of the Gospel of Christ. These are what God expects of you and His Spirit is there to work it in you.

Prayer

 Lord, I pray for a life that is fully committed to You. Amen

Bible Reading Plan:
Exodus 13, Mark 14, Colossians 2

DAY 64  HE OWNS YOUR LIFE

 *"Lord, I know that a man's life is not his own; it is not for man to direct his steps"* (Jeremiah 10:23 NIV).

The principal philosophy of Satanism is, "do what thou will" and "be the master of your own destiny". God owns the human life either by right of creation or twofold by right of creation and right of redemption. God is the rightful owner of the human life. However, many of us live as though our lives belong to us. We make our own choices, take our own decision and live as though there is no account to be given to anyone at the end of the journey on earth. Even professing Christians, make their own plans for themselves, and some go to the extreme of planning the lives of others. It is not for man to direct his steps. We are supposed to live like sheep under the Good Shepherd to avoid going astray.

Prayer

 Father, help me lay hold of the truth that my life is not my own and that it is not for me to direct my steps.

Bible Reading Plan:
Exodus 14, Mark 15, Colossians 3

DAY 65  WHO AM I LIVING FOR

 *"And He died for all, that those who live should no longer live for themselves but for Him who died for them and was raised again"* (2 Corinthians 5:15 NIV).

Who are you living for? Who inspires or validates the choices and decisions you make for your life and the lives of those over whom you are responsible? Remember, the test of authenticity, that you belong to Jesus is Romans 8:14, **"For all who are being led by the Spirit of God, these are sons and daughters of God"**. Not those who lead themselves, but those who have understood that their lives are not their own, and have submitted to the leadership and direction of the Holy Spirit.

Prayer

 Help me, Lord, to live daily as unto You, in everything I do, even in the seemingly insignificant choices and decisions I make.

Bible Reading Plan:
Exodus 15, Mark 16, Colossians 4

DAY 66 THE POWER OF TRUST

 *"But blessed is the one who trusts in the Lord, whose confidence is in Him. They will be like a tree planted by the water that sends out its roots by the stream. It does not fear when heat comes; its leaves are always green. It has no worries in a year of drought and never fails to bear fruit"* (Jeremiah 17:7-9 NIV).

Trust in anything other than the Creator, will lead to a curse and to poverty as the preceding verses to the ones cited here declare. Trust or confidence in the Lord is a key to a blessed and prosperous life:

It spreads its roots by the river: there are rivers of living water flowing from the inside of your innermost being. Trust and confidence in the Lord is what causes you to develop roots that can tap from this endless supply within you.

It doesn't fear when heat comes: it is possible to live a life free from fear that comes because of uncertain and changing external circumstances. No trial, test, or tribulation can cause the one whose trust and confidence are in the Lord to panic

Prayer

 Lord, I choose to trust You. I tap into the endless supply of a life of trust. Amen

Bible Reading Plan:
Exodus 16, Luke 1, 1 Thessalonians 1

DAY 67 THE POWER OF TRUST II

"But blessed is the one who trusts in the Lord, whose confidence is in Him. They will be like a tree planted by the water that sends out its roots by the stream. It does not fear when heat comes; its leaves are always green. It has no worries in a year of drought and never fails to bear fruit" (Jeremiah 17:7-9 NIV).

Its leaves are always green: it is possible to live like an evergreen. When you develop roots to tap from a continuous supply that God provides because of your trust in Him, you do not experience drought when others are complaining of such. This leads us to our next point.

It has no worries in the year of drought: drought represents lack and limited supply. When there is drought you will have a source of supply that others don't have because you are tapping from a deeper source. You know your case is different because your source is different.

It never fails to bear fruit: the ultimate purpose of a tree is to bring forth fruits according to its kind. The constant supply is so that the tree can constantly produce fruit for the one who planted it. If you want a fruitful and productive life, put your trust in the Lord.

Prayer

Lord, help me to live a fear-free and a worry-free life by trusting in You with my whole heart. I want to be like a tree planted by the waters.

Bible Reading Plan:
Exodus 17, Luke 2, 1 Thessalonians 2

DAY 68: THE POTTER AND THE CLAY

 *"Then the word of the Lord came to me. He said, "Can I not do with you, Israel, as this potter does?" declares the Lord. "Like clay in the hand of the potter, so are you in My hand, Israel"* (Jeremiah 18:5-6 NIV).

There are number of life lessons to draw from here. First, like clay in the hands of a potter, so are you in the hands of the Lord. Clay needs to be moistened as the potter works on it, likewise you need to be constantly moistened by the Dew of Heaven so as to remain malleable and flexible in the hands of the potter. Second, it is the potter who determines what to make of the clay. What the potter has determined to make of the clay determines how much time and effort he puts on it. The design determines the process. Third, clay cannot be useless in the hand of the potter. As long as clay is in the hands of the potter, He can make it into whatever he sees fit, even if his intended design was marred for one reason or the other.

Prayer

 Lord, let the Dew of Heaven saturate my life and make me malleable in the hands of the Potter.

Bible Reading Plan:
Exodus 18, Luke 3, 1 Thessalonians 3

DAY 69: INTO ANOTHER VESSEL

"And the vessel that he made of clay was marred in the hand of the potter; so he made it again into another vessel, as it seemed good to the potter to make" (Jeremiah 18:4).

May be you have made some mistakes in your life and you feel you have lost your worth. May be you think some choices you made in the past have frustrated God's plans for your life. I want you to acknowledge that you are just clay in the hands of the Master Potter. Surrender yourself to Him and let Him make you into what He sees fit. God is able to make you into another vessel: better than you can ever imagine. Just surrender to Him. The life that is surrendered in His hands will have the best outcome.

Prayer

Surrender your broken experiences in life and ask Him to take the broken pieces and make the best of it as it seems best to Him.

Bible Reading Plan:
Exodus 19, Luke 4, 1 Thessalonians 4

DAY 70 THE JOURNEY TO ABUNDANCE: THE PHASE OF MEN

 *"You let men ride over our heads; we went through fire and water, but You brought us to a place of abundance"* (Psalm 66:12 NIV).

There seems to be a divinely ordained pattern to bring His children to the place of abundance. There is first the phase where men are allowed to ride over the heads of His children. This is the phase where it appears you are under the rule and control of other human beings. Sometimes, they are appreciative of what you do, other times they are those who are cruel and unappreciative of you. Think of the children of Israel under Pharaoh, or of Joseph in Potiphar's house. May be you find yourself in this phase, it is not meant to be the end of the road. Just maintain a positive attitude, learn what you can, offer the best of the service you can until the Lord takes you to the next phase.

Prayer

 Lord, help me navigate this phase of men to the place of abundance without bitterness

Bible Reading Plan:
Exodus 20, Luke 5, 1 Thessalonians 5

DAY 71: THE JOURNEY TO ABUNDANCE: THE PHASE OF FIRE AND WATER

"You let men ride over our heads; <u>we went through fire and water</u>, but You brought us to a place of abundance" (Psalm 66:12 NIV).

Then there is what I term the wilderness phase in which He takes you through the fire and the water. In this phase the Lord wants to prove to you His faithfulness, and ability to sustain in the midst of adversity. The fire is to purify and the water is to cleanse. You must go through both and experience the Lord fulfil His promise that, **"When you pass through the waters, I will be with you; and when you pass through the rivers, they will not sweep over you. When you walk through the fire, you will not be burned; the flames will not set you ablaze" (Isaiah 43:2 NIV).** Then there is the Promised land phase, where He brings you to a spacious place. The place of abundance. Many people try to reach this place of abundance without the first two phases, which with God is not possible.

Prayer

Take me, LORD, through Your refining fire, and through Your water of cleansing, and bring me to my spacious place

Bible Reading Plan:
Exodus 21, Luke 6, 1 Thessalonians 6

DAY 72 THE COST OF PRESUMPTION

"David and his men reached Ziklag on the third day. Now the Amalekites had raided the Negev and Ziklag. They had attacked Ziklag and burned it, and had taken captive the women and everyone else in it, both young and old. They killed none of them, but carried them off as they went on their way" (1 Samuel 30:1-2 NIV).

In 1 Samuel chapter 29, David had presumptuously committed himself to fight a battle without first of all inquiring of the Lord as his custom was. David's family and that of his men were captured as result. When you go to fight God's battles, He will take care of you and all that concerns you. However, whenever you engage in a battle God has not ordained, you expose yourself and your family to attack. We should learn to seek God before we get into any endeavor; it saves time and energy.

Prayer

Father, may I not engage in any battle You have not ordained for me. Let me learn to inquire of You first before I engage in any battle or endeavour

Bible Reading Plan:
Exodus 22, Luke 7, 2 Thessalonians 1

DAY 73: THERE IS A BLUEPRINT FOR YOUR LIFE

 *"...Your will be done, on earth as it is in heaven"* (Matthew 6:10b NIV).

There is a blueprint kept in heaven for each life, to be revealed to each one of us. You were not created to live by chance. Everything which happens in your life is for a purpose. There is no uncertainty as far as God is concerned in the life of His creatures. If a sparrow will never fall to the ground except at the will of God Almighty (**Matthew 10:29),** then nothing that happens in your life is by chance. All the days of your life here on earth were ordained and written in the book of God's blueprint for your life before you ever started living. If this is so then you must seek to have God reveal to you what that blueprint is all about. He may not reveal it to at once but certainly will do it progressively. Come to God in prayer to seek His will concerning your life and pray the blueprint back to Him. Sometimes, and most often, our prayers are filled with our self-made plans for our lives. No wonder we pray and receive no answers. Your prayers must be in accordance with God's blueprint for you.

Prayer

 Lord, empower me to seek Your blueprint for my life. Help me to pray it into existence

Bible Reading Plan:
Exodus 23, Luke 8, 2 Thessalonians 2

DAY 74 FROM HEAVENLY PLACES TO THE EARTH

 *"Blessed be God and Father of our Lord Jesus Christ, who has blessed us with every spiritual blessing in the heavenly places in Christ"* (Ephesians 1:3).

Prayer is key to releasing in the earthly realm all that God has for us in the heavenly places in Christ. In the Lord's Prayer, the Bible says, **"Your will be done on earth as it is in heaven" (Matthew 6:10).** Thus through prayer, the designs of heaven can become earthly realities. The store house of God is full. But why are we poor spiritually and otherwise. The Lord gives the answer; **"Yet you do not have because you do not ask" (James 4:2).**

If we don't ask, then we will not have. There is a man who learnt to ask: George Mueller. This man operated five orphanages and cared for 10,024 orphans in his lifetime without asking for help from anyone except God. God is faithful and we too are called to ask and receive. Amen

Prayer

 Lord, I pray that I will learn to ask and I will return to a life of asking. Amen

Bible Reading Plan:
Exodus 24, Luke 9, 2 Thessalonians 3

DAY 75 THE WORD AND PRAYER

 *"If you abide in Me and My words abide in you, you will ask whatever you desire and it shall be done for you"* (John 15:7).

Great prayers are born from the word. The basis for true prayer is the word of God. Men whose prayers really shook the world were men whose lives were saturated in the word. Mary, the Queen of Scotland said, **"I fear the prayers of John Knox more than all the assembled armies of Europe"**. Knox's prayers were weighty. He gave the word priority in his life. Knox said the following: **"Let no day slip over without some comfort received from the word of God"**. May we return to word-based praying. This is the key to prayers that carry weight. Amen

Prayer

 Lord, I prayer that my prayers will be grounded and soaked in the word.

Bible Reading Plan:
Exodus 25, Luke 10, 1 Timothy 1

DAY 76 ILLUMINATED PRAYERS

 *"Aaron shall burn on it sweet incense every morning: when he tends the lamps, he shall burn incense on it"* (Exodus 30:7).

In the Old Testament, burning of incense which represent prayers (Revelation 5:8) went together with tending the lamps which represents the word; **"Your word is a lamp to my feet and a light to my path" (Psalm119:105).** So Aaron had to tend the lamps before burning incense. We are to do same; the word has to illuminate, inspire and guide our prayers. Illumination from the word thus precedes prayer. Let's not ask amiss. Stay in the word to be guided with respect to God's mind and direction. Prayers rooted in the word are very much aligned with God's will and are therefore answered.

Prayer

 May the word so saturate our spirits and minds such that our prayers will flow from God's mind and thoughts communicated to us through His word. Amen

Bible Reading Plan:
Exodus 26, Luke 11, 1 Timothy 2

DAY 77 — HE BECAME POOR THAT I MIGHT BECOME RICH

 *"For you know the grace of our Lord Jesus Christ, that though He was rich yet for your sakes became poor, that you through His poverty might become rich"* (2 Corinthians 8:9).

It is the pleasure and will of God that His children prosper. The Bible says, **"Let the Lord be magnified who has pleasure in the prosperity of His servant" (Psalm 35:27).** Before the fall of man, God created every other thing; plant, animal, fish of the sea, birds of the air and all that man needed before creating man on the sixth day **(Genesis 2:8-15).** Today, five represents the number for grace. On the fifth day, God had created all that man needed for life and man was created on the sixth day, to enter into what God had done already. That same grace made Jesus become poor so that we might become rich; **"For you know the grace of our Lord Jesus Christ, that though He was rich yet for your sakes became poor, that you through His poverty might become rich" (2 Corinthians 8:9).**

Prayer

 Lord, I accept and enter into the grace to become rich

Bible Reading Plan:
Exodus 27, Luke 12, 1 Timothy 3

DAY 78: UNDERSTANDING REDEMPTION

"In Him we have redemption through His blood, the forgiveness of our sins according to the riches of His grace" (Ephesians 1:7).

Redemption is the setting free of a person who is held in bondage through the payment of a ransom. We had become slaves and held in bondage by the devil through Adam's sin but through the price paid by Jesus Christ on the cross of Calvary we no longer belong to the devil and not held in bondage by him anymore. We are now the redeemed of the Lord. Our redemption was secured by the Blood of Jesus Christ that was shed on the cross. Dear saint, rejoice in your redemption. You now belong to God eternally. Satan has no claims over your life anymore. You have relocated realms. It is once and for all; it is eternal.

Prayer

Lord, I thank You for Your redemption; I confess I am the redeemed of the Lord. Amen

Bible Reading Plan:
Exodus 28, Luke 13, 1 Timothy 4

DAY 79: REDEEMED FROM SIN AND DEATH

 *"But of Him you are in Christ Jesus, who became for us wisdom from God-and righteousness and sanctification and redemption..."* (1 Corinthians 1:30).

The Lord has redeemed us. What has the Lord redeemed me from?

Dear child of God, you have been redeemed from sin; **"Who gave Himself for us that He might redeem us from every lawless deed..." (Titus 2:14).** Sin should not hold you captive anymore.

Redeemed from Death and its Power; **"I will ransom them from the power of the grave, I will redeem them from death. O Death, I will be your plagues! O, Grave, I will be your destruction! Pity is hidden from My eyes" (Hosea 13:14).** This redemption from bondage of fear of death and its power was accomplished on the cross through the death of Jesus Christ.

Prayer

 Lord, thank you for redeeming me from the power of sin and death

Bible Reading Plan:
Exodus 29 and 30, Luke 14, 1 Timothy 5

DAY 80: REDEEMED FROM THE CURSE OF THE LAW

"For as many as are of the works of the law are under a curse; for it is written, cursed is everyone who does not continue in all things to which are written in the book of the law to do them. But that no one is justified by the law in the sight of God is evident, for the just shall live by faith. Yet the law is not of faith, but the man who does them shall live by them. Christ has redeemed us from the curse of the law, having become a curse for us (for it is written, cursed is everyone who hangs on a tree...." (Galatians 3:10-14).

No one could keep the requirements of the law as a means for justification before God and we were all under a curse as a result. But Jesus became a curse for us by His death on the cross so that the blessing of Abraham might come upon us. We can now be justified before God by faith and also receive the Holy Spirit by faith. Therefore, my justification before God is by faith in the finished work of Jesus Christ on the cross. This the very heart of the protestant reformation. Amen

Prayer

Lord, thank You for redeeming me from the curse of the law and by faith am now justified before You. Amen

Bible Reading Plan:
Exodus 31, Luke 15, 1 Timothy 6

DAY 81: TRANSLATED FROM DARKNESS TO GOD'S KINGDOM

"He has delivered us from the power of darkness and translated us into the Kingdom of the Son of His love, in whom we have redemption, through His blood, the forgiveness of sins" (Colossians 1:13-14).

By virtue of Jesus's death on the cross, the ultimate price for our ransom was paid. That guaranteed our translation from the domain of our captor, Satan to the domain of God's dear Son. Being thus redeemed, we are no more under the sway of the wicked one **(1 John 5:19)** and we are now redeemed unto God **(Revelation 5:9)**. Our "ownership" has changed from the devil to God.

Prayer

Lord, thank You for translating me from the kingdom of darkness into the kingdom of light. The devil has lost hold over my life eternally. Amen

Bible Reading Plan:
Exodus 32, Luke 16, 2 Timothy 1

DAY 82 GLORIFY GOD WITH YOUR BODY

 *"For you were bought at a price; therefore, glorify God with your body and your spirit which are God's"* (1 Corinthians 6:20).

This Scripture is in the context of sexual immorality and Paul was telling the believers in Corinth to glorify God with their bodies and spirit. The Lord says, the body and spirit of the believer are now God's. The believer has therefore lost the right to live anyhow and do whatever with his or her body. The believer has therefore lost the right to use his or body to commit sin or sexual immorality in particular. The Bible says, **"Flee sexual immorality. Every sin that a man does is outside the body but he who commits sexual immorality sins against his own body" (1 Corinthians 6:18).** Am I using my body for sin?

Prayer

 Lord, I pray that I will hold my body in holiness and sanctification.

Bible Reading Plan:
Exodus 33, Luke 17, 2 Timothy 2

DAY 83 MY BODY: GOD'S HABITATION

 *"Or do you not know that your body is the temple of the Holy Spirit who is in you, whom you have from God and you are not your own?"* (1 Corinthians 6:19).

Our body is now the temple of the Holy Spirit. We are not only owned by God; He is also the occupant of our body through His Holy Spirit. The Bible says, **"The heaven and the heaven of heavens cannot contain thee" (1 King 8:27 KJV),** but God through his Spirit has found a habitation in us. What a privilege for divinity to dwell in humanity: in our hearts. Sinning with our bodies is an abuse of that privilege. Our body by virtue of redemption has become God's habitation by His Spirit. To use the body as an instrument of sin is to greatly grieve the Holy Spirit. Continuous sin is a statement of renunciation of one's redemption. Is there any known sin? Will you confess and repent? You can do so now before it is too late.

Prayer

 Lord, I pray that I will use my body to glorify You.

Bible Reading Plan:
Exodus 34, Luke 18, 2 Timothy 3

DAY 84 NO MAN'S SLAVE

"You were bought at a price; do not be slaves of men" (1 Corinthians 7:23)

The Lord paid a very great price for our salvation. We are not to allow any man put us under any bondage. Today, there are many who are slaves of so called men of God or prophets. You are not to be enslaved or let anyone dominate your faith dear child of God. The Bible says, **"Not that we have dominion over your faith, but are fellow workers for your joy; for by faith you stand" (2 Corinthians 1:24).** Paul makes it clear that we are all fellow workers and the work of the man of God is for the joy of the believer and that we stand by faith not by any preacher. No man died for you and me on the cross. Paul had to ask the church in Corinth, **"Was Paul crucified for you?" (1 Corinthians 1:13)**. We are therefore not to be enslaved by men. While we serve and stay under leadership in the church we are aware that the Lord is our Chief Shepherd.

Prayer

Lord, I refuse to let any man dominate my faith or be a slave to any man.

Bible Reading Plan:
Exodus 35, Luke 19, Titus 1

DAY 85 NO MAN'S SLAVE II

 *"You were bought at a price; do not be slaves of men"* (1 Corinthians 7:23)

A.W. Pink speaks on the place of men of God and our attitude to men of God:

"No arbitrary control has been committed to any cleric"

"No man is to be heeded in spiritual matters any further than he can produce a plain and decisive "thus says the Lord' as the foundation of his appeal"

"God does not require the minds and consciences of his children to be enslaved by any ecclesiastical dominion"

A.W. Tozer also spells out what our attitude to men of God should be: **"No free believer should sell his freedom to another. No Christian is worthy to be master of other Christians. Christ alone is worthy to be called Master; there is no other"**

Prayer

 Lord, I pray that I will serve leaders and not be enslaved in any form. Deliver any who are spiritually enslaved. Amen

Bible Reading Plan:
Exodus 36, Luke 20, Titus 2

DAY 86 USEFUL BUT HELD BY FEAR

"Saying, go into the village opposite you, where as you enter you will find a colt tied, on which no one has ever sat. Loose and bring him here. And if anyone ask you why are you loosing him? thus you shall say to him, Because the Lord has need of him" (Luke 19:30-31).

The Lord had wanted to use the donkey for his triumphal entry, but the donkey was tied. The Lord ordered his disciples to loosen it before he could use it. There are many in the Body of Christ or in the Church today with a lot of spiritual potential who are tied like this colt and until they are loosed or delivered they won't be of much use to the Lord. For some, fear is holding them captive. Timothy was one of those held back by the spirit of fear. He was ordained first bishop of the church in Ephesus and as a young man, he could have been afraid of the enormity of such a role. And Paul the apostle had to address that spirit of fear in his life; **"For God has not given us a spirit of fear..." (2 Timothy 1:7).**

Prayer

Lord, I rebuke every spirit of fear holding me back from embracing what you have called me to do.

Bible Reading Plan:
Exodus 37, Luke 21, Titus 3

DAY 87 — USEFUL BUT HELD BY SIN AND GUILT

 *"Saying, go into the village opposite you, where as you enter you will find a colt tied, on which no one has ever sat. Loose and bring him here. And if anyone ask you why are you loosing him? thus you shall say to him, Because the Lord has need of him"* (Luke 19:30-31).

There are many who are held down by guilt. You feel you are not worthy enough to serve Him because of your past life. Dear, saint, if the Lord says, he has need of you, the voice of guilt cannot stand on His way. The blood of Jesus is able to purge your conscience from every dead work so that you can serve the living God or be of use to Him. The Bible says, **"How much more shall the blood of Christ, who through the eternal Spirit offered Himself without spot to God, purge your conscience from dead works to serve the living God?" (Hebrews 9:14).**

Prayer

 Lord, thank You for Your blood that purges my conscience and frees me from every guilt to serve the living God. I let go of every guilt concerning my past life. Amen

Bible Reading Plan:
Exodus 38, Luke 22, Hebrews 1

DAY 88 USEFUL BUT HELD BY SENSE OF INADEQUACY

"Saying, go into the village opposite you, where as you enter you will find a colt tied, on which no one has ever sat. Loose and bring him here. And if anyone ask you why are you loosing him? thus you shall say to him, Because the Lord has need of him" (Luke 19:30-31).

Yours may not be sin but you just feel inadequate for the task or that you don't have the resources for it. Dear, saint, you are not going in your own might or resources. Paul says no one goes to war at his own expense. You can do all things through Christ who strengthens you. The Lord who wants to use you will empower you and make available all you need for the task He is needing you for. Step out in faith. Let nothing hold you back. Amen

Prayer.

Lord, I break free from any entanglement. I make myself available for You and Your purpose. Amen

Bible Reading Plan:
Exodus 39, Luke 23, Hebrews 2

DAY 89 AVAILABLE FOR HIS USE

 *"Then He got into one of the boats, which was Simon's and asked him to put out a little from the land. And He sat down and taught the multitude from the boat"* (Luke 5:3).

There were many boats anchored ashore. The boats were used by the fishermen for their trade or business. The Lord had need of one of the boats as a place from which the gospel will be preached. Peter made his boat available. We all have something the Lord can use for the advancement of the gospel. It may be my position, influence, job, business etc. The question is, will I make it available for the designs and purposes of the Lord? When Peter made his boat available the catch he had almost broke his net.

Prayer

 Lord, I make available all I have for Your use and purposes

Bible Reading Plan:
Exodus 40, Luke 24, Hebrews 3

DAY 90 AVAILABLE FOR HIS USE II

 *"The ark of God remained in the house of Obed-Edom the Gittite three months. And the LORD blessed Obed-Edom and all his household"* (2 Samuel 6:11).

It could be your home. Would you make it available for a house fellowship? Obed Edom made his home available for the ark of the covenant. It was risky doing so: Uzziah had died when the oxen carrying the ark stumbled. Even king David was afraid of the Lord that day. But this man took the risk for God and accepted to keep the ark in his house and the Lord blessed him with eight sons (1 Chronicles 26:4-5). He did one thing: made what he had available for God. And God rewarded him greatly.

Prayer

 Lord, like Obed-Edom and many others, I choose to make available all that I have for Your purpose. Amen

Bible Reading Plan:
Leviticus 1, Acts 1, Hebrews 4

DAY 91 LIFE WITHOUT END

 *"I am the resurrection and the life. He who believes in Me though he may die, he shall live and whoever lives and believes in Me shall never die. Do you believe this?"* (John 11: 25-26).

Our God is eternal in nature **(Deuteronomy 33:27, Psalm 90:2):** from everlasting to everlasting, with no beginning and end, it follows therefore that God's life in us is eternal; life that will never end. In Habakkuk 1:12, the Bible says, "**Are you not from everlasting, O Lord my God, my Holy One? We shall not die**". Our God is from everlasting and because we share His life, we too have life everlasting. We have an endless life; "**Who has come, not according to the law of fleshly commandment but according to the power of an endless life" (Hebrews 7:16).** We are appointed for life that never ends. That life begins now and continues in eternity.

Prayer

 Lord, thank You for life that never ends. Lord, I cherish this life in me. Amen

Bible Reading Plan:
Leviticus 2, Acts 2, Hebrews 5

DAY 92: POWER OVER THE PAIN AND FEAR OF DEATH

 *"He Himself shared in the same, that through death He might destroy him who had the power of death, that is, the devil and release those who through fear of death were all their lifetime subject to bondage"* (Hebrews 2:14-15).

We have conquered the power and pain of death and the fear thereof has been broken in our lives. We are not in bondage anymore to the power of death, for the devil, who had power over death has been defeated. Death no longer has dominion over the believer; **"Knowing that Jesus Christ, having been raised from the dead, dies no more. Death no longer has dominion over you" (Romans 6:9).** Also the pain and horror of death has been taken away by the death of Jesus Christ. The Bible says, **"Whom God raised up, having loosed the pains of death, because it was not possible that He should be held by it" (Acts 2:24).**

Prayer

 Dear saint, rejoice in the Lord. The power and pain of death has been broken over your life.

Bible Reading Plan:
Leviticus 3, Acts 3, Hebrews 6

DAY 93: UNDERSTANDING CORPORATE PRAYER

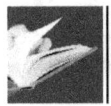 *"These all continued with one accord in prayer..."* (Acts 1:14)

In as much as we do have our private and personal prayer lives, we should also learn to pray with others as there are some results that can only be obtained by corporate prayer. There is power that comes with praying in groups or with another believer. The Early Church understood the power of corporate praying: **"Now Peter and John went up together to the temple at the hour of prayer, the ninth hour" (Acts 3:1).**

The word further says, **"Peter was therefore kept in prison but constant prayer was offered to God for him by the church" (Acts 12:5).** As mighty and great Peter was, the whole church prayed for him before the breakthrough came. Dear saint, pray with others particularly in the local church.

Prayer

 Lord, I pray that I will join other believers in prayer.

Bible Reading Plan:
Leviticus 4, Acts 4, Hebrews 7

DAY 94 CORPORATE WARFARE

 *"And he looked up at the window and said, who is on my side? who? And two or three eunuchs looked out at him. Then he said throw her down. So they threw her down..."* (2 Kings 9:32-33).

There are realms of spiritual warfare that can be waged only at the level of the body of believers. Jehu was anointed to kill Jezebel but he understood that Jezebel was at a realm that needed a two or three scenario. Jezebel was not killed by one person and she was pushed from a height; she was in a certain realm in the spirit. When Jehu arrived where Jezebel was, he first of all looked up at the window (probably saw the realm of Jezebel in the spirit) then, asked twice (knowing that killing Jezebel required corporate warfare), who was with him. The eunuchs were two or three, and the Bible says where two or three are gathered I am in their midst. Esther also mobilized others to join her in the fast. Haman was in a certain realm in the spirit. There are some principalities in cities and in our lives that may only be dethroned by corporate warfare.

Prayer

 Lord, I return to praying and warring with other believers

Bible Reading Plan:
Leviticus 5, Acts 5, Hebrews 8

DAY 95: THE CREATIVE DIMENSION OF THE SPIRIT: KING DAVID

"And the plans for all that he had by the Spirit, of the courts of the house of the LORD, of all the chambers around, of the treasures of the house of the God and of the treasuries for the dedicated things" (1 Chronicles 28:12).

Of all the skills in David's resume presented to Saul when Saul wanted to take him into his service, architectural drawing was not one of them. But in the verse before the passage above, David is giving the plan for the construction of the temple to Solomon his son. But in our text above we learn how David came about the architectural drawings for the temple: he received the plans by the Holy Spirit. Through David's relationship with God, he receives the plans for the construction of the temple. This is the creative and the innovative dimension of the Holy Spirit. Bezalel also operated in this dimension. The Holy Spirit is a Spirit of wisdom and He is at work in all believers to inspire creativity in our jobs, business, studies and work.

Prayer

Lord, I pray that I will begin to experience the wisdom dimension of the Holy Spirit in my life

Bible Reading Plan:
Leviticus 6, Acts 6, Hebrews 9

DAY 96: THE CREATIVE DIMESION OF THE SPIRIT: BEZALEL

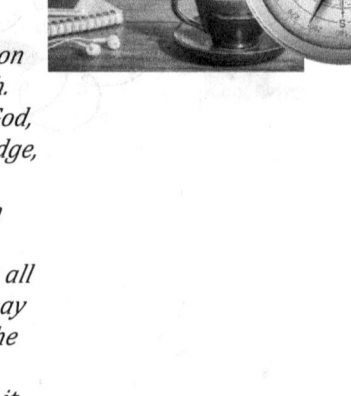

"Then the LORD spoke to Moses, saying; See, I have called by name Bezalel, the son of Uri, the son of Ur, of the tribe of Judah. And I have filled him with the Spirit of God, in wisdom, in understanding, in knowledge, and in all manner of workmanship, to design artistic works, to work in gold, in silver, in bronze, in cutting jewels for setting, in carving wood, and to work in all manner of workmanship......that they may make all that I have commanded you; the tabernacle of meeting, the ark of the testimony and the mercy seat that is on it and all the furniture of the tabernacle" (Exodus 31:1-7).

Bezalel is the first person to be mentioned as filled with the Spirit in the Scriptures: for all kinds of creative work. This is also the work of the Spirit in us. We can thus rely on the Spirit of God for results that are extraordinary and outstanding in our place of work or in all we do.

Prayer

Lord, I enter into the creative dimension by the Holy Spirit who is in me

Bible Reading Plan:
Leviticus 7, Acts 7, Hebrews 10

DAY 97: HEALING IS YOUR INHERITANCE

 *"Who Himself bore our sins in His own body on the tree, that we, having died to sins, might live for righteousness-By whose stripes we are healed"* (1 Peter 2:24)

Healing is the children's bread. Christ bore all our diseases and sicknesses on the cross (**Matthew 8:17).** The Scripture does not say that we shall be healed. The word says we are healed-past tense. It has already happened and the believer has to enter into his or her healing by faith. The apostle John in the opening chapter of his epistle makes a prayer for the believer saying, **"Beloved, I pray that you may prosper in all things and be in health just as your soul prospers" (3 John 2).** Therefore, to be in a state of sickness is not the Lord's wish for you as God's child. By His stripes you were healed-past tense. It is not a promise. It is a spiritual fact and J.C. Ryle says, **Facts are stubborn things".** The Lord has already done that on the cross. Any disease in us is there by our permission. Rise up in faith and enter into your inheritance.

Prayer

 Command every sickness and diseases out of your body in the name of Jesus Christ. Amen

Bible Reading Plan:
Leviticus 8, Acts 8, Hebrews 11

DAY 98 FRUITS OF PRACTICAL RIGHTEOUNESS

 *"For you were once darkness, but now you are light in the Lord. Walk as children of light"* (Ephesians 5:8).

Our actual position is always discovered by the way we act not by the way we talk, says **A. W. Tozer.** Paul tells us that we are now light in the Lord. He doesn't stop there; he further says we should walk in the light. It is common to hear that, I am the righteousness of God in Christ Jesus. This is true. Jesus became sin that we might become the righteousness of God. This is our judicial position. But the story doesn't end there. There is practical righteousness. The Bible says, **"Little children let no one deceive you. He who practices righteousness is righteous, just as He is righteous. He who sins is of the devil, for the devil has sinned from the beginning" (1 John 3:7-8).** May I not settle for judicial righteousness only. May I move to practical righteousness.

Prayer

 Lord, I pray that my life will bear fruits of practical righteousness.

Bible Reading Plan:
Leviticus 9, Acts 9, Hebrews 12

DAY 99: KEYS TO KINGDOM PROSPERITY: WORK THAT HONORS GOD

"And you shall remember the Lord your God for it is He who gives you power to get wealth that He may establish His covenant...." (Deuteronomy 8:18).

God has given us the power to get wealth. We have to engage our hands to unleash the blessing of God. The Bible says, **"And whatever he does prospers"** (Psalm 1:3), "The Lord will command the blessing....in all which you set your hand..." (Deuteronomy 28:8), "He who deals with a slack hand becomes poor but the hand of the diligent makes one rich" (Proverbs 10:4). The Apostle Paul worked and had his tent business while preaching the gospel **(Acts 18:1-4)** and charged or commanded believers in the name of Jesus to work so that they lack nothing; **"That you also aspire to lead a quiet life, mind your own business and work with your own hands, as we commanded you...that you may lack nothing"** (1 Thessalonians. 4:11-12).

Prayer

Lord, I pray for hands that are given to work that honors You

Bible Reading Plan:
Leviticus 10, Acts 10, Hebrews 13

DAY 100 — KEYS TO KINGDOM PROSPERITY: THE WISDOM OF GOD

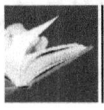 *"O LORD, how manifold are thy works! In wisdom hast thou made them all: the earth is full of thy riches"* (Psalm 104:24 KJV).

God the Father came about all His great works and riches we find on earth through wisdom. What does wisdom here represent? Let's see another passage that talks about the great works of God. The Bible says, **"O Lord, how great are Your works! Your thoughts are very deep" (Psalm 92:5).** Thus through God's thinking and creative ability, he produced the great wealth and works we see today on the face of the earth. We too as His children have access to that wisdom, for Christ became for us the wisdom of God unleashing in us creative abilities and skills necessary to produce that which is relevant in the market place. Joseph and Daniel operated in this realm of prosperity.

Prayer

 Lord, I pray for wisdom to excel and come up with solution to problems that will create value

Bible Reading Plan:
Leviticus 11, Acts 11, James 1

DAY 101: KEYS TO KINGDOM PROSPERITY: SEEK FIRST THE KINGDOM

 *"But seek first the kingdom of God and His righteousness and all these things shall be added unto you"* (Matthew 6:33)

God has ordained that the way to His prosperity is through kingdom focus. The first needs of the believer are kingdom needs. The Israelites did not serve God with gladness of heart and God sent them hunger and all that goes with poverty. The Bible says: **"Because you did not serve the LORD your God with joy and gladness of heart, for the abundance of these things, therefore you will serve your enemies whom the Lord will send against you, in hunger, in thirst, in nakedness and in need of all things..."(Deuteronomy 28:47-48).**

Our desires are linked with degree to which we desire God and his interest; **"Delight yourself in the Lord and He shall give you the desires of your heart" (Psalm 37:4).**

The Scriptures are very clear; our attitude and commitment to God's business and kingdom is a vital key in kingdom prosperity.

Prayer

 Lord, I pray that I will be kingdom focused. Kingdom needs are my first needs. Amen

Bible Reading Plan:
Leviticus 12, Acts 12, James 2

DAY 102: KEYS TO KINGDOM PROSPERITY: ATTITUDE TO GOD'S SERVANTS

"Hear me, O Judah and inhabitants of Jerusalem: Believe in the LORD your God and you shall be established; believe His prophets and you shall prosper" (2 Chronicles 20:20).

God has ordained that some of our blessings will come through men. How we treat them may just be very determinant in that respect. Even our Lord acknowledged that there are rewards from men He has sent. The Bible says, **"He who receives a prophet in the name of a prophet shall receive a prophet's reward. And he who receives a righteous man in the name of a righteous man shall receive a righteous man's reward"** (Matthew 10:41).

God releases His blessings through His servants and our attitude towards those He has sent will determine whether we receive what He has for us. Jesus was despised in His own hometown. He did little there. May we learn to believe in those He has sent.

Prayer

Lord, I pray for the right attitude towards my leaders for You will not bless me through leaders I despise or don't believe in.

Bible Reading Plan:
Leviticus 13, Acts 13, James 3

DAY 103: KEYS TO KINGDOM PROSPERITY: HOLY LIVING

 *"If you return to the Almighty, you will be built up; you will remove iniquity far from your tents. Then you will lay your gold in the dust and the gold of Ophir among the stones of brooks. Yes, the Almighty will be your gold and your precious silver"* (Job 22:23-25).

When man sinned, He fell from abundance in the garden to toiling and sweating for bread. Job was very rich and the greatest man of the people of the East. His story begins with the fact that he was blameless and upright before the Lord **(Job 1:1).** To live in sin is to attract lack, the breaking of the staff of bread as God did to the children of Israel. The Bible says, "**Moreover he said unto me, son of man, behold, I will break the staff of bread in Jerusalem" (Ezekiel 4:16).**

Prayer

 Lord, I pray that I will not live in sin. I embrace the highway of holiness.

Bible Reading Plan:
Leviticus 14, Acts 14, James 4

DAY 104: KEYS TO KINGDOM PROSPERITY: MEDITATING AND OBEYING THE WORD

"But his delight is in the Law of the Lord and in His law he meditates day and night....and whatever he does prospers" (Psalm 1:2-3).

Our delight in the law of the Lord through day and night meditation on His word, is like a tree planted by rivers of water; where it is properly watered for growth and fruit bearing. The word is water. It waters our efforts and makes us flourish in all we do. To neglect the word is to invoke dryness. Joshua's success in taking the promised land was conditioned on his attitude to the word. The Bible says, **"This Book of the law shall not depart from your mouth, but you shall meditate in it day and night that you may observe to do according to all that is written in it. For then you will make your way prosperous and then you will have good success" (Joshua 1:8).**

God promised Joshua good success if he meditated and obeyed all that was written in the word.

Prayer

Lord, I pray for a life lived in meditating and obeying Your word

Bible Reading Plan:
Leviticus 15, Acts 15, James 5

DAY 105: KEYS TO KINGDOM PROSPERITY: HONOURING PARENTS

"Honor your father and your mother, as the LORD your God has commanded you that your days may be long, and that it may be well with you in the land that the LORD your God is giving you"
(Deuteronomy 5:16)

First commandment with a promise attached to it is the command to honor our parents. The apostle Paul re-echoed this commandment in the Book of Ephesians saying, **"Honor your father and mother which is the first commandment with a promise: that it may go well with you and you may live long on the earth" (Ephesians 6:2-3).** The two great things men look for in this life: long life and prosperity is linked to how we honor our parents. Honour relates essentially to giving to our parents. The Lord is against those who instead of giving to their parents they would claim that they have given it to God **(Mark 7:9-13).** Do I give to my parents?

Prayer

Lord, teach me honour. I pray that I will honour my parents to the satisfaction of Your heart

Bible Reading Plan:
Leviticus 16, Acts 16, 1 Peter 1

DAY 106: KEYS TO KINGDOM PROSPERITY: TRUST AND FAITHFULNESS WITH LITTLE

 *"But he who trusts in the Lord will be prospered"* (Proverbs 28:25b)

"And he said to him, well done, good servant; because you were faithful in very little, have authority over ten cities" (Luke 19:17).

Job, a man of immense wealth was a man of unshakeable trust; trust even in the darkest moment of his life; **"Though He slay me, yet I will trust Him...." (Job 13:15).** When all around us is dark, trust in the One who knows what is He doing keeps us going. Trust honors the character of God and He rewards it with abundance.

Also the Lord watches our attitude, when He starts us with little. It determines our promotion. Our faithfulness in little places and beginnings is heaven's gateway to our place of abundance

Prayer

 Lord, I pray that I will trust You even in my darkest moments and I will be faithful in the little beginnings You have started me with.

Bible Reading Plan:
Leviticus 17, Acts 17, 1 Peter 2

DAY 107: KEYS TO KINGDOM PROSPERITY: GIVING AND GRATITUDE OF HEART

"The generous soul shall be made rich and he who waters shall be watered himself" (Proverbs 11:25).

"Let the peoples praise You, O God; Let all the peoples praise You, then the earth shall yield her increase...." (Psalm 67:5-6).

God releases more to the soul that gives. The capacity to give to God and man is the sign of good stewardship. Good stewardship is a requirement for blessing in the kingdom. We are blessed so that we should be a blessing. Those who don't give violate this rule and God cannot trust them with much. God releases increase into a life that shows and exhibits gratitude. Of the ten lepers who were healed only one came to show appreciation and God made him whole. The Lord Jesus multiplied fives loaves and two fishes my showing gratitude to the Father before breaking the bread.

Prayer

Lord, I pray for a heart that gives and shows gratitude to God and men. Amen

Bible Reading Plan:
Leviticus 18, Acts 18, 1 Peter 3

DAY 108: DOUBT NOT YOUR SALVATION

"These things I have written to you who believe in the name of the Son of God, that you may know that you have eternal life and that you may continue to believe in the name of the Son of God" (1 John 5:13).

The way of salvation is clearly laid out in the word of God; **"He who believes the Son has everlasting life and he who does not believe the Son shall not see life but the wrath of God abides on him" (John 3:36).** The word further says, **"He who believes and is baptized will be saved; but he does not believe will be condemned" (Mark 16:16).**

This being so, anyone who has believed as the Bible says is saved irrespective of how they feel. The word says they are saved so far as they have truly repented of their sins and made Jesus their Lord and Saviour. The believer should rest assured that the salvation of God is total and complete. The redemption of God is eternal **(Hebrews 9:12)**. God's forgiveness is not for a few seconds or days or years. It is forever. You are born into God's family and will no longer be born out of it. Don't allow the devil make you doubt your salvation. Amen

Prayer

Lord, thank You for saving me; I renounce every doubt in my heart concerning my salvation

Bible Reading Plan:
Leviticus 19, Acts 19, 1 Peter 4

DAY 109 HE FOREKNEW ME

 *"Before I formed you in the womb I knew you..."* (Jeremiah 1:5)

As a believer you are not a product of some experiment gone wrong or chance. Neither are you a coincidence. God foreknew you and even your salvation was established since the foundation of the world. The Bible says, **"For whom He foreknew, He also predestined to be conformed to the image of His Son, so that He might be first born among many brethren. Moreover, whom He predestined He also called: whom He called, these He also justified; and whom He justified, these He also glorified" (Romans 8:29-30).** Dear child God, Your Father foreknew you even before the very foundations of the world. Your destiny and what you will ever be has been worked out by God. Satan and his demons can do very little. God's purpose for your life shall stand.

Prayer

 Lord, thank You that I am not just an accident that occurred. You foreknew me and predestined me for a glorious life

Bible Reading Plan:
Leviticus 20, Acts 20, 1 Peter 5

DAY 110 HE IS WORKING IN ME

 *"For it is God who works in you both to will and to do according to His good pleasure"* (Philippians 2:13)

God is working in us both to will and to do according to His good pleasure: empowering us by His Spirit to live a life worthy of His holy calling. On our own we can do nothing. Who by his own natural strength and will can meet the standards of God? Moses came with the law but grace and truth came through Jesus Christ. He does not only reveal truth, He also gives us the grace, which is the enabling of God to walk in the truth. All we have to do is to allow the Spirit to work out God's character and holiness in us. Amen

Prayer

 Lord, I pray that I will not hinder Your Spirit's work in me, changing me and conforming me to the image of Christ. Amen

Bible Reading Plan:
Leviticus 21, Acts 21, 2 Peter 1

DAY 111 ASSURED OF SALVATION

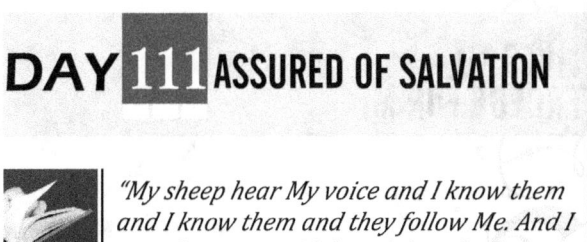
"My sheep hear My voice and I know them and I know them and they follow Me. And I give them eternal life and they shall never perish; neither shall anyone snatch them out My hand. My Father, who has given them to Me is greater than all; and no one is able to snatch them out of My Father's hand" (John 10:27-29).

The Lord Jesus Christ is committed to keeping you; **"All that My father gives Me will come to Me and the one who comes to Me I will by no means cast out" (John 6:37).** Those who have truly come to the Lord Jesus, He says He will not cast them out. You are in the secure arms of Jesus and God the Father **(John 10:27-29).** The believer has double commitment and security from God the Son and the Father. In Colossians the Bible says, **"You are hidden with Christ in God" (Colossians 3:3)**. If you are thus secured in Christ and God, who then can separate you from God? No one dear saint. Hallelujah

Prayer

Lord, thank You for Your commitment to keep me; I am hidden with Christ in God. Amen

Bible Reading Plan:
Leviticus 22, Acts 22, 2 Peter 2

DAY 112 HE LIVES TO INTERCEDE FOR ME

 *"Wherefore He is able to save to them to uttermost that come unto God by Him, seeing He ever liveth to make intercession for them"* (Hebrews 7:25 KJV).

The Lord is making intercession for you dear child of God. Remember when Satan asked for permission to sieve Peter? What did the Lord tell Peter? That I have prayed for you that your faith will not fail. Yes, Peter denied the Lord but because of the intercession of the Lord, he was restored. He is also interceding for you. He is therefore able to save completely. Maybe you live in fear about your salvation or your life in general. Dear saint, Jesus Christ Himself is interceding for you. Fear not; God's purpose for your life will stand. Amen

Prayer

 Lord, I thank You for interceding for me; I live in the assurance that God's designs for me will stand. Amen

Bible Reading Plan:
Leviticus 23, Acts 23, 2 Peter 3

DAY 113 WHAT IF YOU SIN

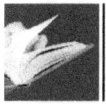 *"If we confess our sins, He is faithful and just to forgive our sins and to cleanse us from all unrighteousness"* (1 John 1:9)

God does not condone sin but He, at the same time pardons sin. Sin need not be suicidal to our spiritual life; where instead of repenting we give up the hope of being able to live a sin-free life and call it quits. Dear saint, don't fall for that trap. Determine you will arise and face your sin and confess it to the Lord and to man where necessary. God has made provision in case you fall. He is a God of second chance. The Blood is our spiritual eraser. Cleaning every sin and spiritual 'mistake' we make.

Prayer

 Lord, I face up to the sin in my life now; I confess it to You. Forgive and cleanse me Lord.

Bible Reading Plan:
Leviticus 24, Acts 24, 1 John 1

DAY 114 STEADFAST AND NOT MOVED AWAY

 *"For we are made partakers of Christ if we hold the beginning of our confidence steadfast unto the end"* (Hebrews 3:14)

Steadfastness is very precious to the Lord. For the Lord to present us blameless in His sight on that day, he expects the believer to continue in the faith and not be moved away. The Bible says, **"In the body of his flesh through death to present you holy and blameless and above reproach in his sight-if indeed you continue in the faith grounded and steadfast and are not moved away from the hope of the gospel which you heard, which was preached to every creature under heaven, of which I Paul, became a minister" (Colossians 1:22-23).** Settle that nothing will make you waver from the hope that is in Christ.

Prayer

 Lord, I pray that I will be steadfast and unmovable in my faith. Amen

Bible Reading Plan:
Leviticus 25, Acts 25, 1 John 2

DAY 115: DILIGENCE FOR SPIRITUAL PROGRESS

"Therefore, brethren, be even more diligent to make your calling and election sure, for if you do these things you will never stumble" (2 Peter 1:10).

Progress in the spiritual life requires effort. The believer has to make every effort or be diligent to add to his or her faith and grow. The Bible says, **"But also for this very reason, giving all diligence, add to your faith virtue, to virtue knowledge, to knowledge self-control, to self-control perseverance, to perseverance godliness, to godliness brotherly kindness and to brotherly kindness love. For if these things are yours and abound, you will be neither barren nor unfruitful in the knowledge of our Lord Jesus Christ" (2 Peter 1:5-8).** The path to a productive spiritual life is constantly adding to our faith. We are either growing or dying spiritually. The question is, am I adding to my faith? Or I am where I use to be 10 years ago? You can arise today and push to new heights in the spiritual life. Amen

Prayer

Lord, I pray that I will work hard to add to my faith and make new heights with You.

Bible Reading Plan:
Leviticus 26, Acts 26, 1 John 3

DAY 116 NO LICENSE FOR SIN

 *"What shall we say then? Shall we continue in sin that grace may abound? Certainly not! How shall we who died to sin live any longer in it"* (Romans 6:1-2)

The grace of God or assurance of salvation is not a license to live in sin. The believer is not to continue in sin. The Bible says, **"For if we sin willfully after we have received the knowledge of the truth, there no longer remains a sacrifice for sins but a certain fearful expectation of judgment, and fiery indignation which will devour the enemies of God.... who has trampled the Son of God underfoot, counted the blood of the covenant by which he was sanctified a common thing insulted the Spirit of grace" (Hebrews 10:26-29).** There is the grace of God that justifies and makes me righteous as though I never sinned **(Titus 3:7)** but there is also the grace that teaches me to deny every form of ungodliness **(Titus 2:11-12).** To continue to live in sin is to abuse the Spirit of grace.

Prayer

 Lord, I pray that I will not abuse Your grace by living in sin deliberately

Bible Reading Plan:
Leviticus 27, Acts 27, 1 John 4

DAY 117 THE CALL TO GOOD WORKS

 *"Thus faith by itself, if it does not have works, is dead"* (James 2:17)

The believer is called to do good works. We are saved and wired for good works. In fact, a genuine salvation experience will flow in good works. In the Book of James, we learn the basic character of lifeless faith: absence of works. While we are not saved by works we are saved to flow in good works. The Bible says, **"We are His workmanship created in Christ Jesus for good works which God prepared beforehand that we should walk in them" (Ephesians 2:10).**

Life outside Christ is not only lived in sin but is also lived outside the purpose and reason God created us. When we return to God through Christ, we are not only saved from sin but we are also restored into the works or purpose God created us. Are you living out those works?

Prayer

 Lord, I commit myself to embrace the works You saved me for in Christ. Amen

Bible Reading Plan:
Numbers 1, Acts 28, 1 John 5

DAY 118 EPISTLE READ BY MEN

 *"You are our epistle written in our hearts, known and read by all men"*
(2 Corinthians 3:2)

The greatest argument for Christianity is a Christian
-C. S. Lewis

Our life speaks the gospel. One believer who lives the gospel is doing more for the kingdom than thousands who just talk. The Bible says our lives are epistles read by men **(2 Corinthians 3:2-3).** One man who lives the life of God and exhibits his character is more valuable to God than a thousand who proclaim His name but whose lives run contrary to the Scriptures. The believer's life matters in the preaching of the Gospel. Light travels faster than sound. Our life speaks more than what we say. In fact, the real and the greatest gospel is the gospel of our lives.

Prayer

 Lord, I pray that men will read Christ and the gospel when they see me.

Bible Reading Plan:
Numbers 2 and 3, 2 John

DAY 119 FIRST THINGS FIRST

 *"Then He appointed twelve that they might be with Him and that He might send them to go and preach"* (Mark 3:14).

In the calling of the twelve, their being with Jesus was primary to their going to preach in His Name. What and who we are is more important than what we say. A man's message is only as strong as his life. The sons of Sceva in Acts 19 learnt their lesson; they wanted to cast an evil spirit using the name of Jesus because they had heard Paul use the name. The result was beatings with the question, Jesus I know, Paul I know, who are you? **(Acts 19:13-16).** The question is, are there questionable areas in my life? Do I have practices in my life that contradict the gospel?

Prayer

 Lord, I pray for a life that pleases You and exhibits the life of Christ. I refuse to be gospel in lips only.

Bible Reading Plan:
Numbers 4 and 5, 3 John

DAY 120: ROUTINES AND SPIRITUAL VISITATION

 *"And as His custom was He went into the synagogue on the Sabbath day and stood up to read"* (Luke 4:16).

The Lord had a custom; a routine. He went to the synagogue every Sabbath to stand up to read. Great men have simple but consistent habits. Greatness is the accumulation of consistent little. The spectacular is born from the regular. The early disciples had a great visitation: on the day of Pentecost. They had to sustain that visitation. They had fixed times to pray. The Bible says, "**Now Peter and John went up together to the temple <u>at the hour of prayer, the ninth hour</u>" (Acts 3:1).** These two, are the leaders of that outpouring; they had a fixed time of prayer. They honoured their time of prayer. They birthed as well as sustained a visitation. May we do same.

Prayer

 Lord, for the discipline to maintain a routine that can trigger and sustain a visitation

Bible Reading Plan:
Numbers 6 and 7, Philemon

DAY 121: ROUTINES AND SPIRITUAL VISITATION II

"And as His custom was He went into the synagogue on the Sabbath day and stood up to read" (Luke 4:16).

The life of Zacharias, the father of John the Baptist was also a life given to fixed spiritual routine; he could trigger a spiritual visitation. The Bible says, **"So it was while he was serving as a priest before God in the order of his division, <u>according to the custom of the priesthood</u>, his lot fell to burn incense when he went into the temple of the Lord. And the whole multitude of the <u>people was praying outside at the hour of incense.</u> Then an angel of the Lord appeared..." (Luke 1:8-11).** The hour of incense, which is the hour of prayer was honored. There was angelic visitation.

Prayer

Lord, I pray that I will be spiritually consistent. I denounce an impulsive spiritual experience

Bible Reading Plan:
Numbers 8 and 9, Revelation 1

DAY 122 ROUTINES AND SPIRITUAL FIRE

 *"And the fire on the altar shall be kept burning on it; it shall not be put out. And the priest shall burn wood on it every morning...."* (Leviticus 6:12).

Spiritual fire is a product of routine. Priesthood is a call to routine. Every morning the priest had to put firewood. We are priests and kings. We have to burn wood every morning. The impulsive cannot birth or sustain a revival. The Moravians had a prayer chain that lasted for 100 years. They shook their time. John Wesley was a product of that movement.

Prayer

 Lord, I pray for Your forgiveness: living an impulsive spiritual life and expecting great visitation. Oh let me return to life changing spiritual routines. Amen

Bible Reading Plan:
Numbers 10 and 11, Revelation 2

DAY 123 LAUNCH INTO THE DEEP

"Those who go down to the sea in ships, who do business on great waters, they see the works of the LORD and His wonders in the deep" (Psalm 107:23-24).

The Lord had asked Peter and his fellow fishermen to launch into the deep. They had fished the whole night with no catch. Peter voiced the hesitation of the group of fishermen initially but later said, nevertheless, at Your word I will let down the net. The result was a catch that was so great that their net was breaking and they had to signal for other partners. The wonders of the Lord are in the deep. Only those who are willing to dare to do business with God on great waters will see and experience His works. As long as we continue to play safe, we lose out on the opportunity to see His wonders. Pastor Nick says **"S.A.F.E is Shallow Attempts For Eternity"**. "Deep calls deep", the Psalmist said. Until we leave the shores of our safe and comfort zones and begin to launch into the deep, all we will get is the fringes of His ways.

Prayer

Lord, I renounce shallow attempts. I launch into the deep

Bible Reading Plan:
Numbers 12 and 13, Revelation 3

DAY 124 — GREAT GOD, GREAT PLANS

 *"...I am doing a great work..."* (Nehemiah 6:3)

God wants to be associated with that which fits His greatness and glory. How shall we ever experience the greatness of God if we don't attempt the great? We are yet to really make a demand on the greatness of God. We dishonor Him by little and small requests and attempts. Men greatly used of God understood this. D. L Moody said, **"If God is your partner, then make your plans BIG"**. William Carey, the pioneer missionary to India said, **"Expect great things from God and Attempt great things for God"**. Professor Zacharias T. Fomum had as goal to make one billion disciples for Christ. Their thinking matched the size of their God. May we do same.

Prayer

 Lord, I pray for deep and great attempts for You. Lord, let me launch into the deep. I want to experience Your greatness and wonders. Amen

Bible Reading Plan:
Numbers 14 and 15, Revelation 4

DAY 125 SPIRITUAL NOBILITY

 *"These were more noble than those in Thessalonica, in that they received the word with all readiness of mind and searched the Scriptures daily whether those things were so"* (Acts 17:11).

Paul was an apostle called by the Lord Jesus Christ in a very distinctive encounter. His apostleship was confirmed by the pillars of the early church. But when he preached, the Berean Jews did not abdicate their own spiritual responsibility of searching the Scriptures for themselves. Their nobility stems from the fact that they did not delegate and surrender their spiritual thinking to an individual. Disaster looms when we hire another to think for us spiritually. **"Over reliance on spiritual authority is evidence of spiritual decline"**, says Emerson.

Prayer

 Lord, I pray that I will search the Scriptures and labour to know You personally.

Bible Reading Plan:
Numbers 16 and 17, Revelation 5

DAY 126 SPIRITUAL NOBILITY II

"These were more noble than those in Thessalonica, in that they received the word with all readiness of mind and searched the Scriptures daily whether those things were so" (Acts 17:11).

In the book, **Warnings to the Churches** by J.C. Ryle, an interesting quote deserve our attention:

"Most men dislike the trouble of thinking for themselves. They like following a leader".

While the minds of the Bereans were ready to receive the word, they also knew that they had to check the word for themselves in order not to be deceived or led astray. Watchmen Nee says, **"If all we believe or know is what another man says, then we are not in the New Testament".** We have to return to the mantra of the Protestant Reformation: **Sola Scriptura**, meaning Scriptures Only, as the final authority. Men however wonderful or great they may be now can always go astray. The history of the church and the Bible reveals so. The safe anchor is the word of God. As we move into the last lap of human history, deception will increase. Only those grounded in the word will survive.

Prayer

Lord, I will not surrender my spiritual responsibility to another. Amen

Bible Reading Plan:
Numbers 18 and 19, Revelation 6

DAY 127: MIGHTY MEN IN HIDING: POOR SELF PERCEPTION

"My clan is the weakest in Manasseh and am the least in my father's house" (Judges 6:15)

Gideon watched the Midianites plunder the produce of the Israelites. Gideon's initial approach was to hide the produce from the Midianites. Gideon saw himself poorly. God saw a mighty warrior; he saw himself as the least person in his household. And as result his approach was protective instead of offensive. The Bible says, "…**While his son Gideon threshed wheat in the winepress in order to hide it from the Midianites (Judges 6:11).** Is God calling you to face that challenge and you think you are not able? Are you rehearsing your weakness or the strength of the Lord in you? Will you renounce poor spiritual self-perception and embrace your calling to fight and win that battle for the Lord?

Prayer

Lord, I refuse to look at myself according to the flesh. I look at Your strength in me. Amen

Bible Reading Plan:
Numbers 20 and 21, Revelation 7

DAY 128: MIGHTY MEN UNLEASHED: GOING IN THE STRENGTH OF THE LORD

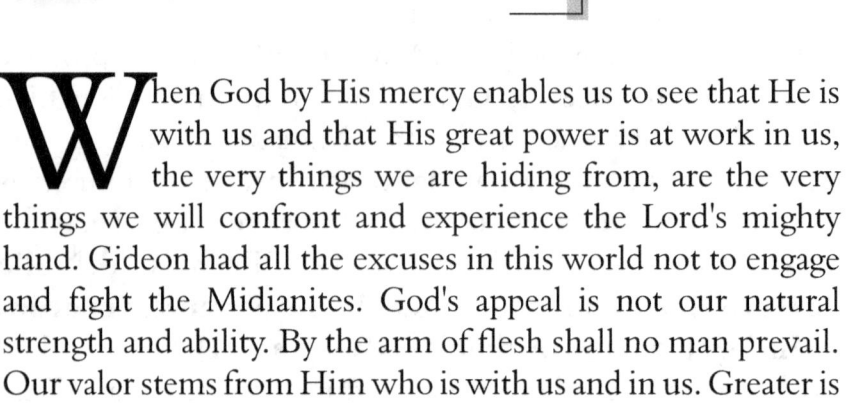

 *"Surely I will be with you and you shall defeat the Midianites as one man"* (Judges 6:16)

When God by His mercy enables us to see that He is with us and that His great power is at work in us, the very things we are hiding from, are the very things we will confront and experience the Lord's mighty hand. Gideon had all the excuses in this world not to engage and fight the Midianites. God's appeal is not our natural strength and ability. By the arm of flesh shall no man prevail. Our valor stems from Him who is with us and in us. Greater is He that is in us than he that is in the world.

Dear saint, great is the ability of God in you. Our power and might is in Christ who is in us, the hope of glory. We can do all things through Christ who strengthens us. Don't hide anymore. Step out and do that thing you have been afraid of all this while.

Prayer

 Lord, in You I can do all things. I refuse to focus on my own weaknesses and inabilities. I look up to You; my strength is in You. I refuse to hide. I go out in Your strength. Amen

Bible Reading Plan:
Numbers 22 and 23, Revelation 8

DAY 129: GOD'S PROCESS OF GROWTH

 *"Most assuredly, I say to you unless a grain of wheat falls into the ground and dies, it remains alone; but if it dies, it produces much grain"* (John 12:24).

Joseph had a dream and according to his dream, he will be in a position where all his family will come and bow down to him. But Joseph kept going down and down. From being thrown into a pit by his brothers, then being sold into slavery in Egypt, accused wrongfully by Potiphar's wife, imprisonment and so on. When we have a dream, God usually subjects that dream to a dark night: the dream will look like its dying. Our temptation will be to doubt our dream and its realization. Saint Athanasius says, **"God writes straight but with crooked lines".** Therefore, do not doubt in the dark what you were convinced of in the light.

Prayer

 Lord, I refuse to doubt when all seems to fall to the ground and die. It is Your growth process

Bible Reading Plan:
Numbers 24 and 25, Revelation 9

DAY 130: PROCESS OF EXPLOSION: SPIRITUAL COMMUNITIES

"Most assuredly, I say to you unless a grain of wheat falls into the ground and dies, it remains alone; but if it dies, it produces much grain" (John 12:24).

This process of falling and death also happens to spiritual communities. These words from Oswald Chambers, capture this truth: **"The work in a community to begin with may be a wondrous delight, then it seems to die out and if you don't know the teaching of the Lord, you will say it is dead; IT IS NOT, but by and by it will bring forth fruit which will alter the whole landscape".**

Dear leader of God's people, when it's like all is about to die please do not lose heart. Remember that before God multiplies, he makes a falling to the ground and allows the seed to die.

Prayer

Lord, I submit to Your process of growth and multiplication; falling to the ground and dying. Amen

Bible Reading Plan:
Numbers 26 and 27, Revelation 10

DAY 131 RELENTLESS

 *"Exhausted but still in pursuit"* (Judges 8:4c)

Gideon had pursued Zeba and Zalmuna, the two kings of the Midianites and was exhausted yet kept the pursuit. This is relentlessness. Some great victories depend on this character attribute. The capacity to press on even against the odds until the finishing line, is the attribute that separates losers from winners. Finishing is always better than starting. Many can start but to press through the challenges, weariness and the exhaustion is the mark of winners. God's purposes and their accomplishment depend largely on those who will not look back in the face of the odds. God detests looking back. Those who relent are not fit for the kingdom. God has entrusted His work in your hands; are you keeping the pursuit or looking back? Will you follow through with that project or course of study? Or drop out along the way? It's in your hands to answer.

Prayer

 Lord, I pray that I will not stop or drop out on the way from that which You have called me.

Bible Reading Plan:
Numbers 28 and 29, Revelation 11

DAY 132: DO NOT GROW WEARY: THE STRENGTH TO KEEP THE PURSUIT

"And let us not grow weary while doing good, for in due season, we reap a harvest if we do not lose heart" (Galatians 6:9).

The goal of weariness is to get us to give up the pursuit. God has given us the key to fight weariness and renew our strength so that we do not relent in our pursuit of that which God has called us to do. The Bible says, **"Even the youths shall faint and be weary and the young men shall utterly fall, but those who wait on the LORD shall renew their strength; they shall mount up with wings like eagles, they shall run and not be weary and they shall walk and not faint" (Isaiah 40:30-31).**

The key is waiting on the Lord. Staying in His presence for infusion of new strength in the inner man by the Holy Spirit so that we do not grow weary and can walk without fainting.

Prayer

Lord, I pray that I will learn to wait on You

Bible Reading Plan:
Numbers 30 and 31, Revelation 12

DAY 133 THE PLACE OF REST AND SOLITUDE

 *"And He said to them, come aside by yourselves to a deserted place and rest a while. For there were many coming and going and they did not even have time to eat"* (Mark 6:31).

Most of us are running on empty and we are now burning out. We keep too busy and we are not refreshed in our bodies. The Lord Jesus understood the need for seclusion and solitude, even away from ministering to people. The Lord who gave six days of work and one full day of rest understands our need for rest. Dear minister, CEO, lecturer etc., is the Lord calling you to take time off to rest and refresh yourself? Will you heed the warning now before it takes its toll on your body and health? If the King of kings could move away from ministry and go to a deserted place for rest and food, how much more of you?

Prayer

 Lord, I recognize the need to take time away, to rest and be refreshed.

Bible Reading Plan:
Numbers 32 and 33, Revelation 13

DAY 134 REAL TIME STRENGTH

"He breathed on them and said to them, Receive the Holy Spirit" (John 20:22)

The Holy Spirit is ever with us and in us. He is there as your Standby, to give you strength in real time. Remember Elijah who outran the chariot of Ahab in the wake of sound of abundant rain? The Bible says, **"The hand of the LORD came upon Elijah and he girded up his loins and ran ahead of Ahab to the entrance of Jezreel" (1 Kings 18:46).** The Holy Spirit is not some distant entity that we have to invoke all day. He is in us and with us to renew our strength in real time; enabling you to keep going without fainting. Amen

Prayer

Holy Spirit breathe on me with strength and life anew. Amen

Bible Reading Plan:
Numbers 34 and 35, Revelation 14

DAY 135 — ORDER: THE WAY OF DOING ALL THINGS

"Let all things be done decently and in order" (1 Corinthians 14:40).

God loves order and God is orderly. Anything done haphazardly in the name of the leading of the Holy Spirit runs contrary to Scripture and the ways of God as seen in Scripture. In the Colossian church, Paul rejoiced not only concerning their zeal but also their orderliness. In fact, he mentions their good order before their steadfastness. The Bible says, **"For though I am absent in the flesh, am with you in the spirit, rejoicing to see your good order and steadfastness of your faith in Christ" (Colossians 2:5).**

The Church should be orderly and run orderly. Paul sent Titus to Crete for one reason: set things in order. The Bible says, **"For this reason I left you in Crete, that you should set in order the things that are lacking......"(Titus 1:5).**

Prayer

Lord, I pray that I will do all You commit into my hands with order for You love order

Bible Reading Plan:
Numbers 36 and Deuteronomy 1, Revelation 15

DAY 136 — ORDER: THE WAY OF MINISTERING THE WORD

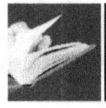 *"And he set bread in order upon it before the LORD, as the LORD had commanded Moses"* (Exodus 40:23).

Luke's account of the gospel of Jesus was an orderly account. **"It seemed good to me also, having had perfect understanding of all things from the very first, to write to you an orderly account...."** (Luke 1:3).

The light of God's word has to be set in order. The Bible says, **"The pure lampstands with its lamps the lamps set in order (Exodus 39:37).** The word is a lamp **(Psalm 119:105).**

The word has to be set in order and rightly divided so that it is understood and makes sense to the believer. There are many believers who are muddled up and in spiritual obscurity today because the word is not rightly set forth before them. When the Lord preached, He was orderly; He started from Moses then to all the prophets **(Luke 24:27).** May we learn order.

Prayer

 Lord, let me be orderly as I minister Your word

Bible Reading Plan:
Deuteronomy 2 and 3, Revelation 16

DAY 137 THE NEED TO UNDERSTAND

"And He opened their understanding that they might understand the Scriptures" (Luke 24:45)

The Bible clearly shows that understanding is the basis for all spiritual turnarounds. What people don't understand they cannot respond to and thus cannot change; **"He has blinded their eyes and hardened their heart, lest they should see with their eyes and understand with their heart, lest they should turn so that I should heal them" (John 12:40).**

We also enter into our riches in Christ through understanding. The Bible says, **"My purpose is that they may be encouraged in heart and united in love so that they may have the full riches of complete understanding" (Colossians 2:2 NIV).** The level of understanding determines the level of riches of the Church. No understanding no riches, partial understanding partial riches and full understanding, full riches.

Prayer

Lord, I pray for full understanding so that I will experience full riches in Christ

Bible Reading Plan:
Deuteronomy 4 and 5, Revelation 17

DAY 138: THE NEED TO UNDERSTAND II

"And He opened their understanding that they might understand the Scriptures" (Luke 24:45)

The Spiritual warfare around the ministry of word is at the level of understanding. Where the word is not understood, it is lost. Ministry without understanding is a waste; **"When anyone hears the word of the Kingdom and does not understand it then the wicked one comes and snatches away what is sown in his heart. This is he who received the word by the wayside"** (Matthew 13:19).

Fruit bearing begins with hearing the word and understanding it. The Bible says, **"But he who received seed on the good ground is he who hears the word and understands it, who indeed bears fruit and produces: some a hundredfold, some sixty and some thirty"** (Matthew 13:23).

Prayer

Lord, I pray that I will always labour to understand Your word so that I can bear fruit.

Bible Reading Plan:
Deuteronomy 6 and 7, Revelation 18

DAY 139 A PRAYER FOR UNDERSTANDING: FOR THE EPHESIAN CHURCH

"That the eyes of your understanding being enlightened; that you may know what is the hope of His calling and what riches of the glory of his inheritance in the saints, and what is the exceeding greatness of His power to us ward who believe..."
(Ephesians 1:18-19).

Paul prayed for the Ephesians that their understanding be enlightened so that they know: the hope of Christ's calling, their riches in glory in Christ and God's power in those who believe. This prayer is also for us today.

Kenneth Hagin said he prayed this prayer for years and he entered another realm in his ministry. May this be our prayer too; for the eyes of my understanding to be enlightened, so that I will know the hope of His calling and the riches of His glorious inheritance in the saints and the exceeding greatness of His power that is in me.

Prayer

Lord, enlighten my understanding

Bible Reading Plan:
Deuteronomy 8 and 9, Revelation 19

DAY 140  NEW HEIGHTS, GREAT FIGHTS

 *"For a great and effective door has opened to me and there are many adversaries"* (1 Corinthians 16:9).

Satan is strategic. Where the stakes are high, there he draws the resistance and opposition line for the child of God. It is important that we understand this so that we don't go to sleep when we are about to enter into a major phase or breakthrough in our lives. This did not only happen to Paul. David had a similar experience. The Bible says, **"Now when the Philistines heard that they had anointed David king over Israel, all the Philistines went to search for David. And David heard and went down to the stronghold" (2 Samuel 5:17).**

The Philistines only came after David, when they heard he had been anointed king. David reacted by going to the stronghold. May we be in a warfare mood in the wake of a major win.

Prayer

 Lord, for spiritual vigilance when am about to or just scored a major victory.

Bible Reading Plan:
Deuteronomy 10 and 11, Revelation 20

DAY 141 NEW HEIGHTS, GREAT FIGHTS II

"For a great and effective door has opened to me and there are many adversaries" (1 Corinthians 16:9).

The Lord Jesus had just been baptized into water and the Holy Spirit and was returning from the Jordan; he was tempted by the devil for forty days and forty nights. The Bible says, **"Then Jesus being filled with the Holy Spirit, returned from the Jordan and was led into the wilderness being tempted for forty days by the devil" (Luke 4:1-2).** After a great spiritual experience, a great period of temptation from the devil followed. The Lord followed his new experience of baptism into water and the Holy Spirit with a forty days fast. Moments of new heights should be our most vigilant moments: the attacks of the devil are ramped up at such moments. Dear saint, when you launch that new business or get that new job or just got married or God opened a door for ministry don't go to sleep. It is time to watch and pray.

Prayer

Lord, I pray that I will be vigilant at the point of a new height and opening in my life. Amen

Bible Reading Plan:
Deuteronomy 12 and 13, Revelation 21

DAY 142 FULFILLED EXPECTATIONS

"Hope deferred makes the heart sick but when the desire comes, it is a tree of life." (Proverbs 13:12).

A lot bitterness is the injury of failure. Unfulfilled expectations injure people, stifles their joy and sickens the heart. Progress or fulfilled expectations is crucial in the spiritual life. The Lord wants us to live a fulfilled and a joyful life;" **... Ask and you will receive and your joy may be full" (John 16:24).** There is need for tangible milestones in a life, without which there is great vulnerability. Let your hopes and expectations become subjects of intense prayer. The Bible says, **"May He grant you according to your heart's desire and fulfill all your purpose" (Psalm 20:4).** Prayer is God's way to avoid deferred hopes and sickness of heart. As we pray, God grants and fulfills our heart's desire. Amen

Prayer

Lord, I pray that my heart' desires will be subjects of prayer so that my joy will be full.

Bible Reading Plan:
Deuteronomy 14 and 15, Revelation 22

DAY 143 BEWARE OF ENVY

"For he knew that because of envy they had Him delivered" (Matthew 27:18).

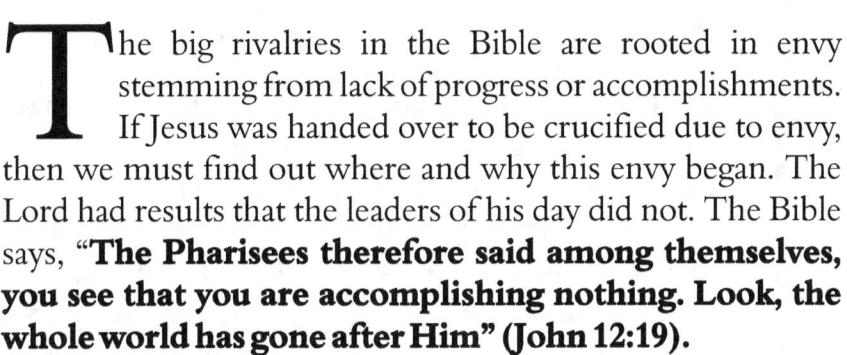

The big rivalries in the Bible are rooted in envy stemming from lack of progress or accomplishments. If Jesus was handed over to be crucified due to envy, then we must find out where and why this envy began. The Lord had results that the leaders of his day did not. The Bible says, **"The Pharisees therefore said among themselves, you see that you are accomplishing nothing. Look, the whole world has gone after Him" (John 12:19).**

Jesus was drawing the crowds more than them. Envy set in and they handed him over. There is a great man of God who worked hard to have big church and when he was asked why he worked so hard, his reply was that he did not want to be envious of those who had larger churches. His answer may look carnal but this man of God must have understood the human heart.

Prayer

Lord, I war against every form of laziness and barrenness in my life and ministry in the name of Jesus. Amen

Bible Reading Plan:
Deuteronomy 16 and 17, Psalm 1

DAY 144 STEADFAST IN CHANGING TIMES

 *"For I am the LORD, I do not change"* (Malachi 3:6)

"And shall intend to change times and law" (Daniel 7:25c)

The LORD does not change but the Anti-Christ as we see in the book of Daniel will intend to change times and laws. It is already happening today and even many in the Body of Christ are using the Bible to rationalize these changes that are coming to the world which are just signs of the emergence of the Anti-Christ. The world may change but the Lord and his word will never change. God will not adjust to the indulgencies of man, it is man that has to change and adopt the ways of God. This is the time to commit oneself to hold on to the standards of God as shown in the Bible and be ready to die for those convictions.

Prayer

 Lord, for the grace to be steadfast in these changing times

Bible Reading Plan:
Deuteronomy 18 and 19, Psalm 2

DAY 145: FOR SUCH A TIME AS THIS

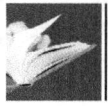 *"Who knows whether you have come in the kingdom for such a time as this?"* (Esther 4:14)

Once we become God's children and become part of God's Kingdom, there is no such thing as coincidence. We are in a particular town or city or local church for a particular reason. God orchestrates the placement of men in places. The Bible says, **"And he has made from one blood every nation of men to dwell on all the face of the earth, and has determined their pre-appointed times and boundaries of their habitations so that they should seek the Lord..." (Acts 17:26-27).**

You are called to be involved and serve in the church with the gifts and talents you have. It may be the ability to play a musical instrument or sing, submit that ability to God and allow Him use it for the edification and the building up of the body. You are in that local church for such a time as this. Make yourself available and useful.

Prayer

 Lord, I refuse to bury my talent or gift or ministry. I decide to use it for Your glory. Amen.

Bible Reading Plan:
Deuteronomy 20 and 21, Psalm 3

DAY 146: FOR SUCH A TIME AS THIS II

 *"Who knows whether you have come in the kingdom for such a time as this?"* (Esther 4:14).

You may be a politician or holding public office or CEO or any job whatsoever; God has placed you there for a purpose. The Lord can use what we do in the secular sphere to advance His purposes. Daniel served before secular kings and God used him greatly. Nehemiah was cup-bearer to the king and God used that position to make a way for Jerusalem and its walls to be rebuilt. William Wilberforce is the perfect example of a Christian who understood his place in politics as orchestrated by God. He fought slave trade and slavery in the British parliament till he died. In fact, he died a few days after it was abolished. He had accomplished his goal.

Prayer

 Lord, I pray that I will use my place in society to advance Your cause

Bible Reading Plan:
Deuteronomy 22 and 23, Psalm 4

DAY 147 RESILIENCE

 *"For a righteous man may fall seven times and rise again..."* (Proverbs 24:16)

There is none of us who is immune to fall or fail. In the spiritual life it is possible to fall or fail. The question is whether we have the comeback ability or resilience when we fail. Those who made it till the end in their spiritual experience were not those who did not necessarily fail. They may have failed but they did not allow that failure to define them.

Peter denied his Lord but sought the restoration of God and later became the man who spoke on the day of Pentecost and 3000 people were saved. Or you have failed that exam or you have had business failure so many times and you think this is the time to stop and avoid further embarrassment. Don't dear saint, always give yourself one more attempt and you will be surprised how things will turn around for the better. Maybe you have had several failed relationships and you want to give up on the idea of marriage. Pick yourself up and try again.

Prayer

 Lord, grant me the capacity to bounce back after failure.

Bible Reading Plan:
Deuteronomy 24 and 25, Psalm 5

DAY 148: LIVING IN EXPECTATION

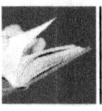 *"According to my earnest expectation and hope that in nothing shall be ashamed"* (Philippians 1:20).

Expectation is the spoon of faith
-A. W. Tozer

God comes to us in response to our expectation. Expectation is faith in earnest; it is proof that we believe what we asked God for and are therefore in expectation of it. True prayer should be accompanied by expectation. The Bible says, **"In the morning, LORD, you hear my voice; in the morning I lay my requests before you and wait expectantly" (Psalm 5:3 NIV).** The Psalmist laid his requests before God and waited expectantly.

Dear child of God, are you in expectation of the answer to the prayers you have made to God? Expectation is the mood to accept what God is about to send. It is the spiritual container to receive what God is sending. That is what Dr. Tozer means by it is the spoon of faith. It is our manifestation of faith and readiness to receive.

Prayer

 May expectation be borne anew in my heart in the name of Jesus Christ.

Bible Reading Plan:
Deuteronomy 26 and 27, Psalm 6

DAY 149 SPIRITUAL PILLARHOOD

 *"He who overcomes, I will make him a pillar in the temple of My God and he shall go out no more"* (Revelation 3:12).

In the face of any kind of tribulation; our spiritual pillar hood is at stake. Our pillar hood has to do with how dependable and stable we become such that God can entrust us with his burdens: whether we have developed shoulders to support the burdens of God. Whether we become a support or a weight, depends on whether we are overcoming what life brings at us. Those who are destabilized by tribulation cannot be pillars in the house of God. They are weights.; they still have to be carried. The overcomer has internal spiritual equilibrium to stand in the face of tribulation, he has therefore graduated to become a pillar. Those who are still tossed by every wind either of doctrine or tribulation, are referred to as children. The Bible says, **"That we should no longer be children tossed to and fro and carried about by every wind of doctrine…." (Ephesians 4:14).** God cannot rely or build on children.

Prayer

 Lord, I pray that I will become a pillar, dependable and stable in Your house

Bible Reading Plan:
Deuteronomy 28 and 29, Psalm 7

DAY 150 HEART ALIVE

"And you who seek God, your hearts shall live" (Psalm 69:32)

Our hearts were made alive when we were saved. But it has to be kept alive by keeping in touch with God; seeking Him daily. Degenerate, reprobate and apostate conditions are late stage spiritual symptoms of failure to keep the heart alive through seeking God. Oswald Chambers has some words in this regard; **"It is impossible for a saint; no matter his experience to keep right with God if he does not take the trouble to spend time with God. In order to keep the mind and heart awake to God's high ideals, you have to keep coming back again and again to the primal source. If you do not, you will be crushed into degeneracy".** You have to keep alive spiritually by seeking God.

Prayer

Lord, I pray that I will always seek You in order to keep the heart alive.

Bible Reading Plan:
Deuteronomy 30 and 31, Psalm 8

DAY 151 HISTORY: A SERVANT OF GOD

 *"This was the Anah who found water in the wilderness as he pastured the donkeys of his father Zibeon"* (Genesis 36:24).

For the Scripture to say, "This was the Anah who found water...", gives the idea that there would have been many Anahs. He distinguished himself among the Anahs of his day and his name received an extra flesh of words in the genealogies. Every life will attract a commentary depending on how it is lived. The bigger the impact of a life the greater the commentary on the life. History has been assigned by God to either preserve or erase memory of men based on how they lived. The Bible says, **"The memory of the righteous is blessed" (Proverbs 10:7).**

Of the woman who came with an expensive perfume to anoint the body of Jesus for burial, the Lord said, **"Assuredly, I say to you, wherever this gospel is preached throughout the whole world, what this woman did will also be spoken of as a memorial to her" (Mark 14:9).**

Prayer

 Lord, I pray that my life will be a memorial; for the impact made in the Kingdom.

Bible Reading Plan:
Deuteronomy 32 and 33, Psalm 9

DAY 152 HISTORY: A SERVANT OF GOD II

 *"This was the Anah who found water in the wilderness as he pastured the donkeys of his father Zibeon"* (Genesis 36:24).

There are men in our day whose lives made impact. The name of a man called John Fletcher comes to mind. John Fletcher had been proposed two parishes to go and serve. One parish had a higher salary and had huge membership and he was even told that he would not have much work in that parish. There was another parish in Madeley with little money and a lot of work to be done there. He chose Madeley instead. He said God forbid that he goes where there is no work and much money. John Fletcher made great spiritual impact in Madeley and today, when he is mentioned, his name is combined with the name of the city; Fletcher of Madeley. We all can live that mark our cities and nations.

Prayer

 Lord, for a life that will mark my city, nation and generation.

Bible Reading Plan:
Deuteronomy 34 and Joshua 1, Psalm 10

DAY 153 — HISTORY: A SERVANT OF GOD III

 *"This was the Anah who found water in the wilderness as he pastured the donkeys of his father Zibeon"* (Genesis 36:24).

What of a Russian girl, Natasha? She proved by her life that God's life in us cannot be destroyed by extreme persecution. She ran towards persecution instead of running away from persecution. This lady will be beaten in one prayer meeting and she will follow the persecutors to the next prayer meeting to the beating again and so on. She did not run. Her persecutors were touched and astounded by this. They concluded that for a person to be beaten for the faith this way then there must be something. One of the KGB agents was led to the Lord as a result. His name is Segei Kourdakov. He later wrote a book titled, Forgive Me, Natasha telling his story: how he came to know Christ and of course the triumphant life of Natasha. Today Natasha's life is immortalized. She stood for her God and her story shines bright for all to read and be inspired.

Prayer

 Lord, I pray that my life will also inspire others.

Bible Reading Plan:
Joshua 2 and 3, Psalm 11

DAY 154 A VERY PRESENT HELP

 *"God is our refuge and strength, a very present help in trouble. Therefore, we will not fear though the earth be removed and though the mountains be carried into the midst of the sea"* (Psalm 46:1-2).

The Lord is not somewhere else before trouble hits us and we have to call him to come. No. He is a **very present help** in the trouble. He is with us all along. Before the trouble happens He is with us and He is with us in the midst of the trouble and will abide with us and in us forever.

The Bible says, **"When you pass through waters, I will be with you; and through the rivers, they shall not overflow thee: when you walk through the fire, you shall not be burned; nor shall the flame scorch you"** (Isaiah 43:2). The Lord is with us when we pass through all these different types of troubles. That is why we are guaranteed to go through them victoriously. Our God is ever present; therefore, we will not fear. He is with you in that trouble to help you.

Prayer

 Lord, thank You for been my ever present help in time of trouble. I will not fear

Bible Reading Plan:
Joshua 4 and 5, Psalm 12

DAY 155: TILL MY CHANGE COMES

 *"I will wait till my change comes"* (Job 14:14)

This is the kind of faith that God will honor and not by-pass. In the heart of the darkest moments of Job's life, he utters these words, that show his determination not to give up on God. The story of Job inspires us today because at some point he made up his mind not to quit, but wait till his change comes. One thing God requires of you too is to be determined like Job: to wait till your change comes. Let these words of Harriet Beecher Stowe encourage you as you stay on till your change comes: **"When you get into a tight place and everything goes against you, till it seems as if you could not hold on a minute longer, never give up then, for that is just the place and time that the tide will turn".**

Prayer

 Lord, I will wait till my change comes. It doesn't matter how long, I will wait. I follow the example of men like Job. Amen

Bible Reading Plan:
Joshua 6 and 7, Psalm 13

DAY 156 LACKING NOTHING

 *"These forty years the LORD your God has been with you: you have lacked nothing"* (Deuteronomy 2:7).

For forty years in the wilderness, God provided for the children of Israel. God is able to make all grace abound toward us for every good work and in every occasion for us today. He is the owner of the cattle in a thousand hills. In its early days, the Dallas Theological Seminary was in a critical need of $10,000 to keep work going. During a prayer meeting, the renowned Bible teacher Harry Ironside, a lecturer at the school prayed, "Lord, you own the cattle on a thousand hills. Please sell some of those cattle to help us meet this need". Shortly after the prayer meeting, a check of $10,000 arrived at the school, from a friend who had no idea of the urgent need. The man simply said the money came from sale of some cattle. Halleluiah. Our God is faithful. Those who seek Him will lack no good thing.

Prayer

 Lord, I pray that I will learn to depend on You for my needs. Amen

Bible Reading Plan:
Joshua 8 and 9, Psalm 14

DAY 157 WITH ALL YOUR MIGHT

 *"Whatever your hands find to do, do it with all your might"* (Ecclesiastes 9:10)

This is about giving and putting in your all in whatever you are called to do for God and even before men. Half-hearted measures will only produce half-hearted and mediocre results. To produce outstanding and enviable results we will have to put in our all. Distinctive results are generated from this all-out effort.

Ralph Waldo Emerson said, **"If a man can write a better book, or preach a better sermon or make a better mouse trap than his neighbor, even if he builds his house in the woods the world will make a beaten path to his door"**.

When we hold back the best we can ever give, we settle for second place results.

Prayer

 Lord, I pray that in all I do I will give my best and my all.

Bible Reading Plan:
Joshua 10 and 11, Psalm 15

DAY 158: BEWARE OF LIFE IN THE CAVE: THE BIRTHING OF SIN

"And he dwelt in a cave he and his two daughters" (Genesis 19:30)

In a cave, light flows only in one direction. This is a linear system in nature. The luxury of all-round perspective is lost. When we are in a cave, sincerity may not help us; our exposure is the limiting factor. Lot and the daughters had just escaped Sodom and Gomorrah: the place of sin. Then they land in a cave. The cave reproduced Sodom and Gomorrah. In verse 31, Lot's eldest daughter says, there are no more men on the face of the earth, so let's get our father drunk and then lie with him. This is how the Moabites and Ammonites come to be: products of incest. Is it true that there were no more men on the face of the earth? What of Abraham and the many servants with him in his household? When we isolate ourselves in our caves, sin is the result. Judah also left his brethren and went to Adullam, and also committed incest (Genesis 38).

Prayer

I pray that I will not cuff of from others so that I don't fall into grave sin.

Bible Reading Plan:
Joshua 12 and 13, Psalm 16

DAY 159 — BEWARE OF LIFE IN THE CAVE: THE SPIRITUAL NARROWNESS

"And he dwelt in a cave he and his two daughters" (Genesis 19:30)

Our perception of spiritual truth is restricted when we are in cave. Apollos was mighty in the Scriptures but he knew only the baptism of John. He was limited in his spiritual knowledge. But when he connected with others: Priscilla and Aquila he got more spiritual light. The Bible says, **"They took him aside and explained the way of the Lord better to him…." (Acts 18:24-27).**

He was 'mighty' till he met Priscilla and Aquila. In our little spiritual corners, our light is limited but when we meet others, we are enriched.

Prayer

Lord, I pray I will connect with others so that I am not limited in my knowledge of the truth.

Bible Reading Plan:
Joshua 14 and 15, Psalm 17

DAY 160 ON ALL FLESH

 *"I will pour out My Spirit on all flesh"* (Acts 2:17)

On the day of Pentecost God sent the Holy Spirit on the 120 gathered in the upper room in Jerusalem that they should be witnesses for Him beyond Jerusalem. The Bible says, **"But you shall receive power when the Holy Spirit comes upon you and you shall be witnesses to Me in Jerusalem, and in all Judea and Samaria and to the ends of the earth" (Acts 1:8).**

The outpouring is on all flesh, no gender or age limitations. If you are a young man, old man, son, daughter, menservants and maidservants, you also listed by the Lord for His outpouring. Aspire to be filled if you have not been filled and the Lord bless you as you do. Wherever you are, it is the Lord that baptizes.

Prayer

 You can cry out to Him and say, Lord, baptize me with the Holy Spirit. He is faithful. He will answer and you will become a faithful witness for Him. Amen

Bible Reading Plan:
Joshua 16 and 17, Psalm 18

DAY 161 THE CALL TO GROW

 *"But grow in the grace and knowledge of our Lord and Saviour Jesus Christ...."* (2 Peter 3:18).

It is obvious from the Scriptures that believing and becoming a new born in the Kingdom of God is not the end game. There has to be growth. Just like in the natural life, the spiritual well-being and growth of the new born will largely depend on the care and nourishment thereafter. God calls us to grow in the grace and knowledge of our Lord Jesus Christ. In the spiritual life, we are either growing or dying spiritually. Stagnation is just a transit zone. We cannot be there for long. You either move from there to a new spiritual height or drop to a lower one. Thus moving from one degree of glory to another, or from faith to faith, strength to strength and grace to grace is of great importance.

Prayer

 Lord, I heed to Your call to grow in the grace and knowledge of Christ.

Bible Reading Plan:
Joshua 18 and 19, Psalm 19

DAY 162 ADD TO YOUR FAITH: GROWTH IN CHARACTER

"But also for this very reason, giving all diligence, add to your faith virtue, to virtue knowledge, to knowledge self-control, to self-control perseverance, to perseverance godliness, to godliness brotherly kindness and to brotherly kindness love. For if these things are yours and abound, you will be neither barren nor unfruitful in the knowledge of our Lord Jesus Christ" (2 Peter 1:5-8).

The apostle says we have to put in all diligence: all the hard work in adding to our faith: virtue (excellence), knowledge, self-control, perseverance, godliness, brotherly kindness and love as the climax for without love we are like a clanging cymbal. Growth is the path to fruitfulness in the spiritual life. If we do not grow, we will be unfruitful in our spiritual life. The life of faith is one of constant addition. It happens by diligence. The lazy cannot grow.

Prayer

Lord, I embrace the diligence for growth. I will keep adding to my faith so that I will not be unproductive in my spiritual life. Amen

Bible Reading Plan:
Joshua 20 and 21, Psalm 20

DAY 163: GUARD THE DEPOSIT IN YOU

"Guard the good deposit that was entrusted to you—guard it with the help of the Holy Spirit who lives in us"
(2 Timothy 1:14 NIV).

To guard means is protect by keeping safe and secure from any form of danger. You only guard what is vulnerable to attack from without, what can be stolen, contaminated, or eliminated. This calls for alertness and watchfulness at all times. You are exhorted to guard the good deposit that God has entrusted in you. There is a good deposit in the inside of you for which you alone as a human being, of course with the help of God, are called to guard. That which has its origin in God can only be truly kept by God. That is why Paul exhorts you to guard it with the help of the Holy Spirit. It is a partnership. He will not do it for you, but will do it with you. You will need to see with his eyes, hear with his ears, and think with his mind. This is only possible as you grow in fellowship with the Spirit.

Prayer

Father, help me guard by the Holy Spirit, the deposit You have entrusted me

Bible Reading Plan:
Joshua 22 and 23, Psalm 21

DAY 164 THE GREATEST FAILURE

"But I have prayed for you, that your faith should not fail" (Luke 22:32)

The greatest failure is the failure of faith. It is the mother of all other failures. Satan knows this so well that he triggers all kinds of tribulations in us and around us in a bid to overwhelm us so that our faith will fail. Faith has failed when what we have gone through produces in use doubt or denial of what we once believed about God and His word. Simply, circumstances have adjusted what you believe instead of faith adjusting your circumstances to line up with the word. While outright denial of the Lord like Peter did is an expression of faith failure, it can also as be as subtle as giving up on a dream God put in your heart because of the circumstances you are going through. Your faith need not fail. Reinforce it by the word, for faith comes by hearing and hearing the word of God and by prayer.

Prayer

Lord, I pray that You uphold my faith; let it not fail even in the face of trial. Amen

Bible Reading Plan:
Joshua 24 and Judges 1, Psalm 22

DAY 165 THE BLESSING OF CONTENTMENT

 *"But godliness with contentment is great gain. For we brought nothing into the world, and we can take nothing out of it. But if we have food and clothing, we will be content with that"* (1 Timothy 6:6-8 NIV).

Contentment is that inner satisfaction that is independent of what one has or does not have. Godliness doesn't automatically bring contentment. It is a fruit that is born by those who through surrender and consecration have come to find their all in the Lord. There are certain marks in the life of the contented: Joy, generosity, gratitude, rest, and the ability to focus. The contented live as simple as possible and concentrate on their God content. They understand that what truly carries one through life is not the volume of his or her possession but his or her God content. The more of God you have the less things you pursue and vice versa. Your God-content depends on your God-pursuit, and your God-pursuit depends on you hunger and thirst for God. And your hunger and thirst of God is inversely proportional to your hunger and thirst for other things.

Prayer

 Lord, I pray for growth in contentment

Bible Reading Plan:
Judges 2 and 3, Psalm 23

DAY 166: THE BLESSING OF CONTENTMENT II

 *For we brought nothing into the world, and we can take nothing out of it. But if we have food and clothing, we will be content with that"* (1 Timothy 6:7-8 NIV).

The secret to contentment is to live with the consciousness that you brought nothing into the world and you will take nothing out of this world. Contentment is being satisfied with the basics. "If we have food and clothing, we will be content with that". When you are satisfied with the basics you can invest in the Kingdom more than you otherwise would. Contentment is being satisfied with one's need being met one day at a time. Contentment makes you put the needs of others and the Kingdom before your wants. It protects you from trying to hoard or amass things for oneself at the expense of the immediate needs of others and of the Kingdom.

Prayer

 Father, teach me to cultivate the fruit of contentment in my life.

Bible Reading Plan:
Judges 4 and 5 Psalm 24

DAY 167 SEEN FROM A DISTANCE

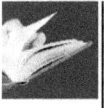 *"But they saw him in the distance, and before he reached them, they plotted to kill him. "Here comes that dreamer!" they said to each other. "Come now, let's kill him and throw him into one of these cisterns and say that a ferocious animal devoured him. Then we'll see what comes of his dreams"* (Genesis 37:18-20 NIV).

Every child of destiny has been seen in a distance by the forces of evil. These forces have plotted your ruin before you reach your goal. They have seen God's deposit in your life and have vowed that you will not accomplish God's purpose for your life. Joseph's enemies said, "Come now, let's kill him and throw him into one of these cisterns ...then we'll see what comes of his dreams." The goal of their hostility was to see what became of Joseph's dreams. But the good news is that the Almighty, omniscient, omnipotent God uses the adversities of life and the ill intentions of the devil to bring into fulfilment the dreams He placed in the inside of you.

Prayer

 Lord, for eyes to see, wisdom to deal with, the traps and snares of the enemy on the pathway to my destiny.

Bible Reading Plan:
Judges 6 and 7, Psalm 25

DAY 168 THE GOD WHO REMEMBERS

 *"Then God remembered Rachel and...... opened her womb"* (Genesis 30:22)

It is always easy to arrive at the conclusion that God has forgotten us when we have prayed and waited for a very long time and there is yet no answer from the Lord. Sarah, had gotten to that point and had given up on the possibility of having a child; since she was way past the age of child bearing. She even laughed when the Angel said she will have a son. But the LORD said, **"Is anything too hard for the LORD? At the appointed time, I will return unto you ...and Sarah shall have a son" (Genesis 18:14).** God has not forgotten about you or your need. God has an appointed time for you and He makes all things beautiful in His time. When that time comes, like Rachel, He will remember you and meet your specific need. Amen

Prayer

 Lord, thank you because You are the God that remembers: at the appointed time You will remember me.

Bible Reading Plan:
Judges 8 and 9, Psalm 26

DAY 169: WHEN YOUR OWN REJECTS YOU

 *"He was in the world, and though the world was made through Him, the world did not recognize Him. He came to that which was His own, but His own did not receive Him"* (John 1:10-11 NIV).

Sometimes people are rejected from the very business they founded. Sometimes ministers are rejected by the congregation they have spent time building. Christ was rejected and crucified by his own creation.

What do you do when you are rejected? Continue to show the love, favor you are called to show even in the midst of the worst rejection. The pathway of rejection is not an easy one to walk but it is the pathway to great accomplishments and great promotions. When God wants to exalt a man He allows him to meet with rejection when he thinks he should be acclaimed and celebrated. When the devil wants to destroy a man permanently he keeps him on the pedestal of worldly applause and acclamations even when he should go through rejection.

Prayer

 Lord, empower me to handle rejection wisely and make the best of the experience

Bible Reading Plan:
Judges 10 and 11, Psalm 27

DAY 170 THE CHIEF CORNERSTONE

"The stone which the builders rejected has become the chief cornerstone"
(Psalm 118:22)

Most times we take rejection from others as a referendum on our worth, whereas it is an indictment on their deep blindness and inability to recognise our worth. Jesus was rejected by the very people who are expecting a Messiah till today. The Messiah lived before them daily but they could not recognise Him. If the Son of God could be rejected by men, how much more of us. The veil that covered the eyes of those back then is still alive and at work today. While we may be tempted to plunge into self-pity, don't forget that rejection is a sign that you carry indispensability that the common cannot handle or recognise: a cornerstone in the making.

Prayer

Lord, open my eye to see the end game of rejection; a cornerstone. Amen

Bible Reading Plan:
Judges 12 and 13, Psalm 28

DAY 171 THE SAFEST PLACE TO BE

"Because the Lord revealed their plot to me, I knew it, for at that time he showed me what they were doing. I had been like a gentle lamb led to the slaughter; I did not realize that they had plotted against me, saying, 'Let us destroy the tree and its fruit; let us cut him off from the land of the living, that his name be remembered no more'" (Jeremiah 11:18-19 NIV).

In a world so full of intrigue, sadly even in the church, where brethren, colleagues, partners etc. spend time plotting against one another for power, position, and prestige, there is a place of safety you cannot afford to do without. You must avoid becoming a victim of wickedness and the corruption of the human heart. It is possible to live in a place of revelation that leads to supernatural knowledge. To be safe in that which you are doing requires avoiding the traps of your enemies. And this can only be done effectively when you place yourself continuously in a position where you are connected to heaven's frequency.

Prayer

Open my spiritual eyes and ears so that I can always see what heaven is showing and hear what heaven is saying to me.

Bible Reading Plan:
Judges 14 and 15, Psalm 29

DAY 172 LACK OF KNOWLEDGE: A DANGER

 *"My people are destroyed for lack of Knowledge"* (Hosea 4:6).

Many people are like "gentle lambs led to the slaughter". Businesses, homes, marriages, ministries, kingdoms, have been destroyed not only because of misplaced trust, but also because the victims were not in a place where divinity could reveal to them what was going on. You cannot afford to live out of touch with heaven., out of the signal of heaven. The Lord Jesus was able to know even the thoughts of men and their plots because he lived consistently in touch with the Father. That is the reason He fulfilled His destiny.

Prayer

 Lord, help me to begin to know the deep things in the realm of the Spirit

Bible Reading Plan:
Judges 16 and 17, Psalm 30

DAY 173: JOURNEY INTO DEPRESSION

 *"I remember my affliction and my wandering, the bitterness and the gall. I well remember them, and my soul is downcast within me.*
(Lamentations 3:19-20 NIV).

When you allow your mind to dwell on certain things, it is bound to lead to a soul that is downcast, that is, a state of despondency. And when this happens long enough, depression becomes the result. The prophet Jeremiah remembered his affliction, his wandering, and the bitter and galling experiences of his life. He allowed his mind to dwell on negative things he experienced and it led him into deep depression such that he cursed the day he was born **(see Jeremiah 20:7-18).** When we unduly focus on what is going wrong, we will be depressed.

Prayer

 Lord, I pray for discipline of the mind not to focus on the negative around me.

Bible Reading Plan:
Judges 18 and 19, Psalm 31

DAY 174: JOURNEY OUT OF DEPRESSION

"Yet this I call to mind and therefore I have hope: Because of the Lord's great love we are not consumed, for his compassions never fail. They are new every morning; great is your faithfulness".
(Lamentations 3:21-23 NIV).

You have the power to redirect your thoughts. The prophet decided to call to mind certain things that gave him hope and that led him out of depression.

Firstly, he called to mind the Lord's great love. Second, he called to mind the compassions of the Lord. Third, he called to mind the great faithfulness of the Lord. Like the prophet, call to mind the good things God has done for you. When you have called the good things to mind, you can go a step further to confess or proclaim them in a consistent manner. In this way the yoke of depression will be avoided or broken.

Prayer

Father, help me to focus my mind on the positive and on You

Bible Reading Plan:
Judges 20 and 21, Psalm 32

DAY 175 ELIMINATE DISTRACTIONS

 *"...Those who buy something, as if it were not theirs to keep; those who use the things of this world, as if not engrossed on them"* (1 Corinthians 7:30b-31a NIV)

One's possessions can either increase or decrease our level of devotion to God and to purpose. There are people, who have refused to possess certain things, not because the things are evil or sinful but because such things will not help them to maximize their time and devotion to God and purpose. One of the world's most renowned architect has denied himself many things so he could have more time to devote to his work. He has no cell phone, does not visit the internet, and does not watch TV etc. It is clear that there are things which if one refuses to possess will not affect one's life in anyway. Each one should be able to determine with respect to his calling and vocation the things which will act as a distraction or time wasters.

Prayer

 Father, grant me the courage to get rid of those things which act as distractions

Bible Reading Plan:
Ruth 1 and 2, Psalm 33

DAY 176: SALVATION NEARER

 *"For now our salvation is nearer than when we first believed"* (Romans 13:11b)

Whatever it is we are believing God for, it is closer today to get to us than when we first believed God for it. Satan tries to lie to us to the contrary so that we get discouraged or slumber or give up just when there is about to be a manifestation or our breakthrough. In the light of eternity too, the coming of the Lord, is a lot closer than when we first believed. We should be all the more alert and watchful not to yield to forces that are asking us, when will all these be fulfilled? Dear saint, stand strong and you will soon see the salvation of the Lord. Amen

Prayer

 Lord, I pray that I will not sleep nor slumber, for my salvation is nearer now than ever before.

Bible Reading Plan:
Ruth 3 and 4, Psalm 34

DAY 177 IT SHALL COME TO PASS

 *"Commit your way to the LORD, trust also in Him and He shall bring it to pass"* (Psalm 37:5).

The Lord wants to see things come to pass in our lives. The way and secret is simple; the word says commit your way to the Lord and trust also in Him and He shall bring it to pass or make it happen. The size of the project doesn't matter. The challenges you face do not matter. Simply obey the Lord and bring that project of yours before Him and say, Lord, I commit this project into your hands; I trust also in you. Make it happen.

Dear saint, once you have done so, leave it there before the Lord. He is able to make it happen. Even if later you see circumstances that run opposite to what you believe, don't panic, only reaffirm your faith in the Lord. God will bring it to pass. Amen

Prayer

 Lord, I commit (Name the project) to You and I trust You to bring it to pass. Amen

Bible Reading Plan:
1 Samuel 1 and 2, Psalm 35

DAY 178 UNMOVED

"But none of these things move me" (Acts 20:24)

The apostle Paul was about to go to Jerusalem and what the Holy Spirit was saying is that, chains and tribulations awaited him. Paul's posture was that none of these things moved him. This is the height of knowledge of God and faith. God is calling all who are His own to get to the place in life where nothing, however bad it is moves us. The Bible says, **"Therefore, my beloved brethren be steadfast, immovable, always abounding in your work..." (1 Corinthians 15:58)**

The Lord, Jesus was asleep in the midst of a storm while the disciples were in frantic care and worry. May we become unmovable and strong; unmoved by situations. Amen

Prayer

Lord, grant me an unshakeable faith in You. Amen

Bible Reading Plan:
1 Samuel 3 and 4, Psalm 36

DAY 179 UNMOVED II

"He alone is my rock and salvation; He is my defense; I shall not be moved"
(Psalm 62:6)

The unshakeable character is a common denominator in the lives of men who knew God. The basis of their unshakeable character is: knowledge of who God is and this is not imparted, it is cultivated over time. The Moravians take the credit of giving us John Wesley. John Wesley's first encounter with the Moravians was in a ship that was in turbulence. All in the ship were in panic except these Moravian Christian brothers. This touched Wesley and later he believed through one of them. The world has heard our voice, but they are also watching to see our poise in the face of challenges. May they see unmoved men and women.

Prayer

Lord, I pray that I will grow deep in my knowledge of You so that nothing in this world will move me. Amen

Bible Reading Plan:
1 Samuel 5, Psalm 37

DAY 180 HE GIVES WHAT IS GOOD

 *"Yes, the LORD will give what is good"*
(Psalm 85:12)

We are used to saying that, a person cannot give what he does not have. God is good and can only give what is good. What makes us not to get things from God at times is not because He is withholding anything from us; God is sparing us from what is not good enough. With our limitations as men, we tend to want some things and God who inhabits eternity and sees beyond what we can see, knows that it is not good enough for us. So, when it appears that God is not giving us what we asked for or desire, bear two things in mind; first it may not be his appointed time and second, what you desire may not be His best for you. God loves his own so much not to surrender them to desires that will not bring them good. Rest assured dear saint, He who is good will give you what is good at His appointed time. Amen

Prayer

 Lord, I give You praise. You are a giver of good and I know You will give what is good

Bible Reading Plan:
1 Samuel 6 and 7, Psalm 38

DAY 181 PRE-HELD SPIRITUAL CONVICTIONS: A POTENTIAL HINDRANCE

 *"But Peter said, "Not so Lord! For I have never eaten anything common or unclean"* (Acts 10:14)

Peter exhibits a great spiritual character; consistency in spiritual convictions like the Rechabites who would not take wine or live in tents. Only that this time, they run contrary to God's move. Most times, our best of convictions can stand in God's way and if we are not sensitive in the Spirit and yielded enough we will be arguing with God or standing on His way as Peter would have eventually done if God did not insist. The apostles up to Acts chapter 10, were preaching to Jews only whereas God had in mind for them to reach the ends of the earth. The destiny of the gentile world in God's plan for salvation was hanging on the pre-held spiritual convictions of Peter. New wine needs new wine skins. May our minds be renewed to accommodate God's move.

Prayer

 Help us Lord, to be flexible and malleable in Your hands. Amen

Bible Reading Plan:
1 Samuel 8 and 9, Psalm 39

DAY 182 PRE-HELD NOTIONS: A POTENTIAL HINDRANCE

 *"And when Saul had come to Jerusalem, he tried to join the disciples but they were all afraid of him, and did not believe that he was a disciple"* (Acts 9:26)

It will amount to been hard on the disciples then if we don't understand their fear for Paul and doubts about his discipleship. This was too good to be true. These disciples were witnesses and victims of the persecution of the church led by Paul. While they were right to have these fears and doubts in that sense, they were wrong in the sense that in their minds they didn't accommodate the idea of the God who does the impossible and can change things in a twinkling of an eye. Thanks to Barnabas, Saul was integrated into the church. What a loss the world would have had if we lost Paul through prejudice of the early church. May God renew our minds.

Prayer

 Lord, renew my mind. Deliver me from prejudice and pre-held notions. I don't want to miss what You want to do in my life and ministry. I pray for an open mind. Amen

Bible Reading Plan:
1 Samuel 10 and 11, Psalm 40

DAY 183 GROW YOUR FAITH: BY USE

 *"And the apostles said to the Lord, increase our faith. So the Lord said, if you have faith as a mustard seed, you can say to this mulberry tree..."* (Luke 17:5-6).

While it appears the Lord was not answering their question; the Lord was actually laying down the foundational principle of growing faith; start by making use of the faith you have for we are all dealt a measure of faith. The path to growing faith is: put to use the faith you already have. It is like growing muscles. We have to exercise them. The great George Mueller said, **"Faith grows with use".** If we are going to exhibit great faith, then we must start using the little we have. Tozer, says **"If we dare to trust Him for something small today, next week or next year you may trust Him for answers bordering on the miraculous".**

Prayer

 Lord, I pray that I will put my faith to use so that it will increase. Amen

Bible Reading Plan:
1 Samuel 12 and 13, Psalm 41

DAY 184 NO ONE CALLS ONE ME

 *"There is none among them who calls upon Me"* (Hosea 7:7)

What an indictment on us His children for our heavenly Father to say, "None calls upon Me". While this is an indictment on us, it is a revelation of the character of our God; a Father who longs to have fellowship with His children and who is very caring and expresses concern that none of His children call upon Him. May this touch our hearts anew and increase our hunger for prayer. Maybe in your mind you are saying, I am not among those who do not call upon Him; the question is do you call upon Him long enough as to fellowship with Him and not just when you need something? Many of us see God as a dispenser. Once we press the button and we have what we need, we are gone. Who are those who really call upon Him? Lord, make me one of such.

Prayer

 Lord, make me one of those who truly calls upon You.

Bible Reading Plan:
1 Samuel 14 and 15, Psalm 42

DAY 185: FEAR: AN UNDERTAKER OF POTENTIAL

"And I was afraid, and went and hid your talent in the ground" (Matthew 25:25)

God's earnest desire is that we live up to our God-given potential. It satisfies the heart of God when we deploy our God-given abilities. The servant in this parable buried his God-given potential because of fear. Fear is an undertaker of potential. There are many who would have amounted to something very great in the purposes of God, but they allowed fear paralyze and freeze them. Such prefer the 'safety' in the shore than dare to venture into the wild. Dr. Walter Okon, a cardiologist in Germany used to say, **"No venture, No success"**. It was his creed and he lived it, going through all the odds to train eventually as a cardiologist. Joan of Arc, the 18-year old girl who commanded the armies of France said, **"I am not afraid. I was born to do this"**. Professor Wole Adedeji says **"Fear is the policeman of the devil"**, arresting the potential of many. May that not be your case and portion; may your potential not be buried. Amen

Prayer

Lord, I refuse to let fear cause the burial of my potential or talent.

Bible Reading Plan:
1 Samuel 16 and 17, Psalm 43

DAY 186: FEAR: AN UNDERTAKER OF THE SOUL

"But the fearful and unbelieving and the abominable and murderers, and whoremongers, and sorcerers and idolaters, and all liars shall have their part in the lake which burneth with fire and brimstone: which is the second death"
(Revelation 21:8 KJV)

In the list of all that could possibly take people to hell or the lake of fire as seen from the passage above, fear tops the list. God is orderly in the presentation of information. Fear is Satan's biggest weapon; employed to create unbelieve. Where fear reigns, there will be tons of reasons not to believe and abominations will follow. There are many who would not accept Jesus because of what people would say: the fear of man being a snare. Or a lady who is taken care of by men; her thoughts will be, if I accept Jesus now, who will pay my rents, who will feed me and so on. Beware of fear; it wants more than your talent. It is after your soul and your eternal destiny. Is there any fear stopping you from obeying God? Can you afford to allow fear, rob you of an eternity with God? Has the fear of suffering, produced a disobedience to God?

Prayer

Lord, I renounce the spirit of fear; I choose to obey You at any cost. Amen

Bible Reading Plan:
1 Samuel 18 and 19, Psalm 44

DAY 187: RATIONALISATIONS OF THE FEARLESS: THE COMMAND NOT TO FEAR

"Fear not, for am with you; be not dismayed, for I am your God. I will strengthen you, yes I will help you, I will uphold you with My righteous right hand" (Isaiah 41:10).

Why must I be free of all fear? The first reason is that God has commanded that I fear not. Theologians say, there are about 365, fear not commands in the Bible: one for each day. Why would God say, fear not? The truth is that there is reason to fear. No sane person can look at life and all what is happening in the world today, and not yield to fear. But the God of the universe, the One who upholds all things by the word of His power says, "fear not". Thus our first rationale for a fearless life is; obedience to God. God has said fear not, why would I act otherwise? Obeying God in this regard is an act of faith. My feelings and environment gives me every reason to fear but by faith in the God who reigns over all the earth and the heavens, I yield to fearlessness. If God, the ruler of the universe has said, fear not, I must as a matter of honor to the King of kings, fear not.

Prayer

Lord, I will obey the command not to fear. You have spoken. I must obey You Lord.

Bible Reading Plan:
1 Samuel 20 and 21, Psalm 45

DAY 188 — RATIONALISATIONS OF THE FEARLESS: GOD IS WITH YOU

"Fear not, for am with you; be not dismayed, for I am your God. I will strengthen you, yes I will help you, I will uphold you with My righteous right hand" (Isaiah 41:10).

Who is with us matters. If the president of your country says he is with you, that is enough to bring great rest to the soul. Now, it is not the president of this world who says he is with you, it is the Immortal God. The Creator of the whole universe; the One whose days are endless, without Beginning and End. He is the God of all flesh; nothing is too hard for Him. The president of your country will not be in power forever. The day he leaves power, your suffering begins. But our God's dominion and kingdom is forever. Your president can only help you in time; but God can help you in time and eternity. This is the God who says, "I am with you". He is not only with you; He is in you; the hope of glory. Amen

Prayer

Lord, thank You because You are with me, I fear not. Amen

Bible Reading Plan:
1 Samuel 22 and 23, Psalm 46

DAY 189: RATIONALISATIONS OF THE FEARLESS: DIVINE STRENGTH AND SUPPORT

"Fear not, for am with you; be not dismayed, for I am your God. <u>I will strengthen you, yes I will help you</u>, I will uphold you with My righteous right hand" (Isaiah 41:10).

In the face of a Goliath-like task and challenge, there is a tendency to yield to fear and chicken out. In most cases, we tend to think that we don't have what it takes to do certain things. God says, he will strengthen you and help you. The Bible says, **"I can do all things through Christ who strengthens me" (Philippians 4:13).** Don't yield to fear, God says He will help. Don't look at your material resources, look at Him who owns the cattle in a thousand hills. Don't look at your natural abilities; look at Him who is the Omniscient and Omnipotent God. That work for God or business or school project or house project you are building will be realized; God will strengthen and help you. Go ahead without fear. Don't allow Satan freeze your efforts through fear.

Prayer

Lord, thank You for Your strength and help; I will not fear.

Bible Reading Plan:
1 Samuel 24 and 25, Psalm 47

DAY 190 RATIONALISATIONS OF THE FEARLESS: THE RIGHT HAND OF GOD

 *"Fear not, for am with you; be not dismayed, for I am your God. I will strengthen you, yes I will help you, <u>I will uphold you with My righteous right hand</u>"* (Isaiah 41:10).

The RSV talks of His victorious right hand. His right hand is in reference to His authority and victorious power. God is saying, you need not fear the powers of darkness and enemies all around. You have been lifted up with Christ in the right of God in the heavenly places, far above every dominion. As a believer, you are in a realm unreachable by the forces of darkness. You have been translated from the kingdom of darkness to the kingdom of God through the redemption that is in Christ. Satan has lost every claim and power over you. Not only so, the Bible says, 'you are hidden with Christ in God'. You need not walk in fear. He has given you authority to trample on snakes and scorpions and to overcome all the power of the enemy. Amen

Prayer

 Lord, I walk in the consciousness of my place of authority in Christ; I therefore fear no evil. Amen

Bible Reading Plan:
1 Samuel 26 and 27, Psalm 48

DAY 191 RATIONALISATIONS OF THE FEARLESS: FEAR IS NOT OF GOD

 *"For God has not given us a spirit of fear, but of power and of love and of a sound mind"* (2 Timothy 1:7).

God has not given us a spirit of fear. Therefore, fear is not of God. The believer has the duty not only to hate but to renounce violently anything that is not of God. Just as the believer should violently deal with immorality or theft, so should the believer be vexed in spirit against fear. The vexation of the believer is: why should I harbor in my spirit that which is not of God? My body and spirit by right of redemption belong to God and is the temple of the Holy Spirit. The believer has to rise up and take authority over the spirit of fear; casting it out of his or her life in the name of Jesus.

Prayer

 Lord, I take authority over the spirit of fear and I launch out to accomplish Your plan and purpose by deploying the talents You have placed in me in the name of Jesus Christ. Amen

Bible Reading Plan:
1 Samuel 28 and 29, Psalm 49

DAY 192 THE MIND TO WORK

"For the people had a mind to work"
(Nehemiah 4:6)

Those who have written their names in the sands of time and are a beacon of hope to us were men who gave their all in whatever area they had chosen. Their results inspire us but we hate the drudgery that produced the enviable results. Hard work has been one of the common denominators of outstanding men. D.L. Moody was a great preacher in his day and his words and the story of his life still inspires us today. It is said that he was a workaholic and used to work until his co-workers would pray saying, **"Lord, let Moody be tired"**, so that they could also rest. He accomplished great things for his God. He worked tirelessly. Tireless work has been amongst others the separator of men. Henry Wadsworth Longfellow was right to have said that, **"The heights great men reached and kept were not attained by sudden flight, but they, while their companions slept, were toiling upward in the night"**.

Prayer

Lord, for a mind to work

Bible Reading Plan:
1 Samuel 30 and 31, Psalm 50

DAY 193 WORK: THE KEY TO SPIRITUAL DISTINCTION

"But by the grace of God I am what I am: and His grace toward me was not in vain; but I laboured more abundantly than they all, yet not I, but the grace of God which was in me" (1 Corinthians 15:10)

The example of the apostle Paul is there for us all to see. He accomplished a lot and wrote almost half of the books of the New Testament. He was a late comer in a certain sense but continued and ended the story of the Acts of the Apostles. In the Book of Romans, Paul mentions many who were in Christ before him **(Romans 16:7).** Many came to know the Lord before Paul, but he accomplished great things for the Lord than most if not all of them. The question is what was the secret of Paul? Paul laboured more than them all. Laziness is a vow of spiritual obscurity and oblivion. Wake up oh sleeper and Christ will shine on you.

Prayer

Lord, grant me a mind to work and work very hard. I renounce the ways of laziness in the name of Jesus Christ. Amen

Bible Reading Plan:
2 Samuel 1 and 2, Psalm 51

DAY 194 — THE HALLMARK OF HONOR: WHO WE ARE AND WHAT WE BECOME

"That you may approve the things that are excellent" (Philippians 1:10)

We should be and become the best for God. God as our master deserves the best of us. There are many who still hold the idea that, the church is a place for rejects and the world's dumping ground. Professor Zacharias Tanee Fomum thought differently. This great man was a professor of organic chemistry and even attained the rank of DSc (Doctor of Science) in the same field. His academic record as an undergraduate took many years to be broken. His undergraduate scores were so high that he was admitted to do PhD direct without sitting for a master's degree. But this man gave himself without reserve for the cause of Christ and the Gospel. His efforts with his co-workers in his homeland of Cameroon birth a missionary movement with missionary outposts in many countries. He valued excellence; in his studies and development knowing that God deserves the best men. Are you becoming the best that you can ever be?

Prayer

Lord, I commit myself to be excellent

Bible Reading Plan:
2 Samuel 3 and 4, Psalm 52

DAY 195: THE HALLMARK OF HONOR: WHAT WE GIVE AND DO

 *"That you may approve the things that are excellent"* (Philippians 1:10)

Excellence is of God. God demands excellence. If earthly kings can ask for the best, how much more the King of kings and Lord of lords. Cain did not give out his best and God rejected him and his offering. God did not only reject his offering, he rejected Cain as a person **(Genesis 4:1-7)**. It is a serious matter. It is better not to give than to give God trash. In the Book of Malachi, we see the hallmark of dishonor of God. What could not be accepted by the governor was offered to God **(Malachi 1:6-8).** Not giving our very best for God and His purpose is evil. Malachi gave a simple test for the quality of what we offer to God: can it be offered to the governor of your state, region? If not, how much more does it fall below the standards and approval of the King of kings.

Prayer

 Lord, I repent for service rendered to You that has not met the standard of the King of kings. I pray for the spirit of excellence in all I do in the name of Jesus Christ. Amen

Bible Reading Plan:
2 Samuel 5 and 6, Psalm 53

DAY 196 EXCELLENCE: PENETRATION OF THE HIGH PLACES FOR GOD

"Do you see a man who excels in his work? He will stand before kings; he will not stand before unknown men"
(Proverbs 22:29)

Excellence is a key instrument in penetrating the high places for the gospel. We can be so good in what we do such that kings will have no choice but to hire us and that will be an opportunity to bear witness for the gospel. We determine our audience and who will hire us. Daniel was hired by the greatest king of his time. He was excellent. He served in high places and brought the counsel of God to Babylon and spiritually influenced Nebuchadnezzar. Excellence opened the door. May we see excellence as a tool in God's hands for the gospel.

Prayer

Lord, may I render service that attracts the favor of heaven and takes me to high places, serving before kings and prominent men. Amen

Bible Reading Plan:
2 Samuel 7 and 8, Psalm 54

DAY 197 — LAZINESS: A DEEP SPIRITUAL PITFALL

 *"But his lord answered and said to him, 'You wicked and lazy servant...'"* (Matthew 25:26)

It should frighten us all that wickedness and laziness follow each other and lie side by side. Our religious understanding of wickedness borders largely on the obvious evils of the flesh like drunkenness, sexual immorality, murder and many other evils that we are a lot familiar with. But our Lord has made it clear that laziness is wickedness. Laziness is self-orchestrated jeopardy. While the fearful fail to deploy potential, the lazy fail to multiply 'deployed' potential. Multiplication is God's first command to man **(Genesis 1:26).** Laziness is an attack on that commandment.

There is a lot in us that is waiting to be unleashed for the benefit of a dying world and in the Body of Christ. For most of us laziness stands on the way. Do I need to change?

Prayer

 Lord, I pray that laziness will not be part of my life; I want to multiply Your potential in me.

Bible Reading Plan:
2 Samuel 9 and 10, Psalm 55

DAY 198 — LAZINESS AND WORK: THE PROTESTANT THINKING

 *"But his lord answered and said to him, 'You wicked and lazy servant...'"* (Matthew 25:26)

How and why did protestant nations prosper and flourish should be a subject of interest to the modern day Christian. In book, the **Protestant Ethic and the Spirit of Capitalism**, Max Weber reveals why protestant nations prospered compared to non-protestant nations and how the believers in those nations shaped western civilization. He started studying the theology and teaching of the different shades of the protestant movement. He noticed amongst other things, that they had a very a robust and developed theology against idleness, waste of time and unnecessary leisure: **"Waste of time is thus the first and in principle the deadliest of sins. The span of human life is infinitely short and precious to make sure of one's own election. Loss of time through sociability, idle talk, luxury, even more sleep than is necessary for health, six to at most eight hours, is worthy of absolute moral condemnation"**. How many today, want to be rich materially and spiritually but waste time and are in idleness?

Prayer

 Lord, I pray for greater shunning of laziness and idleness

Bible Reading Plan:
2 Samuel 11 and 12, Psalm 56

DAY 199 — LAZINESS AND WORK: THE PROTESTANT THINKING II

We continue to x-ray the spiritual thinking that projected protestant nations:

Laziness or a person's attitude to work in protestant thinking was indicative of spiritual condition. They had these words in that respect: **"Unwillingness to work is symptomatic of the lack of grace"**.

Doggedness and unrelenting efforts was a religious duty: **"The perseverance of the individual in the place and within the limits which God had assigned to him was a religious duty."**

How many of us see the unwillingness to work or the laziness in us as a spiritual condition or how many of us see a problem in the character of not seeing things through when we start them? Most people will throw the towel when they meet the slightest challenge; even claiming that the obstacles are a sign that God is not in the project.

Prayer

Lord, opens my eyes to see the spiritual bankruptcy in laziness and lack of perseverance along the line of a chosen endeavour.

Bible Reading Plan:
2 Samuel 13 and 14, Psalm 57

DAY 200 — LAZINESS AND WORK: THE PROTESTANT THINKING III

Taking advantage of opportunities and choosing the most profitable way, provided it did not affect one's relationship with God was highly encouraged among the protestants. It was considered part of Christian stewardship: **"Hence the faithful Christian must follow the call by taking advantage of the opportunity. If God shows you a way in which you may lawfully get more than in another way (without wrong to your soul or to any other), if you refuse this, and choose the less gainful way, you cross one of the ends of your calling, and you refuse to be God's steward, and to accept His gifts and use them for Him when He requireth it: you may labour to be rich for God, though not for the flesh and sin."**

These nations prospered, communities flourished not by praying for prosperity but by work and shunning idleness and taking advantage of most profitable opportunities.

Prayer

Lord, awaken in me a strong work ethic, doggedness and an eye for opportunities.

Bible Reading Plan:
2 Samuel 15, Psalm 58

DAY 201: THEY BEGAN TO MAKE EXCUSES

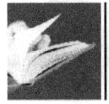 *"The slothful man says, there is a lion in the road! A fierce lion is in the streets"* (Proverbs 26:13).

There is no challenge-free path. There is no task that was accomplished without the odds of failure. Therefore, there can always be excuses or reasons for not doing something. The Wright Brothers who pioneered flying had every reason not to try. All the 'big' men of science of their day were against them. In fact, Lord Kelvin who was president of the Royal Society of Science at the time said, **"It is impossible to fly a metallic object"**. Today we know that it is possible to fly a metallic object. Fools and the lazy see the obstacles, magnify them, then get overwhelmed and call it quits. But the brave and hardworking, find a way and reasons for the task to be accomplished. They are like Hannibal the Carthaginian General who said, **"We will either find a way, or make one."** Those who fail see reasons why they should not succeed and make decisions based on that. Those who succeed see reasons why they should not fail and make decisions on that basis.

Prayer

 Lord, I pray that I will find solutions, not make excuses

Bible Reading Plan:
2 Samuel 16 and 17, Psalm 59

DAY 202: GOD WILL NOT TAKE EXCUSES

"...So that they are without excuse"
(Romans 1:20)

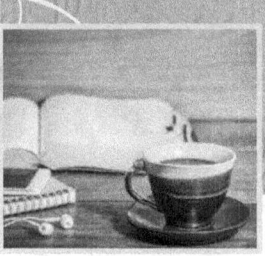

Every age has those who will challenge the excuses they will produce for their failure to live up to what God demanded. For those who will complain that they sinned because of the strength of the temptation they faced, the Lord will ask them if the resisted sin unto bloodshed (**Hebrews 12:4**) or you plunged into prostitution because you didn't have anybody to help you; on the last day you will find a person or persons who stood for God in conditions far worse than that or those who will say that they didn't have preachers close to them, Queen Sheba will rise up on that day to make useless their excuse as she came from the ends of the earth to hear the wisdom of Solomon **(Luke 11:31).** But now, one greater than Solomon is here. Men shall be without any excuse. Is there any excuse you are making right now? Will you do what the Lord is asking of you?

Prayer

Lord, let me not fall into the trap of excuses.

Bible Reading Plan:
2 Samuel 18 and 19, Psalm 60

DAY 203 — AM ONLY A CHILD: LET NOT AGE BECOME A CAGE

 *"Then said I, ah, Lord GOD! behold, I cannot speak: for I am a child..."*
(Jeremiah 1:6 KJV)

For some, age has become a cage; they are either too young or too old. But those who have accomplished great things disregarded their age. The famous Kentucky Fried Chicken (KFC), known for their wonderful fried chicken all over the world, was started by colonel Harland Sanders at age sixty-five. Alexander the Great had conquered countries at age eighteen and by age thirty-two had conquered almost all the known world of his time. Joan of Arc at seventeen was commanding the armies of France. Blaise Pascal at age nineteen had invented the calculator. Charles Spurgeon was already preaching at age fifteen and at age sixteen accepted his first pastorate. The fact that he had no formal education did not stop him. He went on to school himself in puritan theology, natural history, Latin and Victorian literature.

Prayer

 Lord, I refuse to use age to limit myself. I yield to what You have assigned me to do.

Bible Reading Plan:
2 Samuel 20 and 21, Psalm 61

DAY 204 DO NOT DESPISE LITTLE BEGINNINGS

"For who has despised the day of small things?" (Zechariah 4:10)

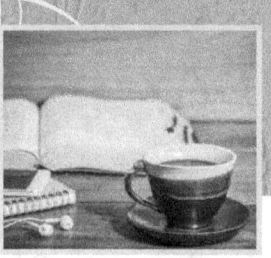

King David started with a few sheep. David's brother made us know that his initial assignment was in a small place. The Bible says, **"...and Eliab's anger aroused against David and he said, why did you come down here? And with whom have you left those few sheep in the wilderness?" (1 Samuel 17:28).** David started in a small place. The few sheep experience also enabled David to learn invaluable lessons on shepherding which was very needful in shepherding God's people when he eventually became king in Israel; **"He also chose David His servant and took him from the sheepfolds; from following the ewes that had young he brought him, to shepherd Jacob His people and Israel His inheritance. So He Shepherded them according to the integrity of his heart and guided them by the skillfulness of his hands" (Psalm 78:70-72).** Let's not despise our 'little' place and assignment.

Prayer

Lord, give me a heart to serve You wherever You place me and however small the assignment

Bible Reading Plan:
2 Samuel 22 and 23, Psalm 62

DAY 205: MASTERING DELAY: THE ART OF KEEPING HOPE ALIVE

"But if that evil servant says in his heart, my master is delaying his coming and begins to beat his fellow servants, and to eat and drink with drunkards, the master will come when he is not looking for him and at an hour that he is not aware of" (Matthew 24:48-50)

The evil servant had stopped expecting his master. He had judged his master as delaying. Spiritual and moral chaos followed. Once we stop expecting the Lord's visitation whether in temporal or eternal perspective of things, spiritual vigilance is lost and we plunge into spiritual recklessness. To serve faithfully in our place of assignment, we need to be in it for the long haul knowing that no one knows when the Lord will visit. The Lord Himself asked, If the Son of Man comes will he find faith on the earth?

Prayer

Lord, I pray that You help me to hang in there even when there is delay.

Bible Reading Plan:
2 Samuel 24 and 1 Kings 1, Psalm 63

DAY 206: THE POWER OF A LIVING HOPE

 *"Beloved, now we are children of God; and it has not yet been revealed what we shall be, but we know that when He is revealed, we shall be like Him, for we shall see Him as He is. And everyone who has this hope in Him purifies himself, just as He is pure"* (1 John 3:2-3).

The hope of His coming inspires our purity as He is pure. Without a living hope of seeing the Lord on the last day, there can be no true purity. The hope of our seeing Him fuels our drive for ever increasing purity. The believer or a church that loses its expectation of seeing the risen Lord, is headed for compromise and spiritual complacency. May we never lose sight of His coming. The Lord is not slow in keeping His promise. The Bible says, **"The Lord is not slack concerning His promise as some count slackness..." (2 Peter 3:9).** He may return sooner than expected.

Dear saint, keep the hope of His coming and our being changed alive; may this inspire new levels of purity in your walk with the Lord. Amen

Prayer

 Lord, teach me to keep hope alive. May this hope birth in me purity of heart as You are pure.

Bible Reading Plan:
1 Kings 2 and 3, Psalm 64

DAY 207 AS TO THE LORD

 *"And whatever you do, do it heartily as to the Lord and not to men, knowing that from the Lord you will receive the reward of the inheritance; for you serve the Lord Christ"* (Colossians 3:23-24).

There are two foundations of service: service as unto the Lord and service as unto men. A lot of spiritual passivity will be dealt with today if we served as unto the Lord and that the Lord will reward what we do; be it in our place of work or business or in church.

Those who serve as unto the Lord, will go on serving even when they are resisted, unappreciated, opposed or even misunderstood by other believers. Their eyes are focused on the Lord who called them. Why do many abandon their place of assignment at the slightest provocation from other believers or even church leadership? Their service was as unto men. Is my service as to the Lord or men? How you react when you are unappreciated or opposed says a lot.

Prayer

 Lord, I pray that my service will be as unto You

Bible Reading Plan:
1 Kings 4 and 5, Psalm 65

DAY 208 THE TRAGEDY OF AN INDEPENDENT SPIRIT

 *"But his citizens hated him and sent a delegation after him, saying, we will not have this man reign over us"* (Luke 19:14).

If there is one thing the church suffers from today is the spirit of independence. What we forget is that God still works through men. The destinies of most of us are tied to the men we are endlessly laboring to be independent from. Many have missed and will miss their God-given destiny and purpose in life because they will not submit to God-ordained leadership in their life. When next we think that being on our own is the way forward, may these words from our Lord spare us from the insanity of independence. The Bible says **"And if you have not been faithful in what is another man's, who will give you what is your own?" (Luke 16:12).** The Lord Jesus makes clear that what God has for us will come through others; our faithfulness in serving others is the key that unlocks what God has in store for us.

Prayer

 Lord, let not independence rob me of that which You have in store for me.

Bible Reading Plan:
1 Kings 6 and 7, Psalm 66

DAY 209 — MISSING GOD'S COUNSEL

 *"But the Pharisees and lawyers rejected the counsel of God for themselves not having been baptized by him"* (Luke 7:30)

Our purpose will be tied to men God will place on our way and in our generation. The Pharisees where so self-absorbed that they missed God's design for their lives. According to them, all that pertained to God revolved exclusively around them. They missed it greatly. They rejected God's purpose or plan by refusing to be baptized by a man sent by God. God imparts us through men. In the Book of Romans, Paul says, **"For I long to see you, that I may impart to you some spiritual gift, so that you may be established" (Romans 1:11).** May the Lord correct our attitude towards men. Amen

Prayer

 Lord, I pray that my attitude towards the men You have sent will be correct. Let me not miss what You have to impart in my life through them.

Bible Reading Plan:
1 Kings 6 and 7, Psalm 67

DAY 210 SUBMISSION AND SPIRITUAL WARFARE

"Therefore submit to God. Resist the devil and he will flee from you" (James 4:7).

The spirit of independence was very manifest in Lucifer. Even men in the liberal world acknowledge his independent spirit and lack of submission: the book, **Rules for Radicals** by Saul Alinsky, is dedicated to Lucifer, as the first one to rebel and win a kingdom of his own. When we live in independence, we cannot resist the enemy and put him to flight; we lose our authority to do so. The Bible says, **"Therefore submit to God. Resist the devil and he will flee from you" (James 4:7).** Submission is a fundamental condition for victory in spiritual warfare. Let's beware of independence, for we can only punish every disobedience when our obedience is complete **(2 Corinthians 10:6).** Are you resisting submission?

Prayer

Lord, I embrace Your way of submission and I renounce an independent spirit. Amen

Bible Reading Plan:
1 Kings 8 and 9, Psalm 68

DAY 211 SPIRITUAL APPRENTICESHIP

 *"And the things that you have heard from me among many witnesses, commit these to faithful men who will be able to teach others also"* (2 Timothy 2:2).

Any system, be it Christian or secular owes its survival and perpetuation in its ability to transfer its core values to the next generation. This does not happen by wishing. There must be a deliberate system in place to foster continuity. The failure to effect this transfer will eventually usher decay and collapse. Karl Marx the founder of Communism said that, **"The quickest way to destroy a nation is to block the transfer of values from one generation to the next."** The apostle Paul understood the critical nature of transfer of spiritual values. He did not only groom the likes of Timothy, Titus, Silas and many others but also urged Timothy to make sure it moved on to others. Are you grooming others? I am being groomed? Will your ministry end with you?

Prayer

 Lord, I pray that I will give myself to grooming others and to be groomed by others.

Bible Reading Plan:
1 Kings 10 and 11, Psalm 69

DAY 212 NOT A BURDEN

"So because they were of the same trade, he stayed with them and worked; for by occupation they were tent makers" (Acts 18:3).

Paul's trade and skill was very important for his ministry. He was not a burden to anyone and even met the needs of others through the use of his skill and trade **(Acts 20:33-35).** The apostle who worked and preached the gospel did more for the gospel than many who claim to be doing full time. Our Lord Jesus acquired his own skill serving the father. In the Scriptures we see Him being referred to as the carpenter's son and later as the carpenter. As a carpenter's son he learnt from his father and later, he himself became a carpenter. In Matthew 13:55, the Bible says, Is this not the carpenter's son? And in Mark 6:3, it is said, Is this not the carpenter? Am a burden to the saints when I can use my own hands and work?

Prayer

Lord, I refuse to be a burden to others; You worked as a carpenter, as an example to follow

Bible Reading Plan:
1 Kings 12 and 13, Psalm 70

DAY 213 A GLORIOUS INHERITANCE

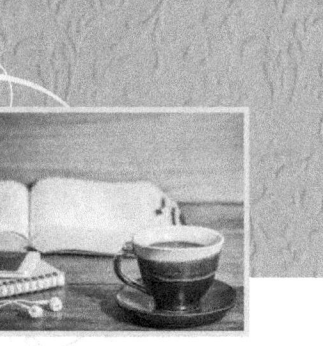

 *"A good man leaves an inheritance for his children's children"* (Proverbs 13:22)

While material inheritance may be the case mentioned here, there is nothing as powerful as a man's investments in the gospel to shape the destiny of his future generations. The Bible reveals that every spiritual act of ours also involves our unborn generations. Though unborn but in our loins they are partakers of any spiritual act of ours and enters into their future for their good; **"Even Levi, who receives tithes, paid tithes through Abraham, so to speak, for he was still in the loins of his father when Melchizedek met him" (Hebrews 7:9-10).** This should make us careful about what we do for, we involve the next generations for blessing or curse. When we do the work of God, our children reap glory. The Bible says, **"Let your work appear to Your servants and Your glory to their children" (Psalm 90:16).** Am I investing for a glorious inheritance?

Prayer

 Lord, I pray for the consciousness that my actions will definitely influence the next generation; may this lead me to invest wisely.

Bible Reading Plan:
1 Kings 14 and 15, Psalm 71

DAY 214 A GLORIOUS INHERITANCE II

Below is an example of two families and their generations. One of the families had as their father a preacher and the other an atheist. The results as preserved by Dr. Winship are startling:

"**The father of Jonathan Edwards was a minister and his mother was the daughter of a clergyman. Among their descendants were, fourteen presidents of colleges, more than one hundred college professors, more than one hundred lawyers, thirty-six judges, sixty physicians, more than a hundred clergy, missionaries and theology professors and about sixty authors.... The contrast is presented in the Jukes family which could not be made to study and would not work and is said to have cost the state of New York a million dollars. Their entire record is one of pauperism, crime, insanity and imbecility. Among their twelve hundred known descendants, three hundred and ten were professional paupers, four hundred and forty were physically wrecked by their own wickedness, sixty were habitual thieves, one hundred and thirty were convicted criminals, fifty-five were victims of impurity, only twenty learned a trade (and ten of these learned it in state prison), and this notorious family produced seven murderers**".

Am I investing towards a glorious inheritance?

Prayer

Lord, I pray that I will make great investments that will affect the next generation for good.

Bible Reading Plan:
1 Kings 16 and 17, Psalm 72

DAY 215 — UNLOCKING DOORS OF FAVOUR: THE REWARD OF FAITHFUL SERVICE

"The king's favor is toward the wise servant" (Proverbs 14:35)

As we serve diligently and in faithfulness, favor opens up to us before God and man. Imagine a servant sharing an inheritance among brothers; that is the kind of favor that true service opens us to; **"A wise servant will rule over a son who causes shame and will share an inheritance among the brothers" (Proverbs 17:2).**

Eliezer had served Abraham so well that, Abraham had started considering him as his heir if God will not answer his prayer for a child. He had even presented Eliezer to God as possible heir. That is the favor of true servant hood. The Bible says, **"But Abram said, LORD God, what will you give me, seeing I go childless and the heir of my house is Eliezer of Damascus? Then Abram said, look you have given me no offspring; indeed, one born in my house is my heir" (Genesis 15:2-3).** Am I serving? Will I offer to serve someone? Favours are unlocked by service to men.

Prayer

Lord, I choose to serve and serve faithfully; show me one leader or saint(s) I should serve in a distinctive way

Bible Reading Plan:
1 Kings 18 and 19, Psalm 73

DAY 216 — MODEL FOR SPIRITUAL LEADERSHIP

 *"Whoever desires to become great among you, let him be your servant; and whoever desires to be first among you, let him be your slave"* (Matthew 20:26-27).

Servanthood is God's model of effective and lasting leadership. Leadership that will make impact is leadership that serves and does not seek to be served. The Lord Jesus Christ showed this model of leadership by the washing of the feet of the disciples **(John 13:12-15)**. The Chief Shepherd served, so we too should not expect to be served but rather serve. Can I go as low as washing the feet of others? Am I only expecting to be served? Is there a clear way in which I am serving God's children? Tabitha had a clear service to God's children and it spoke for her when she died. Prayers from the women her life touched rose up to heaven and she was raised to life.

Prayer

 Lord, I pray that I serve others in a very distinct and clear way. I change from expecting to be served to actually serving others.

Bible Reading Plan:
1 Kings 20 and 21 Psalm 74

DAY 217: THE ESSENCE OF GOD CONCEPT

 *"Then he who had received the one talent came and said, Lord I knew you to be a hard man...."* (Matthew 25:24).

The way you view God will eventually show up in the way you live your life, says **A. W. Tozer.** Our conception of God is very important in our service for Him. The man who buried his talent had a certain idea about God. His wicked and lazy attitude flowed from his distorted thinking about God; he saw God as a hard man. He therefore buried his talent. The apostle Paul said, **"for I know whom I have believed" (2 Timothy 1:12).** Paul knew whom he served. He gave his all and held nothing back. But before he got to say that I know whom I have believed, he had prayed, **"that I may know Him"**. Could this be the reason why Paul worked tirelessly for the gospel, risking his life daily? Those who don't Him will not serve with their talents. May we pray like Paul; **That I may know Him**.

Prayer

 Lord, may I know You ever so increasingly and as result give myself to You without reserve. Amen.

Bible Reading Plan:
1 Kings 22 and 2 Kings 1, Psalm 75

DAY 218 GOD'S ORDER

 *"For there stood by me this night an angel of the God to whom I belong and whom I serve"* (Acts 27:23)

Paul the apostle didn't just say the God whom I serve. He would have been correct after all, to just say, the God whom I serve. But interestingly, the apostle takes the trouble to lay out a spiritual order that is greatly overlooked today: The God to whom I belong and whom I serve. It is clear that our belonging and spiritual birth precedes our service to God. And it is very easy to ascertain our belonging. The Bible has a simple test. If we are living in a known sin, then we are certainly not His and our service is a waste of time. The Bible says, **"He who sins is of the devil" (1 John 3:8).** No one who continues in sin has any basis to claim that he or she is a child of God. I am in any known or continued sin?

Prayer

 Lord, let there be no sinful way in me. I repent and seek Your mercy for sin in my life.

Bible Reading Plan:
2 Kings 2 and 3, Psalm 76

DAY 219 RESULTS WITHOUT GOD

 *"For Israel has forgotten His Maker and has built temples; Judah has multiplied fortified cities"* (Hosea 8:14).

In prophet Hosea's time, temples went up and cities were multiplied but God was forgotten and was out of the picture. Imposing and magnificent spiritual structures have no direct relationship with desire for God. There may be great external progress in ministry without God. The church in Laodicea had no need but Jesus was outside knocking the door of the church. The Lord Jesus Christ warned those who cared a lot about what they did as opposed to who they are before God. In Matthew seven from verse twenty-one to twenty-three, the Lord was saying not all who call Him, Lord, Lord shall enter the kingdom of heaven. These people prophesied, casted out demons and did many wonders in the Lord's name but the Lord would have nothing to do with such. They were workers of iniquity.

Prayer

 Lord, I pray that I will not be deceived by results; there can results without You

Bible Reading Plan:
2 Kings 4 and 5, Psalm 77

DAY 220 STAYING ON FIRE

 *"Fervent in spirit, serving the Lord"* (Romans 12:11)

Every service to God, be it preaching the word or serving in very practical things requires a vibrant spiritual condition. The believer does not only have to retain the initial fire at birth but must labor to make sure that the fire keeps burning and glows even brighter. We are to keep our lamps burning; **"Let your waist be girded and your lamps burning" (Luke 12:35).** The girding of the waist refers to our holding fast to the word which is the belt of truth. To be trim and vibrant for our God we have to be filled with the word. The Bible says, **"Let the word of Christ dwell in you richly" (Colossians 3:16).** Men and women who have made impact for God have always invested greatly in the word. It is said that Catherine Booth (Catherine Mumford before she married William Booth), the wife of the founder of the Salvation Army, had read her Bible eight times from Genesis to Revelation by age twelve. Watchman Nee read the New Testament once every week. How much are you investing in the word?

Prayer

 Lord, I pray that I will remain on fire; with the word richly dwelling in me.

Bible Reading Plan:
2 Kings 6 and 7, Psalm 78

DAY 221 STAYING ON FIRE II

"Fervent in spirit, serving the Lord"
(Romans 12:11)

The burning lamps has to do with the fire of the Holy Spirit in us. The Bible says, **"The spirit of man is the lamp of the LORD searching all the inner depths of his heart" (Proverbs 20:27).** To keep our spirits (the lamp of the Lord) burning we must keep party with the Holy Spirit.

Being filled with the Holy Spirit is a basic requirement to serve even in practical things in the body. In the Acts of the Apostles, the fullness of the Spirit was required even for men chosen to distribute food; **"Therefore, brethren, seek out from among you seven men of good reputation, full of the Holy Spirit and wisdom, whom we may appoint over this business" (Acts 6:3).**

The believer should therefore not grieve or put out the fire of the Spirit; but remain filled with the Holy Spirit.

Prayer

Oh Lord for a lamp with oil and fire always. Help me maintain in filling with the Holy Spirit.

Bible Reading Plan:
2 Kings 8 and 9, Psalm 79

DAY 222 UNDERSTANDING GOD'S WISDOM

 *"Who then is that faithful and wise servant"* (Matthew 24:45)

The execution of the Lord's business or any task that is entrusted to us will require the employment of wisdom, which is the ability to apply relevant knowledge in an insightful way, especially to different practical situations. God's design is that through us, the church, His wisdom will be made manifest in the world as an opportunity to witness. The wisdom of God in us is multifaceted and should find expression now, in this world in the way we run our businesses, do our jobs, operate the church and build our homes. In whatever God assigns to be done, there are two important components and dimensions: the spiritual and the wisdom or practical dimension. The wisdom dimension is very practical, requiring the use of even science, technology and managerial abilities to carry out God's design. The Lord is calling us to begin to exercise that wisdom as a tool of our dominion mandate as kings doing extraordinary exploits.

Prayer

 Lord, I pray that I will recapture Your wisdom mandate for my calling and assignment.

Bible Reading Plan:
2 Kings 10 and 11, Psalm 80

DAY 223 — AUTHENTIC SERVANTS

 *"Servants obey in all things your masters according to the flesh"* (Colossians 3:22)

It will be inconceivable to think of servanthood without obedience. In fact, the idea of a disobedient servant is oxymoronic. Servants obey their masters. In the book **Spiritual Authority**, Watchman Nee says, **"another name for believers is obeyers"**. Saul was anointed by God to serve as king of Israel. God gave him specific instructions to destroy everything of the Amalekites, sparing nothing. The Bible says, **"Now go and attack Amalek and utterly destroy all that they have and do not spare them. But kill man and woman, infant and nursing child, ox and sheep, camel and donkey" (1 Samuel 15:3).**

Saul, instead of obeying God, rationalized the instructions of God; He went for convenient and partial obedience. Everything worthless was destroyed but what could be of some material gain was spared. This is convenient obedience. Saul was rejected as king for partial obedience.

Prayer

 Lord, I pray that I will obey fully.

Bible Reading Plan:
2 Kings 12 and 13, Psalm 81

DAY 224: THE GLORIES OF A SELFLESS LIFE

"He must increase and I must decrease" (John 3:30)

There are many whose efforts have been frozen because the credit for the results will not directly come to them. It takes true humility to labor and not bother who gets the credit. It is even more so when we serve and we know from the start that the glory will go exclusively to another. Many are like Ornan; waste it if it will benefit another. The Bible says, **"And Judah said to Ornan, go in to your brother's wife and marry her, and raise up an heir for your brother. But Ornan knew that the heir would not be his; and it came to pass, when he went in to his brother's wife, that he emitted on the ground, lest he should give an heir to his brother." (Genesis 38:8-9).** The selfless are wired differently. They see the big picture; the overall interest of God and His kingdom. Charles Spurgeon said, if he does not bother which church the souls he wins go to, when those churches filled up, they will eventually overflow to his own church. Can I still give myself to serve even if the credit goes to another?

Prayer

Lord, I pray that I will be selfless, putting my all even if the credit goes to another.

Bible Reading Plan:
2 Kings 14 and 15, Psalm 82

DAY 225 A PROFILE IN SELFLESNESS: JOHN THE BAPTIST

 *"He must increase and I must decrease"* (John 3:30)

John the Baptist's role by definition was to make way for another. The greatness of this man is that he never for once tried to share the glory of Christ. He would have exploited the fact that people kept asking him, if he was the Messiah or the Christ. His replies and answers reveal his servant state of heart. Very few can serve in the order of John the Baptist; our entire call being that of making the way for another. Many came to test his selflessness; **"And they came to John and said to him, Rabbi, He who was with you beyond the Jordan, to whom you have testified-behold, He is baptizing, and all are coming to Him!" (John 3:26).** These people were simply saying to John that, the man you baptized now has the attention of people more than you. What will you do about that it? Doesn't that concern you? But John was a true servant: he was selfless. He replied, **"He must increase and I must decrease".**

Prayer

 Lord, I pray for a selfless life and grace to serve even when another gets the credit

Bible Reading Plan:
2 Kings 16 and 17, Psalm 83

DAY 226 — LET THIS MIND BE IN YOU

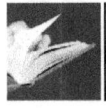 *"Let this mind be in you which was also in the Lord Jesus Christ"* (Philippians 2:5)

"I implore Euodia and I implore Syntyche to be of the same mind in the Lord" (Philippians 4:2)

Minds have to meet for a sustainable and successful service to God or man. Those who must serve God through a spiritual leader must align to the vision of God for that house. They must be of the same mind. Servanthood ends where there is loss of spiritual like-mindedness.

Oneness of mind is very important to God. The Bible says, **"That you may with one mind and one mouth glorify the God and Father of our Lord Jesus Christ (Romans 15:6).** From our passage, we see that, one mind will produce one mouth. This condition is very crucial for God's visitation. God is glorified in oneness of mind and mouth. Am I a source of division?

Prayer

 Lord, I pray that I will not be a source of division in the body

Bible Reading Plan:
2 Kings 18 and 19, Psalm 84

DAY 227 — TIMOTHY: A LIKE-MINDED SERVANT

"But I trust in the Lord Jesus to send Timothy to you shortly, that I also may be encouraged when I know your state. For I have no one like-minded, who will sincerely care for your state. For all seek their own, not the things which are of Christ"
(Philippians 2:19-20).

Timothy served the Lord as a son to Paul in the Gospel. The apostle had witnessed many of his fellow co-workers desert and abandon him. But Timothy stayed with the apostle till the end. The like-mindedness of Timothy with Paul the apostle was key to the success of Timothy's service with Paul in the gospel.

The apostle was saying that Timothy shares his thinking on sincerely caring for the state of the believers. Paul and Timothy were thus united in sincere care for the condition of the saints and the things that are of Christ. The others, the apostle says, were seeking their own. Like the Devil they would not align. There are many today, who think that aligning with leader makes them less spiritual and not having a mind of their own. May we learn alignment with others and leadership.

Prayer

Lord, grant me humility to align with spiritual leadership and those placed over me.

Bible Reading Plan:
2 Kings 20 and 21, Psalm 85

DAY 228 UNAVAILABLE SHOULDERS: THE TRAP OF REPUTATION AND STATUS

"Next to them the Tekoites made repairs; but their nobles did not put their shoulders to the work of the Lord" (Nehemiah 3:5).

Many are in the clutches of their reputation and it is holding them back from serving the Lord. The nobles of the Tekoites did not put their shoulders to the work of the Lord. They were too big to make repairs like their fellow Tekoites. Those who truly know the Lord, will do anything for Him and in His name: such count their earthly status as nothing. Jesus Christ made Himself of no reputation, though He was God. He could therefore take the form of a servant. He did not only make Himself of no reputation. He accepted to die on the cross for our sins. Dear saint, are you too big to put your hands or shoulders to the Lord's work?

Prayer

Lord, I pray that reputation and status will not stand on my way; I count all as nothing. I will put my shoulders to Your work. Amen

Bible Reading Plan:
2 Kings 22 and 23, Psalm 86

DAY 229: GOD'S PATHWAY TO GREATNESS

 *"Then He came to Capernaum. And when He was in the house, He asked them, what was it you disputed among yourselves on the road? But they kept silent, for on the road they had disputed among themselves who would be the greatest. And He sat down and called the twelve and said to them, if anyone desires to be first, he shall be last of all and servant of all"* (Mark 9:33-35).

The Lord did not to 'rebuke' His disciples for having such a dispute and rivalry. Meaning the matter of greatness is a healthy topic. From the Lord Jesus, we learn that it is not wrong to desire to be great and that the path to greatness is to become servant of all. God's way is serving others. Do you aspire greatness before God and men, God's way? If you do, then embrace the life of a servant; putting yourself at the disposal of others.

Prayer

 Lord, I give myself to seize every opportunity to serve others.

Bible Reading Plan:
2 Kings 24 and 25, Psalm 87

DAY 230 SPIRITUAL AMBITION

 *"And do you seek great things for yourself? Do not seek them"* (Jeremiah 45:5).

The word ambition is neutral. It can only be condemned or accepted based on qualification. Baruch's ambition centered on himself and such ambition is unworthy. And the Lord asked him not to seek such. But the ambition which God sanctions is of another set and scale of values. The glory of God is its sole aim, tinged with self-abnegation and self-sacrifice. The wrong lies not in wanting to be great but the inspiring motive for our quest for greatness. Men who were sold out for God and the good of others aspired for the heights. For example, the motto of William Carey, the father of modern missions was; **"Attempt great things for God. Expect great things from God"**. Paul the apostle said, **'I press toward the mark for the prize.'** These men like many others were not content with the spiritual lowlands but wanted the best of all that God had for them in Christ and they knew that, there is nothing which God will not do for the man whose ambition is for His greater glory.

Prayer

 Lord, for the desire to also press for the upward call in service to You and others in the name of Jesus Christ. Amen

Bible Reading Plan:
1 Chronicles 1 and 2 Psalm 88

DAY 231: PROVEN CHARACTER FOR CHRISTIAN SERVICE

 *"But you know his proven character, that as a son with his father, he served with me in the gospel"* (Philippians 2:22).

It has been said that, **"The greatest fraud of our time is religion without character"**.

The testimony of Timothy by the local churches was that of proven character. It was on that basis Paul offered to take Timothy into the ministry. The Bible says, **"Then he came to Derbe and Lystra. And behold a certain disciple was there named Timothy, the son of a certain Jewish woman who believed, but his father was Greek. He was well spoken of by the brethren, who were at Lystra and Iconium. Paul wanted to have him go with him. And he took him and circumcised him……. And as they went through the cities…" (Acts 16:1-4).** Paul did not take Timothy because of any spiritual gift; it was proven character. What is your basis for taking people into ministry? Those who enter without character, will not last.

Prayer

 Lord, I pray that I will place importance on character development; it is Your basis for ministry.

Bible Reading Plan:
1 Chronicles 3 and 4, Psalm 89

DAY 232 THE FAITHFUL LIFE

 *"Who then is a faithful and wise servant, whom his master made ruler over his household, to give them food in due season?"* (Matthew 24:45).

Faithfulness is precious before the Lord. The Bible even acknowledges that it is hard to find the faithful; **"…But who can find the faithful man?" (Proverbs 20:6).** Faithfulness implies loyalty which is a firm resistance to any temptation to desert or betray. In the Book of Matthew, the Lord presents an example that pictures for us faithfulness. Faithfulness borders on carrying out our assignment, when we are supposed to and to continue to do so come what may and however long that will take. The Bible says **'Blessed is that servant whom his master, when he comes, will find doing so" (Matthew 24:46).** The faithful will be found doing what they are supposed to do and when they are to do it. Time, in terms of how long they have to do it will not change their commitment to the task entrusted to them. Have you left place of your calling?

Prayer

 Lord, I pray that I will stick to my assignment, come what may.

Bible Reading Plan:
1 Chronicles 5 and 6 Psalm 90

DAY 233 DAILY MANNA

 *"Then the Lord said to Moses, behold, I will rain bread from heaven for you and the people shall go out and gather a certain quota per day"* (Exodus 16:4)

There is no spiritual experience for one day that will take care of all our days. We have to seek God and feed on His word daily. There are many who practice saltation in their spiritual lives: they skip like Kangaroos, reading one chapter today and read another after one week. Such persons will not walk in spiritual strength or keep their spiritual fire. The spiritual food of yesterday may not suffice for today's needs. It will pay the believer well to be spiritually consistent with little than to be intermittent with too much. One long fast is wonderful but if the next one only comes after six months, it may not be of impact as a person who fasts three days every week and is faithfully doing so all year round like Charles Finney did. He experienced great power. He lived the fasted life.

 Lord, may I be disciplined to pick the manna daily and be consistent.

Bible Reading Plan:
1 Chronicles 7 and 8 Psalm 91

DAY 234 — HE IS ABLE TO KEEP YOU

"Now to Him who is able to keep you from stumbling and present you faultless before the presence of His glory with exceeding joy" (Jude 1:24).

There is nothing the sincere believer is afraid of like stumbling or backsliding and betraying their Lord. With all the pressures in the world and the increase in iniquity of all kinds the average believer seeks God's assurance and grace to be able to stand and not stumble when that hour of trial comes. Jude, makes us know that God is able to keep us from stumbling and present us faultless before Him on that day. What a comforting word for the believer. Dear saint, fear not. God is able to keep you. All you have to do is to entrust yourself into His hands; He will not fail. We have no strength and power of our own. Let's not be like the Galatians who were bewitched: they started by faith and later wanted to continue in the flesh. Look up to Him who is the author and finisher of your faith. Amen

Prayer

Lord, thank You for the assurance that You are able to keep me from stumbling. I give myself to You.

Bible Reading Plan:
1 Chronicles 9 and 10 Psalm 92

DAY 235 — MORE THAN CONQUERORS

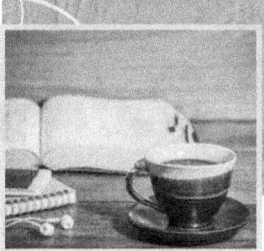

 *"Yet in all these things we are more than conquerors through Him who loved us"* (Romans 8:37)

We are more than conquerors not by ourselves but through Him who loved us. Without Him the trials and pressures of this life would drown even the most powerful of us. His life in us has empowered us to live above all that the enemy can release against us. Pastor Nick without hand and legs, lives a joyful life and is moving around the world to encourage others. Indonesia is a Muslim country that would not allow the gospel. But when they saw a man without legs and hands but so joyful, they said come, you can preach to us. The life of God in us triumphs over all that Satan can release from hell. Saint, you are more than a conqueror not by your power but by Him who loved you. Don't be afraid of any circumstance; rise and say, in the name of Jesus, I am more than a conqueror, I overcome you. Amen

Prayer

 Lord, thank You for making me more than a conqueror; no situation can bring me down. Amen

Bible Reading Plan:
1 Chronicles 11 and 12, Psalm 93

DAY 236 SPIRITUAL BRILLIANCE

 *"Arise, shine; for your light has come!"* (Isaiah 60:1)

Shine only comes after arise. Light shines at the expense of something; something must burn for there to be light. No brilliant spiritual career can be forged by sleepers. God is no man's favorite. He is fair enough to have given His word to the world and we all know what He requires; waking up from sleep and experience spiritual illumination. No one can wish his way into a noble spiritual experience. The Lord Himself was not a sleeper. He would wake up well before daybreak to go to a solitary place to pray. Will I pay the price for a new level with God? Before John the revelator got the revelation of Jesus as revealed in the book of Revelation, the Lord said, **"come up here and I will show the things which must take place" (Revelation 4:1b)**. May we move up for greater things.

Prayer

 Lord, I pray that I will arise and move up so that I can experience Your glory in a greater way. Amen

Bible Reading Plan:
1 Chronicles 13 and 14, Psalm 94

DAY 237 GREATER THINGS

 *"Call to Me, and I will answer you and show you great and mighty things, which you do not know"* (Jeremiah 33:3)

Jeremiah had just been shut into prison when the Lord, is asking Jeremiah to call to Him for greater and mighty things. Sometimes for the Lord to take us into deeper and mighty things, He would have to shut us out of all even if that means imprisonment. Sometimes, the greatest of divine studies can be made only when we are in custody. In such tight corners God is sure to have all our focus as never before. Sometimes when we are navigating these tight places, while we are thinking about our comfort and so on, God is thinking about His purpose through us. May we not yield to offense during such period. May the Holy Spirit open our eyes in such moments, to see that the Lord is about to use our situation for mighty things.

Prayer

 Lord, I pray that my heart will heed the call for greater and mighty things. I will trade my pain for the greater things of God.

Bible Reading Plan:
1 Chronicles 15 and 16 Psalm 95

DAY 238 — WE LOOK FOR ANOTHER

 *"Are You the coming One or do we look for another?"* (Matthew 11:3)

It is John the Baptist who announces and presents to us the Messiah; **"Here is the Lamb of God who takes away the sin of the world" (John 1:29).** John was convinced of who the Messiah was. But trouble came and John was imprisoned. Jesus, the Messiah is not coming to rescue John. John the Baptist begins to doubt the Messiah; He asks, are you the one coming or should we expect another? It is possible to doubt in the dark what we were once convinced of in the light. Maybe like John, you have a crisis and God has not showed up; this has made you start to doubt the goodness and the reality of God. Dear saint, doubt not His love and goodness. Sometimes in a crisis, it is not the goodness of God that is on trial any more than our faith is on trial. The question before you is; will you remain faithful to Him even if He does not solve your problem? Remember Job, who had said though He slay me I will yet trust Him. He was ready to go on with God even though he had been bruised by all kinds of affliction.

Prayer

 Lord, I pray that I will not yield to doubts when the night is so dark; I will still trust You

Bible Reading Plan:
1 Chronicles 17, Psalm 96

DAY 239: FORGETTING THOSE THINGS THAT ARE BEHIND

"Forgetting those things which are behind and reaching forward to those things which are ahead" (Philippians 3:13)

Sometimes the greatest thing we can do for ourselves is to walk past our past and if we don't do, it has a way of robbing us of the great future that God has for us. However painful and useless our past is, God can still have access to our past, redeem it so that we experience a great future. All the sins a man is asking forgiveness for were committed in the past. You may have committed murder, abortion or you stole and that led to the loss of your job. You are so full of shame and you feel you cannot face life anymore. We want to assure you that the stories of the Bible are stories of how God took the worst of men or women and made them into saints; do you know Moses was a murderer turned law giver and prophet? Do you know Paul was a murderer and persecutor turned apostle with more than half of New Testament books to his name? Seek the Lord's mercy; He is able to make a glorious future out of your horrible past. Amen

Prayer

Lord, I refuse to let the past hold me down; I look forward to the great things You have in store for me

Bible Reading Plan:
1 Chronicles 18 and 19, Psalm 97

DAY 240 LOOKING UP TO JESUS

 *"Looking unto Jesus, the author and the finisher of our faith..."* (Hebrews 12:2a)

Adelaide Proctor said, **"For every one look at myself, I take ten looks at Jesus"**. We become what we behold. As we behold Him who is the bright morning star, the brightness of that star radiates in our life the light of God and we are transformed from one degree of glory to another. In us is no good thing found; our goodness is in Him who became sin that we might become the righteousness of God in Christ Jesus. Every good thing in us stems from the goodness that is Christ. We dare not trust our sweetest frame. The Bible says, **"That the sharing of your faith may become effective by the acknowledgement of every good thing which is in you in Christ Jesus" (Philemon 1:6).** The only good thing in me is that which is Christ Jesus. I therefore, have to look up to Him.

Prayer

 Look I choose to look up to You; for all my goodness is in You and from You. Amen

Bible Reading Plan:
1 Chronicles 20 and 21, Psalm 98

DAY 241 A RULE FOR MINISTRY

 *"For I will not dare speak of any of those things which Christ has not accomplished through me, in word and in deed"*
(Romans 15:18)

What degree of humility in the life of the apostle: not to speak anything that had not become part of his personal experience? There is great temptation today to speak from the Bible truths that are not yet life in us. In ministry we do not only communicate, we transmit what we are. If we are not living in the reality of a particular truth, we cannot birth the reality of that truth in the life of another saint. Ministry as Watchman Nee puts it, is life. The more life we have the more ministry we can render others. May we arise with renewed honesty and humility in the ministry of the word. May we seek the Lord, so that our lives radiate that which we want the saints to enter into.

Prayer

 Lord, I pray that I will grow in depth and new dimensions with You; so that ministry is not words only but a life that lives in the reality of the word.

Bible Reading Plan:
1 Chronicles 22 and 23 Psalm 99

DAY 242 BEYOND BELIEVING

"He who believes and is baptized will be saved; but he who does not believe will be condemned" (Mark 16:16)

To be saved, one has to believe. There is no hope of salvation, to start with, without a person believing. However, once I believe, does the matter end there? Is there more I should know?

After believing, we are called to suffer for Him. We are not only to believe in Him, we are also to suffer for Him; **"For it has been granted for Christ's sake, not only believe in Him, but also to suffer for Him" (Philippians 1:29).**

We have to endure till the end to be saved. The Bible says, **"But he who endures to the end shall be saved" (Matthew 24:13).** The early believers were made to know that**, "We must through tribulations enter the kingdom of God" (Acts 14:22).** Go beyond believing; be reader to suffer and endure.

Prayer

Lord, thank You for showing me that I must not only believe but must also suffer and endure

Bible Reading Plan:
1 Chronicles 24 and 25 Psalm 100

DAY 243 ARMING THE MIND

"Therefore, since Christ suffered for us in the flesh, arm yourselves with the same mind..." (1 Peter 4:1)

The mind has to be armed and that involves spiritual preconditioning of what it takes to go all the way with the Lord. Zac Poonen told of a story of Corrie ten Boom's visit to the churches in China. When she arrived China, she was told by local pastors that the missionaries that came to China, did not prepare the believer's mind for persecution; they never told the believers about the suffering that could come as a result of their faith in Christ. All they expected was that Jesus will come before any tribulation; Jesus has not returned and the Communist came and have been there ever since; many of the believers fell away. As Christ suffered so we should expect to suffer for Him for there will trouble as a result of our faith in Christ sooner or later. We must suffer many tribulations in order to enter the kingdom of God **(Acts 14:22).**

Prayer

Lord, arm my mind to suffer persecution for the sake of the gospel and Your name.

Bible Reading Plan:
1 Chronicles 26 and 27 Psalm 101

DAY 244 ALWAYS IN TRIUMPH

"Now thanks be to God, who always leads us in triumph in Christ" (2 Corinthians 2:14)

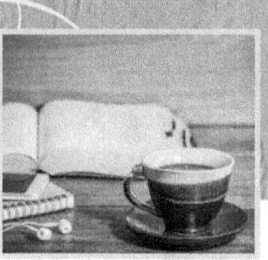

This is great news. God always leads us in triumph in Christ. It doesn't matter what we suffer, what we go through; God has guaranteed your triumph. Sometimes, the devil starts by having the upper hand, but the final triumph is with us. The devil is like a team that opens the score but eventually loses the game by five to one goal. Don't be frightened by the initial 'upper hand' of the kingdom of darkness. They are destined to fail. The last laugh is with you dear saint. Amen

Prayer

Lord, I praise You: You have guaranteed triumph for me always irrespective of the situation. I give You praise; I give You adoration. Amen

Bible Reading Plan:
1 Chronicles 28 and 29, Psalm 102, Daniel 1

DAY 245 THE STAGNATION CYCLE

 *"It is eleven days' journey from Horeb by way of Mount Seir to Kadesh Barnea...On this side of the Jordan, in the land of Moab, Moses began explaining the law, saying, the Lord spoke to us in Horeb saying you have dwelt long enough at this mountain"* (Deuteronomy 1:2-6).

The Israelites were eleven days' worth of travel time to get into the Promised Land. But they ended up spending forty years in the wilderness. What could have caused such stretch in their journey time? Complaining and murmuring against God as seen in Numbers 14. The Bible says, **"How long will I bear with this evil congregation who murmur against Me? I have heard the murmurings which the children of Israel murmur against Me" (Numbers 14:27).** The consequence of their complaining and murmuring was 40 years of stagnation; **"And your children shall wander in the wilderness forty years and bear your whoredoms...." (Numbers 14:33 KJV).**

"Remember, we cannot go to the next level if we are complaining about the one we are currently in" said Joyce Meyer. May I not complain but praise God in all situations.

Prayer

 Lord, I refuse to settle for complaints; I will praise You in all situations

Bible Reading Plan:
2 Chronicles 1 and 2, Psalm 103, Daniel 2

DAY 246 — THE STAGNATION CYCLE II

"Then he who had received the one talent came and said, Lord I knew you to be a hard man...." (Matthew 25:24).

The Israelites had opted for a place close to the Promised Land: a place just eleven days to the Promised Land. Sometimes stagnation is caused by our satisfaction with what looks close to what God is taking us into. We tend then to sacrifice the best for the better and we settle. Closest to the best replaces the best. Soren Kierkegaard the Danish theologian said, **"People settle for a level of despair they can tolerate and call it happiness"**. This is stagnation by accommodation of that which is nearest to the best. The believer must not settle for the nearest best or closest to the best. God's best is what we must go for in all areas of our life. It should be God's best or nothing. May we not be content with a substandard spiritual experience.

Prayer

Lord, I refuse to settle for the nearest to the best. I go for the best You have for me in life and ministry. Amen

Bible Reading Plan:
2 Chronicles 3 and 4, Psalm 104, Daniel 3

DAY 247 HE CARES FOR US

 *"Casting your care unto Him for He cares for you"* (1 Peter 5:7).

While in this life, we face many challenges and pressures that burden our hearts. God does not intend that we carry these burdens and weights in our hearts. He cares enough for us and He desires that we cast these cares unto Him. Nothing needs to scare us for we have a God who cares for us. In the Psalms He also says, **"Cast your burden on the Lord and He shall sustain you: He shall never permit the righteous to be moved" (Psalm 55:22).** It is a deliberate act by the believer to cast his or her burdens on the Lord. We are not to be weighed down by loads of care for our Lord is a giver of rest; **"Come to Me, all you who labor and are heavy laden and I will give you rest" (Matthew 11:28).** We should not be like the man who entered the vehicle and still carried his load on his head. Let the Lord bear your burdens for He is very able to carry them.

Prayer

 Lord, I cast every burden this day to You for You care for me

Bible Reading Plan:
2 Chronicles 5 and 6, Psalm 105, Daniel 4

DAY 248 — BEWARE OF CARES: AN ETERNAL PERSPECTIVE

 *"But take heed to yourselves, lest your hearts be weighed down with carousing, drunkenness and the cares of this life and that Day come on you unexpectedly"* (Luke 21:34).

Cares can be snares in the spiritual life if they are not properly dealt with and are allowed to overwhelm us. In the parable of the sower, the seed of the word was choked by the cares of this life. The Bible says, **"Now he who received seed among the thorns is he who hears the word and the cares of this world and the deceitfulness of riches choke the seed of the word and he becomes unfruitful" (Matthew 13:22).** The cares of this world choke the word of God in us and impact our ability to be spiritually fruitful. Even more significantly, the cares of this life weigh us down and they dampen our expectation and preparedness for the coming of the Lord.

Prayer

 Lord, I commit myself not to allow the cares of this life to overwhelm my soul and weigh me down

Bible Reading Plan:
2 Chronicles 7 and 8, Psalm 106, Daniel 5

DAY 249 THE PLACE OF ENCOURAGEMENT

 *"Therefore, encourage one another with these words" (1 Thessalonians 4:18)*

Encouragement is so important in the body of believers such that the apostles in the early church had to name someone son of encouragement: Barnabas who was initially called Joses **(Acts 4:36)**. Encouragement involves words to edify and comfort the saints. The Bible says, **"Now Judas and Silas, themselves being prophets also, exhorted the brethren with many words and strengthening them" (Acts 15:32).** Paul says all believers can prophesy; thus should be encouragers; **"For you can all prophesy one by one, that all may learn and all may be encouraged" (1 Corinthians 14:31).** A prominent servant of God once said, **"If I had to do my ministry all over again, I will give myself entirely to the encouragement of the believers"**. Discouragement is a very strong weapon in the hands of the enemy **(Ezra 4:4 NIV)**. None of us is immune to discouragement. Even Elijah was discouraged and needed encouragement. Our journey is great and full of tribulations. Encourage someone today. Speak words of encouragement and comfort to others; it strengthens and edifies.

Prayer

 Lord, I give myself to the encouragement of the saints. I renounce the urge to criticize. Amen

Bible Reading Plan:
2 Chronicles 9 and 10, Psalm 107, Daniel 6

DAY 250 READ OR LEAVE THE MINISTRY

"Till I come, give attendance to reading"
(1 Timothy 4:13)

Men who have impacted the world for God and other domains have been men of books. The love for books and study is one common denominator of great men. We begin by looking at the example of our Lord Jesus Christ; His life as a student of the word and as a learner. The Bible speaks of Jesus saying, **"The Lord God has given Me the tongue of the learned, that I should know how to speak a word in season to him who is weary. He awakens Me, morning by morning, He awakens My ear to hear as the learned" (Isaiah 50:4).** Our Lord was a reader. He always asked and challenged the Pharisees, **"Have you not read?"** (Matthew 12:3, 5, Matthew 19:4, 22:31, Mark 12:10, 26). Our Lord was a committed learner and we too should. Not just when we have to minister but as a way of life: morning by morning.

Prayer

Lord, I pray that I will be a reader of Your word and good books

Bible Reading Plan:
2 Chronicles 11 and 12, Psalm 108, Daniel 7

DAY 251 — READ OR LEAVE THE MINISTRY II

The apostles, men of the generation past and those who made impact in our time were men of books. The apostle Paul stands tall in this regard. In 2 Timothy 4:13, he tells Timothy, **"Bring the cloak that I left with Carpus at Traos when you come and the books especially the parchments"**. Paul called for his books to be brought to him. Charles Spurgeon the "Prince of Preachers" has this commentary on Paul concerning the passage above: **"He (Paul) was inspired, yet wants books. He had been preaching for 30 years and yet he wants books. He had wider experience than most men do and yet wants books. He had been caught up in the third heavens and had heard things that it was not lawful for man to utter yet he wants books. He had written a major part of the New Testament and yet wants books. Paul cries, "Bring the books, and join in the cry".**

Prayer

Lord, make me a life-long learner

Bible Reading Plan:
2 Chronicles 13 and 14, Psalm 109, Daniel 8

DAY 252 READ OR LEAVE THE MINISTRY III

Another man in generations past who made a mark and gave himself to study was Charles Spurgeon. He was a 17th century preacher of the famous Metropolitan Tabernacle with about 5000 plus members. He began pastoring in his teenage years, and helped found about 66 organizations. He still had time to read about 6 books per week. His library had about 5100 volumes and authored over 50 plus books. He had this to say about reading for ministry: **"Give yourself to reading. The man who never reads cannot be read; he who never quotes will never be quoted. He who will not use the thoughts of other men's brains, proves that he has no brains of his own. You need to read".**

Prayer

Lord, I pray for more fire for Your word and books

Bible Reading Plan:
2 Chronicles 15 and 16, Psalm 110, Daniel 9

DAY 253 MASTERY: A SPIRITUAL REQUIREMENT

"Sing to Him a new song. Play skillfully" (Psalm 33:3.)

To be sloppy in the name of God is a shame. **"Slovenliness is an insult to the Holy Spirit"**, says Oswald Chambers. The word speaks of David saying, **"So he shepherded them according to the integrity of his heart and guided them by the skillfulness of his hands"(Psalm 78:72.)** To master anything and be skillful at it is a matter of work and practice. Men who made impact mastered their trade. Ezra became a skilled scribe by preparation; **"For Ezra had prepared his heart to seek the Law of the LORD and to do it and to teach its statutes and ordinances in Israel"(Ezra 7:10).** Luke's writing to Theophilus flowed from his perfect understanding of the life and ministry of Jesus Christ. He did not package garbage. Luke says, **"It seemed good to me also, having had perfect understanding of all things from the very first, to write to you........." (Luke 1:3).** Are we striving for mastery in all we do? Or we are packaging garbage?

Prayer

Lord, I pray that I will strive for mastery in all I do; making sure it is well done

Bible Reading Plan:
2 Chronicles 17 and 18, Psalm 111, Daniel 10

DAY 254 — MASTERY: A SPIRITUAL REQUIREMENT II

There can be no mastery without drudgery and it is the drudgery involved that scares many. I may not be a minister but in what I do, am I putting in all the effort to master my craft? Will I settle for mediocre performance which is an expression of lack of mastery stemming from the evasion of drudgery? Paderewski, the great Pianist had once played before the queen of England. The queen came to him after the performance and said, 'Mr. Paderewski, you are a genius'. Paderewski replied saying, 'yes, before I became a genius I was a drudge'. No mastery without drudgery. Will you pay the price for mastery or settle for mediocrity?

Prayer

Lord, may I embrace drudgery. I renounce the way of mediocrity and lack of mastery in whatever I do. Amen

Bible Reading Plan:
2 Chronicles 19 and 20, Psalm 112, Daniel 11

DAY 255 STRENGTHENED WITH MIGHT IN THE INNER MAN

 *"In the day when I cried out You answered me and made me bold with strength in my soul"* (Psalm 138:3).

All crumbling begins from inside and it is determined by the state of the soul. If the soul is exerting a strength less than that of the pressures without, the result will be a fall or spiritual failure. Prayer has a bearing on the state of the soul: whether strong or weak. In the Bible, strength is always related or measured in respect to our posture in the face of adversity. The Bible says, **"If you falter in a time of trouble, how small is your strength" (Proverbs 24:10 NIV).** What brings us down is not necessarily the size of our trouble but the size of our strength. If we work on our internal strength, Satan can let the whole of hell lose for all we care. We can now understand why the Lord kept telling His disciples, **"Watch and pray so that you will not fall into temptation" (Matthew 26:41 NIV).** Prayer is key to internal strength or soul might. Give yourself to pray; to strengthen your soul.

Prayer

 Lord, I give myself to pray; let my soul be strengthened daily.

Bible Reading Plan:
2 Chronicles 21 and 22, Psalm 113, Daniel 12

DAY 256 — STRENGTHENED WITH MIGHT IN THE INNER MAN II

In the events leading up to the arrest and crucifixion of Jesus, the Lord had admonished his disciples to stand with him in prayer, but they all slept. When the trial moment came, all ran and Peter of all denied his Lord before a little servant girl. But the Lord retreated to pray during that period. The Bible says he prayed three times saying the same words. When the moment came, he did not faint. He could stand strong and be subjected to the most horrible treatment that can ever be given to an individual. Prayerlessness is the prelude to soul anemia: weakness of the soul. The fatal result is falling or fainting in the face of adversity. Prayerlessness is a harbinger of a fall. Those who do not pray are preparing their soul to fall to a level where they will deny Christ in the face of pressure. Many take prayer for granted and their souls are lean and weak. It need not be so. Heed the call to pray.

Prayer

Lord, I will follow Your pattern; give myself to prayer in quiet and turbulent times.

Bible Reading Plan:
2 Chronicles 23 and 24, Psalm 114, Hosea 1

DAY 257 AN IMPACTFUL MINISTRY

 *"For My mouth has commanded it and His Spirit has gathered them"* (Isaiah 34:16).

Soul winners are first of all soul weepers -Charles Spurgeon.

The Spirit and the word must work for there to be any true work of God in the hearts of men. Even in the creation, we see the same pattern in operation. The Spirit of God was hovering over the deep and God said let there be light and there was light **(Gen.1:2-3).** There must be fire without which we have just empty words and to have that fire power behind our message, our hearts have to be filled with the Spirit of God. Preaching is aimed at the initial and progressive winning of the hearts of men to God. To do so, we have to wrestle in prayer for them, so that the power of the Holy Spirit will reach their hearts and produce lasting change. Our rule should be not to talk to people about God without talking to God about the people.

Prayer

 Lord, I pray that I will be a soul weeper, crying out to You for the saving of the souls of men

Bible Reading Plan:
2 Chronicles 25 and 26, Psalm 115, Hosea 2

DAY 258: AN IMPACTFUL MINISTRY II

The Lord Jesus is a perfect example in this regard; ministry flowing from prayer. The Bible says, **"Now in the morning having risen a long while before daylight, He went out and departed to solitary place: and there he prayed.........But he said to them, "Let us go into the next towns that I may preach there also, because for this purpose I have come forth and He was preaching in their synagogues throughout all Galilee and casting out demons" (Mark 1:35-38).** So, the Lord prayed before he proceeded to preach. We should do same. The apostle preached sanctification but prayed that the believers be sanctified **(1 Thessalonians 4:3-7, 5:23).** Our preaching should be backed by prayer. Every subject of preaching should be a subject of intense praying on behalf of the saints and the unsaved. The minister should edify himself, praying in the Holy Spirit so that he too can build others up **(Jude 1:20).** This could explain why Paul said, **"I thank my God that I speak in tongues more than you all" (1 Corinthians 14:18).** He built himself up in order to build others.

Prayer

Lord, I commit myself to ministry that is soaked in prayer and Your presence. Amen

Bible Reading Plan:
2 Chronicles 27 and 28, Psalm 116, Hosea 3

DAY 259 — THE PURPOSE DRIVEN LIFE

 *"When he came and had seen the grace of God, he was glad and he encouraged them all that with purpose of heart they should continue with the Lord"* (Acts 11:23).

Our God is a God of purpose; **"And as I have purposed it, so it shall stand" (Isaiah 14:24).** God does things for a purpose and you are in the kingdom for such a time as this because God wants to accomplish His plan for your church or city or nation through you **(Esther 4:14).** The Lord Jesus Christ was also purpose driven. He had a reason why He came forth. The Bible says, **"But he said to them, "Let us go into the next towns that I may preach there also, because for this purpose I have come forth" (Mark 1:38).** The Holy Spirit too inspires plans and purposes; **"And all the plans for all that, he had by the Spirit" (1 Chronicles 28:12).** Paul also experienced the Holy Spirit in this area of purpose and plans for the Lord; **"When these things were accomplished, Paul purposed in the Spirit......to go to Jerusalem saying, after I have been there, I must also see Rome" (Acts 19:21)**. And Paul did get to Rome, dwelt there for two full years in his own rented apartment and preaching the gospel **(Acts 28:16, 30-31).** May we also be purpose driven in our lives.

Prayer

 Lord, I pray that I will live a purpose driven life; accomplishing Your plans for my life.

Bible Reading Plan:
2 Chronicles 29 and 30 Psalm 117, Hosea 4

DAY 260: THE LIFE THAT ILLUMINATES

 *"You are the light of the world"* (Matthew 5:14)

The life of God in us constitutes the principle of development or light in us that enables us to set the pace in a world enveloped by darkness **(Isaiah 60:1-3).** The Bible says, **"In Him was life and the life was the light of men" (John 1:4).** Light here stands for development and thus we can say, in Him was life and that life was the development of men. Because we represent this principle of development, believers are the city set on hill, setting the pace and standard for a fallen world in all respects and areas of life. We are to do good and great works in the face of men that bring glory to the Father. The believer is thus a productive person in life. The life of God in you is light that inspires good works that bring glory to God in the face of men. Paul the apostle says, **"This is a faithful saying and these things I want you to affirm constantly, that those who have believed in God should be careful to maintain good works. These things are good and profitable to men" (Titus 3:8).** Our lives are to inspire good works.

Prayer

 Lord, I pray that my life will inspire good works; for I am the light of the world

Bible Reading Plan:
2 Chronicles 31 and 32 Psalm 118, Hosea 5

DAY 261 THE LIFE THAT ILLUNINATES II

The matter of doing works that profit men is a very important theme in the Bible. The word of God says, **"And let our people also learn to maintain good works, to meet urgent needs, that they may not be unfruitful" (Titus 3:14).** This is why a lot of what has helped in the progress of society and even alleviate human suffering has been the work of men of faith. In education for example, men of light have contributed greatly. Prestigious universities today like Harvard, Yale, Princeton and many others was the work of people of light. The ending of slave trade was the work and fight of William Wilberforce, a man of faith. Great businesses and institutions like the Barclays Bank, Quaker Oats, Cadbury, Colgate, the Red Cross and many others. We too have the life in us that inspires light for great works. God counts on you to bring glory to Him through good works.

Prayer

Lord, I will let my light shine and do good works to bring glory to Your name.

Bible Reading Plan:
2 Chronicles 33 and 34 Psalm 119, Hosea 6

DAY 262 OUTSTANDING UNDERSTANDING

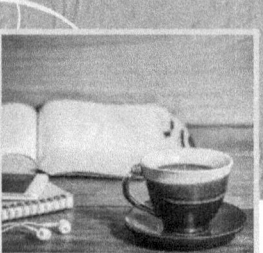

 *"My purpose is that they may be encouraged in heart and united in in love so that they may have the full riches of complete understanding"* (Colossians 2:2).

The understanding of unbelievers is darkened because they are alienated from the life of God **(Ephesians 4:18)** and so the things of the kingdom and other secrets of God are hidden from them. But for the believer who has the life of God in him or her, the capacity to understand God and His word is imparted. This entitles the believer to unravel the things of God and the Spirit. The Bible says, **"And we know that the Son of God has come and has given us an understanding, that we may know Him who is true......(1 John 5:20)** The Word further says **"But there is a spirit in man and the breath of the Almighty gives him understanding" (Job 32:8).** The impartation of the breath of life in us brings with it, divine capacities to understand all things. Amen

Prayer

 Lord, thank You for the blessing to understand the mysteries of the Kingdom.

Bible Reading Plan:
2 Chronicles 35 and 36 Psalm 120, Hosea 7

DAY 263 OUTSTANDING UNDERSTANDING II

God also imparts supernatural understanding for exploits and extraordinary results in life. Daniel experienced this level of supernatural understanding and this distinguished him in Babylon. The Bible says, **"I have heard of You, that the Spirit of God is in you and that light and understanding and excellent wisdom are found in you" (Daniel 5:14).** This capacity to understand is the believer's inheritance as we do have the Mind of Christ **(1 Corinthians 2:16).** This understanding also gives the believer capacity for outstanding exploits in life. According to E. W Kenyon, **"Wherever men have received Eternal Life, the next generation of that people, whether it is Christian or not, receives something that makes it produce inventors, discoverers, students, scientists and educators. The intellectual Renaissance of Germany followed Luther's teaching of the New Birth. The mechanical Renaissance of England followed the Wesleyan and Whitefield revivals."** The new life imparts this understanding for exploits; giving solutions to complex problems like Daniel in Babylon. An enlightened understanding is your inheritance in Christ; No subject or discipline of study need be a challenge. You have an anointing to know all things **(1 John 2:20).**

Prayer

Lord, I unleash the understanding for exploits in my job, business, studies and all I do. Amen

Bible Reading Plan:
Ezra 1 and 2 Psalm 121, Hosea 8

DAY 264 A LIFE THAT WINS

"Yet I all these things we are more than conquerors through Him who loved us" (Romans 8:37).

Jesus is not a convenient option or the Christian faith is not a convenient religion. There will be challenges and troubles. Our guarantee in Christ is not advantageous circumstances but advantageous character and life. The life in us is an abundant life; far more than anything the world can do. The life of God in you is an overcoming life; a life that comes out victorious in the face of any challenge or circumstance. We have been imparted a winner's spirit. Nothing in this life can be able to separate us from the love of God. The word shows us a lot about our power to overcome in the face of challenges. The Bible says, **"You are of God, little children and have overcome them because He who is in you is greater than he who in the world" (1 John 4:4).**

When the treasure of God's life is in us, no situation will bring us down **(2 Corinthians 4:7-9)**. We are more than conquerors through Christ who loved us and we are victors and winners. We surrender to none and nothing except to our Father in Heaven. We are called to reign in life through Jesus Christ **(Romans 5:17),** thus let nothing bring you under its power.

Prayer

Lord, thank You for an overcoming life; a life that wins in the face of tribulation

Bible Reading Plan:
Ezra 3 and 4, Psalm 122, Hosea 9

DAY 265 HE IS MY SANCTIFICATION

 *"But of Him you are in Christ, who became for us wisdom from God-and righteousness and sanctification and redemption"* (1 Corinthians 1:30)

Christ is our sanctification. So once we accept Him as Lord, we are sanctified not by our own work but by what Jesus obtained for us through His death and resurrection. If regeneration has to do with our nature, justification with our standing before God, and adoption with our position, then sanctification has to do with our character and conduct. In justification we are declared righteous in order that in sanctification we may become righteous. Justification is what God does for us, while sanctification is what God does in us. Justification puts us in right relationship with God, while sanctification exhibits the fruit of that relationship-a life separated from a sinful world and dedicated unto God. On the cross, Jesus Christ became for us sanctification. Hallelujah. He is your sanctification; count on Him to produce in you new heights and greater depths in holy living. Amen

Prayer

 Lord, I praise Your name; You became my sanctification so that I can live a holy life in Your own power and strength. Amen

Bible Reading Plan:
Ezra 5 and 6 Psalm 123, Hosea 10

DAY 266 SEATED IN THE HEAVENLY PLACES

 "But God, who is rich in mercy, because of His great love with which He loved us, even when we were dead in sins and trespasses, made us alive together with Christ (by grace you have been saved) and raised us up together and made us sit together in the heavenly places in Christ Jesus"(Ephesians 2:4-6).

We are seated with Christ in the heavenly places, far above all principalities and power. The Devil does not have access to the believer. The believer is not of the earth; he or she is born from above. The believer has every reason to rejoice: for we are seated in the heavenly places while the devil has been cast down into the earthly realm with great wrath. We are not only seated in the heavenly places, we are also hidden with Christ in God, beyond Satan's reach. The Bible says, **"For you died and your life is hidden with Christ in God" (Colossians 3:3).** We are not only hidden with Christ in God, the word says, Christ is our life **(Colossians 3:4).** This wonderful and marvelous.

Prayer

 Lord, I rejoice in my place of authority in the heavenly realms. Glory to Your name. Amen

Bible Reading Plan:
Ezra 7 and 8 Psalm 124, Hosea 11

DAY 267 SEATED IN THE HEAVENLY PLACES II: KEEPING OUR PLACE OF AUTHORITY

To retain our place of authority in the heavenly places, the Bible gives us some vital keys:

Seek the things which are above: **"If the you were raised with Christ, seek those things which are above, where Christ is sitting at the right hand of God" (Colossians 3:1).**

Set the mind on things above: **"Set your mind on things above not on things of the earth" (Colossians 3:2).**

Put to death that which is of the earth: **"Therefore put to death your members which are of the earth: fornication, uncleanness, passion, evil desire and covetousness, which is idolatry" (Colossians 3:5).** Sin is of the earth. When we live in sin, we are changing dimensions and realm for sin is of the earth. The quickest way for Satan to get the believer is to get the believer to sin and bring the believer to the earthly dimension. In the case of Balaam and Balaak in their attempt to curse Israel, Balaam could not curse Israel until Israel was seduced into sexual immorality, idol worship and the anger of the Lord was aroused **(Numbers 23:21, 25:1-3, 16-18).**

Prayer

 Lord, I refuse to descend to the earthly dimension through sin, where Satan can have access to my life. Amen

Bible Reading Plan:
Ezra 9 and 10 Psalm 125, Hosea 12

DAY 268: NOT IGNORANT OF HIS DEVICES: THE REALITY OF WARFARE

 *"For we are not ignorant of his devices"* (2 Corinthians 2:11)

As we labor to do God's work and fulfill his plan for our lives, we also have an adversary whose mission is not only to oppose our efforts, but to, in subtle ways seduce us into things that will move us away from what God has called us to do for Him or to get us into sin and bring discredit to our life and ministry. Spiritual warfare is real and the Bible makes it clear that we have an adversary. The Bible says, **"Be sober and vigilant; because your adversary the devil walks about like a roaring lion, seeking whom he may devour. Resist him, steadfast in the faith knowing that the same sufferings are experienced by your brotherhood in the world" (1 Peter 5:8-9).** If you are a child of God know that you have an adversary. The day you said yes to Jesus, two things happened; friendship with God and enmity with the devil. The days of play are over. This calls for vigilance and watchfulness.

Prayer

 Lord, thank You for making it clear to me that there is an adversary; I renounce the life of ease and playfulness

Bible Reading Plan:
Nehemiah 1 and 2, Psalm 126, Hosea 13

DAY 269 — NOT IGNORANT OF HIS DEVICES II: BEING VIGILANT AND WATCHFUL

The Lord calls us to be vigilant and watchful. Our capacity for spiritual resistance is all the more required in the times in which we live. The Devil only moves away temporarily. After the temptation of the Lord Jesus, the Bible says, **"Now when the Devil had ended every temptation, he departed from Him until an opportune time" (Luke 4:13).** The Christian life is living to fight and resist another day. Perpetual watchfulness and 'eternal' vigilance is the winning strategy. There is no single prayer or fast that will send Satan away once-and-for-all. In the Christian life there is no once-and-for-all spiritual inoculation that will now usher us into a holiday mood. We have to watch daily and be vigilant for the devil is a chance taker and an opportunist.

Prayer

Lord, I enroll into a life of perpetual vigilance and watchfulness

Bible Reading Plan:
Nehemiah 3 and 4, Psalm 127, Hosea 14

DAY 270 — NOT IGNORANT OF HIS DEVICES III: GIVE NO PLACE TO THE DEVIL

The word says, **"Nor give place to the devil" (Ephesians 4:27).** If we give him place, he will take it. The very reason the devil is walking about is to take available places, spaces and exploit vulnerabilities. He had lost his home or place in heaven. He will occupy every unoccupied place and space. Space matters to the devil; **"When an unclean spirit goes out of a man, he goes through dry places, seeking rest and finds none. Then he says, I will return to my house from which I came. And when he comes, he finds it empty, swept, and put in order. Then he goes and takes with him seven other spirits more wicked than himself and they enter and dwell there..." (Matthew 12:43-45).** Let's beware of spiritual emptiness. Satan will enter empty places. This is a time for our lamps to be filled with oil. Judas had created space. The devil entered him. He moved from an apostle to a traitor. The Bible says**, "Then Satan entered Judas, surnamed Iscariot, who was numbered among the twelve" (Luke 22:3).** May we not give place to the devil; may we be filled with the word and Holy Spirit.

Lord, I refuse to give place to the devil: I will remain filled with the word and Your Spirit

Bible Reading Plan:
Nehemiah 5 and 6, Psalm 128, Joel 1

DAY 271 NOT IGNORANT OF HIS DEVICES IV: BEWARE OF DISCOURAGEMENT

A strong weapon of the enemy against God's elect is discouragement. Once we realize this, our initial spiritual instinct towards God's children will be to encourage and say words of comfort and edification. The Bible says, **"Then the people of the land tried to discourage the people of Judah. They troubled them in building and hired counselors against them to frustrate their purposes for all the days of Cyrus king of Persia, even until the reign of Darius king of Persia" (Ezra 4:4-5 NIV).** Satan is relentless in the game of frustration. These are the days of stamina and capacity to resist him and put him to flight. The capacity to encourage ourselves in the Lord like David did will **(1 Samuel 30:6)** be very important going forward. There will be trouble as we labor to build and Satan will have us think we are not called that's why we are facing all we are facing, but we have to stand strong and not quit. May God raise many Jonathans and Barnabas' in the body for the strengthening and encouragement of the saints.

Prayer

Lord, I give myself to encourage the saints; teach me also to encourage myself like David did

Bible Reading Plan:
Nehemiah 7 and 8, Psalm 129, Joel 2

DAY 272 — NOT IGNORANT OF HIS DEVICES V: GREAT OPPOSITION

The devil will not only try to discourage; he will also place great opposition in the face of opportunities that God has given us. The Bible says, **"For a great and effective door has been opened for me, and there are many adversaries" (1 Corinthians 16:9).** Opportunities will be contested. That is not a time for surrender. We have to arise and war. Great openings will attract an onslaught of satanic opposition. The child of God must be a contender and fighter. Of all the lands that Joshua took in the Promised Land, only one was taken without a fight **(Joshua 11:19).** There will be resistance of promised possessions. The believer must therefore have stamina for sustained warfare **(Joshua 11:18).**

Prayer

 Lord, I pray for stamina for sustained spiritual warfare

Bible Reading Plan:
Nehemiah 9 and 10, Psalm 130, Joel 3

DAY 273 NOT IGNORANT OF HIS DEVICES VI: DISTRACTIONS

Beware also of distractions. They are the hall mark of our generation and time. They will come and but we should be focused on what the Lord has entrusted in our hands to do for Him. The Bible says," **That Sanballat and Geshem sent to me saying, Come, let us meet together in one of the villages in the plain of Ono. But they thought to do me harm. So I sent messengers to them saying, I am doing a great work, so that I cannot come down. Why should the work cease while I leave it and go down with you? But they sent the message four times, and I answered them in the same manner" (Nehemiah 6:2-4).** We thank God for the likes of Nehemiah. We need such men today, for whom the devil knows what to expect even if he comes a thousand times. Nehemiah conquered distractions and succeeded to rebuild the wall. We too, if we must realize our God-given assignment, we need matchless focus.

Prayer

Lord, I embrace focus and the ability to stand strong in the face of opposition. Amen

Bible Reading Plan:
Nehemiah 11 and 12, Psalm 131, Amos 1

DAY 274 THE TEST OF SINCERITY

"Servants obey in all things your masters according to the flesh, not with eye-service, as men pleasers, but in sincerity of heart, fearing God." (Colossians 3:22)

Elijah had performed seven miracles, Elisha fourteen miracles; double that of Elijah. A lot was at stake in the success of Gehazi; not only the possibility of more miracles but most importantly continuity of a great spiritual 'mantle' and prophetic tradition. Elisha died with his anointing. Even his dead bones brought a dead person back to life **(2 Kings 13:20-21).** He did not transfer this power. The gifts of God are without repentance or they are irrevocable. But how did this tragic thing happen? We have the story in 2 Kings chapter five. Gehazi runs after Naaman who had been healed of leprosy by Elisha and falsely uses Elisha's name to collect material gifts **(2 Kings 5:20-26),** and lies to his master about his where about. He had in fact, ran after the Syrian but when his master asked, he replied that he had gone nowhere. He failed the test of sincerity. He lost a prophetic mantle in the process. Dear saint, forget your title for a while. Are there areas of dishonesty in your life or ministry? Would you repent and renounce the ways of shame?

Prayer

Lord, I pray that I will live a life full of honesty and sincerity

Bible Reading Plan:
Nehemiah 13 and Esther 1, Psalm 132, Amos 2

DAY 275 — STRENGTHENED IN THE INNER MAN: THE WORK OF THE HOLY SPIRIT

 *"That He would grant according to the riches of His glory, to be strengthened with might by His Spirit in the inner man"* (Ephesians 3:16).

Inner strength is very important and we had discussed inner strength as a function of prayer. In this meditation we want to explore the work of the Holy Spirit in strengthening us from inside. Why do we need strength on the inside? The Bible shows us why; **"Strengthened with all might, according to his glorious power, for all patience and long-suffering with joy" (Colossians 1:11).** It is clear from the above Scripture that the purpose for the inner strengthening of the Holy Spirit is for birthing in us the inner capacity to go through difficult times and days without losing our joy and peace. When you meet a person who retains his joy in the midst of great suffering then you are in the face of one in whom the Holy Spirit has strengthened with might from within.

Prayer

 Lord, let your Spirit strengthen me with might in my inner man today. Amen

Bible Reading Plan:
Esther 2 and 3, Psalm 133, Amos 3

DAY 276 — STRENGTHENED IN THE INNER MAN II: HOW JESUS ENDURED THE CROSS

The Lord Jesus endured great suffering on the cross. The Bible says, **"Looking unto Jesus the author and finisher of our faith; who for the joy set before Him endured the cross" (Hebrews 12:2).** What could have provided the Lord with the strength within to go through the great ordeal on the cross. It is clear from the Scriptures that it is through the work of the Holy Spirit that the Lord offered Himself up on the cross; **"How much more shall the blood of Christ, who through the eternal Spirit offered Himself without spot to God…" (Hebrews 9:14).** Therefore, the Lord offered Himself to God through the help and strengthening of the Holy Spirit. May be you are going through very hard and difficult times. Dear saint, know that the Holy Spirit is the one who stands by you and is also within you to strengthen you from within so that what you are going through does not crush you.

Prayer

Lord, let Your Spirit dwell in me and strengthen me in a mighty way, for all endurance

Bible Reading Plan:
Esther 4 and 5, Psalm 134, Amos 4

DAY 277 — STRENGTHENED IN THE INNER MAN III: ACCESSING THE HOLY SPIRIT

The strengthening supplied by the Holy Spirit can be accessed through prayer. Prayer is the channel through which we access heaven for the release of the Spirit. As we pray, God pours and allows to flow into us His Spirit in greater measure, giving us the strength we need for all patience and long-suffering. The Bible says, "**Now when all the people were baptized, it came to pass that Jesus also was baptized; and <u>while he prayed, the heaven was opened and the Holy Spirit</u> descended in bodily form like a dove upon Him…" (Luke 3:21-22).** Prayer ushers the descent of the Holy Spirit. As we pray, heaven opens for the Holy Spirit to infuse in us strength in the inner man for patience and long-suffering with all joy. Adopt the routine of asking the Holy Spirit each new day for strength in the inner man. This will preserve your spirit from been crushed by the pressures of the day.

Prayer

Lord, thank You for showing me the inner strength that is available to me by the agency of the Holy Spirit. Lord, I pray that I will embrace a life of prayer, for a release of your Spirit in me.

Bible Reading Plan:
Esther 6 and 7, Psalm 135, Amos 5

DAY 278 RENEWING OF THE MIND

 *"And do not be conformed to this world but be transformed by the renewing of the mind"* (Romans 12:2)

God will not put new wine into old wineskins. If God is about to do a new thing in our lives and our minds are not renewed, we will miss it or worst still, resist it. The teachers of the law in Jesus' day are an example in this regard. Their minds were stuck. Remember Peter resisting God's command to kill and eat and argues that he has never eaten anything unclean before. God wanted to do a new thing; open up the gospel to the Gentiles but Peter was still stuck in his old mindset of reaching only Jews with the gospel. Renewal of mind is key to perceiving God's will in any situation. As we renew our minds, we will be able to prove or know or perceive as expressed in other versions of Scripture God's mind and will in any given situation.

Prayer

 Lord, I pray that I will seek renewal of the mind so that I don't miss or resist Your move.

Bible Reading Plan:
Esther 8 and 9, Psalm 136, Amos 6

DAY 279 RENEWING OF THE MIND: THE WORD AND THE WORK OF THE SPIRIT

We have to renew our minds or grow in our minds and this can be achieved through: God's word for the Bible says, **"The law of the Lord is perfect, converting the soul" (Psalm 19:7).** As we study and meditate on the word of God, our minds are transformed (converted) and renewed to fit the mold and mind of God. Meditation is a kind of mentality transmission. It is transmitting kingdom mentality into the mind: We are soaking into the mind of God through his word. Also through the working of the Holy Spirit in us our minds are renewed; **"Not by the works which we have done but according to his mercy he saved us, by the washing of regeneration and <u>renewing of the Holy Spirit</u>" (Titus 3:5).** God's thoughts are higher than our thoughts but if we meditate on the word and allow the Holy Spirit to work in us, our thoughts can align with God's and we can be able to perceive his designs in our lives and not miss His move.

Prayer

Lord, I pray that I will allow Your word and the Holy Spirit renew my mind

Bible Reading Plan:
Esther 10 and Job 1, Psalm 137, Amos 7

DAY 280: PURITY OF HEART AND SPIRITUAL INSIGHT

"Blessed are the pure in heart for they shall see God" (Matthew 5:8)

Purity fosters spiritual clarity. Impurity on the flip side fosters spiritual obscurity. When there are no more visions like in Eli's time then sin has become the order of the day. As the lens of heart gets cleaner, we begin to see the things of God clearer and clearer. Picture a dusty glass window. It is hard to see through such a window but when it is wiped clean, we begin to see clearer through it. Isaiah was a man of unclean lips. It therefore means his heart was also unclean for out of the abundance of the heart the mouth speaks. When God cleansed him, he perceived God's call and one of the greatest prophetic ministries of all time was born **(Isaiah 6:1-8).** Insight is the reward for purity. Daniel is an example in this regard. The Bible says, **"Daniel purposed in his heart that he will not to defile himself with the portion of king's delicacies…." (Daniel 1:8)**. The reward was great insight and capacity for visions that speak till today; **"As for the four young men God gave them knowledge and skill in all literature and wisdom; and Daniel had understanding in all visions and dreams" (Daniel 1:17)**.

Prayer

Lord, I pray for life of purity; I desire to walk in depth of insight in all I do

Bible Reading Plan:
Job 2 and 3, Psalm 138, Amos 8

DAY 281 PURITY OF HEART AND SPIRITUAL INSIGHT II

The greater the purity, the greater the spiritual perception and insight. Access to new things is reserved for the pure. The Bible says, "**They <u>sang a new song</u> before the throne, before the four living creatures and the elders: and no one could learn that song except the……from the earth. These are the ones who were <u>not defiled with women</u>, for they are virgins….and <u>in their mouth was found no deceit</u>, for they are <u>without fault before the throne of God</u>" (Revelation 14:3-5).**

Purity is an exclusive club for access to keys that crack the codes of some divine mysteries. Only those who had kept themselves from women could access the insight into the new song. Impurity blocks access to divine mysteries and inspiration. Even the Scriptures were given but to holy men. May we arise to new levels of purity in our individual lives and in the church.

Prayer

May a new day of visions and deep revelations be born in my life as embrace new levels of purity and faultlessness before the throne of God. Amen

Bible Reading Plan:
Job 4 and 5, Psalm 139, Amos 9

DAY 282 GIVING MY ALL AND BEST

"Of all of your gifts you shall offer up every heave offering due to the LORD, from all the best of them..." (Numbers 18:29.)

The apostle Peter lays out what our attitude should be whenever we have an assignment to do for God; **"If anyone speaks, let him speak as oracles of God. If anyone ministers let him do it with the ability which God supplies, that in all things God may be glorified through Christ..." (1 Peter 4:11).**

Serving the Lord and the brethren is a call to give our all. In fact, it's all or nothing. God will not accept less than the best. It is a curse to hold back the best from God; **"But cursed be the deceiver who has in his flock a male and makes a vow, but sacrifices to God what is blemished-for I am great King, says the LORD of hosts and My name is to be feared among the nations" (Malachi 1:14).** Am I giving my best?

Prayer

Lord, I pray that I will give You the best; I will hold back nothing that I have.

Bible Reading Plan:
Job 6 and 7, Psalm 140, Obadiah 1

DAY 283 — GIVING MY ALL AND BEST II: THE LORD DID NOT HOLD BACK ANYTHING

The Lord did not hold back His best from us. He gave us His only begotten son Jesus Christ. We therefore as much as we know should hold nothing back from Him. The British missionary C.T. Studd said, **"If Jesus Christ be God and died for me, then no sacrifice can be too great for me to make for Him".** He lived true to his creed and thinking. He gave all for Christ and served Him as a missionary in China, India and Africa after abandoning what would have been a brilliant career in Cricket.

What of the great apostle Paul? For Paul, to live was Christ and to die is gain. The apostle said, **"Yet indeed I also count all things loss for the excellence of the knowledge of Christ Jesus my Lord, for whom I have suffered loss of all things and I count them as rubbish, that I may gain Christ" (Philippians 3:8).** He saw the excellency of Christ and all else paled into insignificance. He could suffer loss of all in order to win the Christ.

Prayer

Lord, may I behold Your excellence so that nothing will be too great to sacrifice for Your name and gospel. Renew my vision of You. I want to serve You better. Amen

Bible Reading Plan:
Job 8 and 9, Psalm 141, Jonah 1

DAY 284: JUSTIFIED AND MADE RIGHTEOUS

 *"But you were washed, but you were sanctified, but you were justified in the name of the Lord Jesus and by the Spirit of our God"* (1 Corinthians 6: 11)

Justification is the rendering of a guilty person not guilty before a judge. Our sin, made us guilty before God but through the death of Jesus on the cross, He made it possible for us to stand before God as if we never sinned. This justification is an act of God through the redemptive work of Christ Jesus on the cross. It is not based on what any man could do or it cannot be attained by works of the flesh or by trying to keep the law. The word says, **"Therefore by the deeds of the law no flesh shall be justified in His sight, for by the law is the knowledge of sin" (Romans 3:20).** The law can only open our eyes to our sin but cannot remove it. How then are we justified? The Bible says**, "Being freely justified by His grace through the redemption that is in Christ" (Romans 3:24).** Glory to Jesus Christ for His grace. Today I can stand as though I have never sinned because of the free justification that is in Christ. Amen

Prayer

 Glory to Your Name Lord for the price You paid for my justification. Be exalted King of Glory.

Bible Reading Plan:
Job 10 and 11, Psalm 142, Jonah 2

DAY 285 PLANS THAT PREVAIL

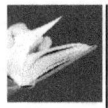 *"Many are the plans in a person's heart, but it is the LORD's purpose that prevails"* (Proverbs 19:21).

As children of God, we have plans, we dream and have visions. Some actually take their dreams and hopes beyond just dreaming. They do this by making plans. The wise man knows that it is the Lord's purpose that prevails. Fruitless efforts result from dreams, hopes and plans that are not in line with God's purpose. Some see their dreams and hopes shattered by some unplanned event and turn around to blame God. Was it in line with God's purpose in the first place? If, for example, I marry someone out of God's purpose then I can only blame myself for any failures in that marriage. So, as a child of God, in everything I do I must first strive to know God's purpose. Once I know it, I then line up my dreams, hopes, plans, efforts, and investments in that direction. It is the simplest path towards success in everything I do.

Prayer

 Lord, may I constantly line up my dreams, hopes, aspirations, plans, investments, and efforts towards Your purpose for my life in Jesus' Name. Amen.

Bible Reading Plan:
Job 12 and 13, Psalm 143, Jonah 3

DAY 286 HIS PROMISES ARE YEA AND AMEN

 *"God is not a man, that He should lie, nor a son of man, that He should repent. Has He said, and will He not do? Or has He spoken, and will He not make it good?"* (Numbers 23:19)

Men lie about the age; they falsify birth certificates to play international football and/or to spend many years in the civil service. Some people lie about their past lives, past relationships and many other things. On the contrary, telling the truth is God's nature. God is not a liar and cannot tell lies. All His promises to us are "Yes" and "Amen". This means that whatsoever God says in His Word is true. Whatsoever He has promised to us (His children), He will do. He cannot promise a thing and not do it. He cannot say a thing and it does not come to pass.

May be you have been waiting for a promise of God to come to pass in your life. Dear saint, do not lose heart. The One who promised is the faithful and true. In His own appointed time, it shall come to pass.

Prayer

 Lord, teach me to believe Your Word as the truth, and help me stay fixed without wavering as I wait to see Your promise come to pass in my life.

Bible Reading Plan:
Job 14 and 15, Psalm 144, Jonah 4

DAY 287 BE ANXIOUS FOR NOTHING

 *"Be anxious for nothing, but in everything by prayer and supplication, with thanksgiving, let your requests be made known to God"* (Philippians 4:6).

Anxiety is defined **as** a feeling of worry, nervousness, or uneasiness about something with an uncertain outcome or a strong desire or concern to do something or for something to happen. Whatever the source of the anxiety or stress is, God is saying here that it's root cause is the absence of prayer, supplication and thanksgiving. Someone who is under the effect of stress, whether coming from his/her job, studies, marriage, thoughts of the future and so on is simply a prayerless person. In prayer we offer up all the challenges that are sources of stress to God and receive the **"peace of God that surpasses all understanding" (verse 7)**. A prayerful and thankful person will see the hand of God in every circumstance and will expect God to move in His time and bring the situation under control. May be right now there is a burning issue that is a subject of worry and anxiety in your life. Can you go on your knees wherever you are and present the matter to God with thanksgiving? God will surely answer you.

Prayer

 Lord, I pray that I will always counter anxiety with prayer and thanksgiving

Bible Reading Plan:
Job 16 and 17, Psalm 145, Micah 1

DAY 288 THE GREAT GAIN

 *"Now godliness with contentment is great gain. For we brought nothing into this world, and it is certain we can carry nothing out"* (1 Timothy 6:6-7).

Life on earth is temporal and every success and achievement obtained on this earth is only temporal. Everyone is born naked, meaning that we all entered the world with nothing. The greatest leaders of this world were all born naked. Even when they die, they carry nothing along. Recently, the rich president of the United Arab Emirates, who built Dubai out of desert sands died. He was wrapped in a bed sheet and thrown into a hole in the sand. He had no chance to take any cars, sky scraper houses, private jets, wives or money along. We often get surprised why men often forget this reality and live life as though they were the owners of life itself. In verse 6, we see two recipes for true happiness in life; godliness and contentment. When there is no contentment, the love of money invades the soul leading to incalculable losses in time and in eternity **(1 Timothy 6:10).** Once the love of money invades the soul, faith in God starts exiting the soul.

Prayer

 Lord, I pray that I will live in godliness and contentment in Jesus Name.

Bible Reading Plan:
Job 18 and 19, Psalm 146, Micah 2

DAY 289 THE LITTLE HAND IN THE CLOUD

 *"Then it came to pass the seventh time, that he said, there is a cloud, as small as a man's hand rising out of the sea"* (1 Kings 18:44)

Most times God starts the heavy down pour with the small cloud like a man's hand. The small cloud was the harbinger of the heavy down pour. God announces our great with little. Let us not despise the small victories and results. In Genesis Chapter one we see how God created the universe in a step-wise gradual process. The world didn't come to be by just one sudden act of God that put all things in place. This manner of working by God runs all through the Scriptures. The Lord asked the Israelites to take the Promised Land little by little. When Elijah prayed for rain, before the heavy down pour, it was a cloud as small as a hand that first appeared and that was at the seventh time of praying to God. Rockefeller, the billionaire's first job was 50 cents. But today he is so rich that his money is managed in a trust. He was so grateful for that job such that he celebrated it all the days of his life as, **"Job Day"**. Don't despise small beginnings

Prayer

 Lord, help me see the little hand in the cloud as Your sign for the heavy down pour. Let me not despise the little victories and successes.

Bible Reading Plan:
Job 20 and 21, Psalm 147, Micah 3

DAY 290: CAN GOD? OR GOD CAN

 "Yes, they spoke against God; they said, can God prepare a table in the wilderness? Behold, He struck the rock, so that waters gushed out, and the streams flowed. Can He give bread also? Can He provide meat for His people?" (Psalm 78:19-20).

The God of all flesh had asked, **is there anything too hard for the LORD? (Genesis 18:14).** Each man has to answer this question and the answer we give will determine whether we say, **can God? or God can.** This pattern of always putting God's ability to question each time there is challenge is the hallmark of the lack of spiritual back bone. Each time the Israelites faced a challenge or a need, God's ability faced a renewed scrutiny. David was different. A new challenge resurrected his faith all the more in God but for the Israelites challenges buried their faith. May we be like David. He used previous breakthroughs to reinforce his faith in God's ability to deal with present challenges. The Israelites on the other hand used previous victories to assess if God's ability could rise up to the present challenge.

Prayer

 Lord, let me not call to question Your ability in the face of a challenge; I affirm that You Can.

Bible Reading Plan:
Job 22 and 23, Psalm 148, Micah 4

DAY 291 FIREBRAND

"Let your waists be girded and your lamps burning" (Luke 12:35).

The Lord calls us to be on fire; to keep our lamps burning. God requires us to keep our lamps perpetually burning particularly in today's world where Satan is doing all to freeze men's love for God. The Bible says, **"And the fire on the altar shall be kept burning on it; it shall not be put out. And the priest shall burn wood on it every morning…."** (Leviticus 6:12).

The word of God is fire; **Is not My word like a fire? Says the Lord, and a hammer that breaks the rock in pieces? (Jeremiah 23:29, 20:9).**

Professor Zacharias Tanee Fomum, our father in the Lord used to say that he is a spiritual log, and that he will burn and burn and burn. That he kept in his office toilet a devotional of Oswald Chambers to read and meditate while in the toilet and that he had read about fifteen books just by using judiciously his time while in the convenience. May we develop flexible ways to remain on fire.

Prayer

Lord, I pray that I will keep the fire burning: through Your word.

Bible Reading Plan:
Job 24 and 25, Psalm 149, Micah 5

DAY 292 — FIREBRAND II: UNDERSTANDING IMPARTATION AND CULTIVATION

Public ministry from leadership provides impartation but for us to stay on fire and burning for the Lord, we have to embrace cultivation and fanning into flames the spiritual deposit imparted to us by those God has placed above us. The Bible says, **"For this reason I remind you to fan into flames the gift of God which is in you through the laying on of my hands" (2 Timothy 1:6).** Paul imparted by the laying on of hands and he is asking Timothy to cultivate by fanning into flames the spiritual deposit. Take responsibility for how much fire is burning in you. Develop flexible and creative ways to feed your spirit with the word. This can happen anywhere and anytime: in airport lounges, in the plane, in restaurants etc. The Lord will come for a church whose lamp is burning. Stay on fire. Become a firebrand today.

Prayer

Lord, I commit myself to put wood on the fire of the altar of my heart daily. Amen

Bible Reading Plan:
Job 26 and 27, Psalm 150, Micah 6

DAY 293 BUT: THE PUNCTUATIONS IN THE LIFE OF THE FAITHFUL

 *"And they were both righteous before God, walking in all the commandments and ordinances of the Lord blameless. But they had no child…"* (Luke 1:6-7).

Zacharias and the wife Elizabeth were faithful to God. They were not only righteous; they were also blameless before the Lord and were keeping all His commandments. We should expect that in return, their desires should be met; even the desire for a child. With all this positive spiritual resume, there was a BUT in their lives. There was no child. Not only so, they were well advanced in years and Elizabeth was barren. All was stacked against this couple. The BUT was a great one. However, this couple remained faithful in their service to God. Zacharias still kept his routine and order of service as priest. The Bible says, **"So it was that while he was serving as priest before God in the order of his division according to the custom of the priesthood, his lot fell to burn incense when he went into the temple of the Lord" (Luke 1:8-9)**. Faithfulness does not mean all will be rosy all the time. The life of the faithful can have contradictions and God knows why He allows them. Trust Him and remain faithful.

Prayer

 Lord, thank You for opening my eyes to see that even in faithfulness there can be contradictions in my life.

Bible Reading Plan:
Job 28 and 29, Micah 7

DAY 294 — BUT II: POSTURE IN THE FACE OF PUNCTUATIONS AND WAY OUT

The posture and way out of our contradictions is to remain faithful to the Lord; our solution meets us in the place of faithfulness. As a rule, the punctuations in our lives should never be allowed to introduce a punctuation in our service and commitment to God. The big trick of the enemy is to make us move away from the place of service to God and miss out on God's visitation. Zacharias kept his order of service in the temple as priest. The angel of the LORD that brought the answer to Zacharias' cry for a child met him in the place of service: the place of faithfulness. The Bible says, **"Then an angel of the Lord appeared to him, standing on the right side of the altar of incense…But the angel said to him, do not be afraid, Zacharias, for your prayer is heard; and your wife Elizabeth will bear you a son and you shall call his name John. And you will have joy and gladness and many will rejoice at his birth" (Luke 11-14).** Maybe you are also having a BUT in your own life. Dear, saint, stay faithful to God and the service He has called you. God's angel is coming with a greater answer to your need.

Prayer

Lord, teach me to stay faithful in my service to You even in the midst of the BUTS in my life.

Bible Reading Plan:
Job 30 and 31, Nahum 1

DAY 295: BUT III: WHEN THE DELAY IS LOADING SOMETHING BETTER

"And they were both righteous before God, walking in all the commandments and ordinances of the Lord blameless. But they had no child..." (Luke 1:6-7).

If God could not withhold His Son Jesus from us, then there is nothing that He would not freely give us **(Romans 8:32).** God did not spare Jesus Christ for our sake. God will therefore not withhold anything good from those whose walk is blameless **(Psalm 84:11).**

Therefore, when God seems to withhold the good thing, then He has something higher and better for us. God uses delay to align us with the very best. Lazarus was sick and his sisters had sent for Jesus. He did not show up immediately. He came when Lazarus was already in the grave for four days; corpse already smelling. Did the Lord come late? Why didn't He heal him? The Lord had greater in mind. Lazarus and his sisters were privileged to be used by heaven to show that Jesus is the resurrection and the life; that the resurrection is not an event but is embodied in the Person called Jesus. Hallelujah.

Prayer

Lord, I celebrate Your delays in my life; You are using them to work something better for me.

Bible Reading Plan:
Job 32 and 33, Nahum 2

DAY 296 — BUT IV: PROPHETIC IMPLICATIONS OF DELAY

"Then he who had received the one talent came and said, Lord I knew you to be a hard man...." (Matthew 25:24).

We return to our story concerning John the Baptist and the parents. Their delay and BUT had huge prophetic significance and implications. Some delays are mandated by heaven in order to align us with God's agenda. God was about to use their son to close a major spiritual dispensation and introduce another one. The son of Zacharias and Elizabeth was not just going to be like any other son; He will be great in the sight of the Lord, will be filled with the Holy Spirit from birth and will turn many to God **(Luke 1:15).** John will therefore be the first person or one of the first persons to be filled with the Holy Spirit from birth: by-passing spiritual protocol.

Finally, he will have the rare privilege of being the person to introduce the Messiah to the world **"This is the Lamb of God that takes away the sin of the world"**. Wow. What a task? What a great privilege? Could God be using your delay and BUT to align you to something bigger? Dear saint look beyond your personal need. The Lord may be considering you for something greater than your personal quest. Stay faithful. Stay blameless. The Lord has the best. Celebrate the delay. God is using it for something greater. Amen

Prayer

Lord, open my eyes to see delay as a tool for spiritual alignment with Your greater purposes

Bible Reading Plan:
Job 34 and 35, Nahum 3

DAY 297 YOU HAVE NEED OF ENDURANCE

 *"You have need of endurance so that having done the will of God you may inherit the promise"* (Hebrews 10:36).

The Lord is committed to supplying all our needs according to His riches in glory. If there is one need that we all must crave for today is our need for endurance. As we engage in the Lord's work and even in our personal lives, there will be moments of trial and testing. We will go through periods with great temptations to give up or call it quits. God may not and usually doesn't intervene as we would expect. This will require endurance on our part. Endurance keeps us in the game till the Lord shows up. There are many who were close to their miracle and breakthrough but gave up just when there was about to be a turnaround. If we give up, God will not show up. May be you are going through a very difficult time now and you are tempted to quit. Please don't quit. Approach the throne of grace so that God meets your need for endurance. The Bible says, **"Let us therefore come boldly unto the throne of grace, that we might obtain mercy and find grace to help in time of need" (Hebrews 4:16).**

Prayer

 Lord, grant me the grace to endure so that after doing the will of God I will inherit the promise.

Bible Reading Plan:
Job 36 and 37, Habakkuk 1

DAY 298 — CULTIVATING ENDURANCE: THE PLACE OF VISION

 *"But recall the former days in which after you were illuminated, you endured a great struggle with sufferings"* (Hebrews 10:32).

Endurance is not a gift per se. It is a fruit of the Spirit. It is therefore cultivated. There are therefore spiritual dynamics of endurance. The first one we see today is illumination: a vision of something greater and worth the need to bear the unbearable. The stakes must be high enough to support the unbearable. What would have made a Moses to abandon the palace of Pharaoh and rather suffer with the Israelites in the wilderness? The Bible says, **"By faith he forsook Egypt, not fearing the wrath of the king: for he endured as seeing Him who is invisible" (Hebrews 11:27).** He saw Him who was invisible: he could endure. His vision of the invisible One and the treasures in Christ inspired his endurance. The Lord Jesus also endured the cross. His vision of the joy set before Him inspired His endurance; **"Looking unto Jesus the author and finisher of our faith: who for the joy set before Him endured the cross" (Hebrews 12:2).** The Lord endured because of the joy that was set before Him. Behind every great display of endurance is clear vision.

Prayer

 Lord, grant me a clear vision of You. Let me truly see You

Bible Reading Plan:
Job 38 and 39, Habakkuk 2

DAY 299 — CULTIVATING ENDURANCE: THE PLACE OF VISION II

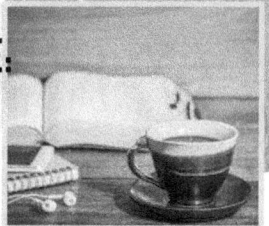

Failing capacities to endure are always products of fading visions. No one who has seen the glories of the age to come will fail to endure. How did a Stephen bear the stoning in the Early Church as the first martyr? The Bibles, **"But he being full of the Holy Spirit gazed into heaven and saw the glory of God and Jesus standing at the right of God....and they stoned Stephen as he was calling on God saying, Lord Jesus, receive my spirit. Then he knelt down and cried out with loud voice, Lord, do not charge them with this sin. And when he had said this he fell asleep" (Acts 7:55-60).** His vision of God and the throne was real. He could endure the stoning. Could it be why the Lord insisted on the mount of transfiguration encounter with the three, knowing this would leave a life-changing impact on their lives and affect their witness and stand for Him in the face of persecution? Peter never forgot that encounter in the mount **(2 Peter 1:16-18).** That encounter affected their attitude in the face of persecution **(Acts 4:19-20).** They had not only heard about Jesus; they had seen Him. Men who have seen Him, is the need of the hour.

Prayer

Lord, rekindle my vision of You. Let me see You in majesty in the name of Jesus Christ. Amen

Bible Reading Plan:
Job 40 and 41, Habakkuk 3

DAY 300 TRIBULATION WORKS PATIENCE

 *"My brethren count it all joy when you fall into various trials, knowing that the testing of your faith produces patience"* (James 1:1-2).

If there is one thing God uses to produce endurance or patience or perseverance in us, is the trials we face. The apostle Paul, writing to the Romans also shows how trials are used to produce the character of endurance in us. The Bible says, **"And not only that, but we also glory in tribulations, knowing that tribulation produces perseverance; and perseverance character; and character, hope" (Romans 5:3-4)**. When I am going through tribulation, I should rejoice and thank God in them and for the tribulation. God is using the little tribulations of today to equip us for the great days when only those who will endure till the end will be saved. He is interested in our character than in our comfort. Endurance has a crown: the crown of life **(James 1:12)**. Am I glorying in the face of tribulation? Or am I complaining and in offence?

Prayer

 Lord, let me glory in tribulation, knowing You are using it to shape my character and life

Bible Reading Plan:
Job 42 and Isaiah 1, Proverbs 1, Zephaniah 1

DAY 301: TRIBULATION WORKS PATIENCE II: FOR HIGHER SPIRITUAL STAKES

When we go through little tribulations our approval is on the line and the Lord is using them to forge in us greater capacities to endure when the stakes will be higher. As we endure little trials so our capacity to endure even greater trials will increase. The first verse of the hymn, Yield Not to Temptation puts it better; **"Yield not to temptation for yielding is sin. Each victory will help you, some other to win"**. Each victory will help some other to win. As we endure the little trials of today, it forges more capacity to endure in greater occasions with higher stakes. In the time of the great tribulation, God appeals to the patience and endurance of the saints. The Bible says, **"Here is the patience and faith of the saints" (Revelation 13:10c, 14:12).** May we cooperate with the Holy Spirit and the tribulations we go through to learn and rehearse patience and endurance now. We will need it in the greater tribulation. Like Zac Poonem says, **"If we sweat in the time of peace, we will bleed less in the time of war"**. May these days be days of preparation.

Prayer

Lord, I rejoice in the tribulations I go through. I rejoice that You are forging in me the great virtue of endurance. Amen

Bible Reading Plan:
Isaiah 2 and 3, Proverbs 2, Zephaniah 2

DAY 302 YET WILL I TRUST

 *"Though He slay me, yet will I trust Him"* (Job 13:15)

The dealings of God most times leave us with no choice but to say, Lord I trust. The foundation for trust under those circumstances is our knowledge of God. Trust that will defy the odds against us is rooted in our knowledge of God. The Bible says, **"And those who know Your name will put their trust in You; For You, LORD have not forsaken those that seek You" (Psalm 9:10).**

Trust flows from the knowledge of God: the knowledge of His name. The name of God here refers to his character. Can God be therefore trusted based on what we know about His nature and character? God can be trusted.

God is not a liar **(Numbers 23:19).** His promises are Yea and Amen in Christ Jesus.

His name is the Faithful and True **(Revelation 19:11).** He can therefore be relied upon.

His Plans and thoughts towards me are good. Even if it appears that things are looking bad, the one who has good thoughts and plans is piloting me to my expected end **(Jeremiah 29:11, Romans 8:28).** God is reliable; trust Him even in the dark days like Job.

Prayer

 Lord, grant me the faith to still trust even when it appears I am being slain.

Bible Reading Plan:
Isaiah 4 and 5, Zephaniah 3

DAY 303: THE WRATH OF MEN: GOD'S INSTRUMENT FOR OUR GOOD

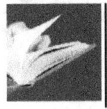 *"Surely the wrath of man shall praise You"* (Psalm 76:10)

At some point in our life, we would have been treated badly by men or people around us. They may have done so with the intention to inflict pain on us out of jealousy or sheer wickedness. But the word of God opens our eyes to see that the wrath of men will end in praise to God on our behalf. All what men do against us, will only lead us to where God is taking us to. The wrath of men are the visible chariots used by God to transport us to our place of destiny. One person in the Scripture whose life really captures this truth is Joseph. All the wrath of his brethren only pushed him to the place of destiny: eventually becoming prime minister of Egypt.

Dear saint, the wrath of men in whatever form it comes to you will turn in praise to God. Trust your heavenly Father to turn it around and your final words when you look back at all that happened will be like what Joseph said to his brothers; **"But as for you, you meant evil against me; but God meant it for good...." (Genesis 50:20).**

Prayer

 Lord, thank You for the wrath of men; You are using it to help me reach my place of destiny

Bible Reading Plan:
Isaiah 6 and 7, Proverbs 3, Haggai 1

DAY 304 NEVER TRY THIS

 *"In return for my love they are my accusers, but I give myself to prayer. Thus they have rewarded me evil for good, and hatred for my love"* (Psalm 109:4-5).

One thing we should never do is to betray another; returning evil for good. In the last days, betrayal will be common: many will betray and hate one another **(Matthew 24:10-11)**. Let's beware. Betraying others puts us in the company of Judas Iscariot. How does the Bible define betrayal? It is rewarding evil for good. Judas rewarded evil for good. Jesus made him one of His apostles and appointed him treasurer of the greatest rescue operation in the history of man. Judas was God's treasurer. But he chose to deliver Him to the authorities of the day for His eventual crucifixion. Psalm 109 reveals the curses on Judas Iscariot and his entire generation. Verse 6-20 of Psalm 109 are all about the curses on Judas Iscariot and all would be traitors. Fourteen verses of Scripture, all for curses. Is there someone I have betrayed? Will I repent if need be?

Prayer

 Lord, I pray that I will never return evil for good.

Bible Reading Plan:
Isaiah 4 and 5, Proverbs 4, Haggai 2

DAY 304 INTENT ON PRAISING HIM: DEDICATING TIME TO PRAISE GOD

"At midnight I will rise to give thanks to You" (Psalm 119:62)

Smith Wigglesworth said, "**First thing every morning, when I get out of bed, I jump out. I don't just drag out, but I jump out! And when my feet hit the floor I say, 'Praise the Lord!' And I praise God every morning**".

We have to create time to praise God. King David had dedicated time to express gratitude to God **(Psalm 119:62).** The prophet Daniel had a custom of prayer and giving of thanks to God. The Bible says, **"Now when Daniel knew that the writing was signed, he went home. And in his upper room, with his windows open toward Jerusalem, he knelt down on his knees, three times that day and prayed and gave thanks before his God as his custom was since early days" (Daniel 6:10).** This was Daniel's custom since early days. It was not a frantic reaction to the signed decree. Three times a day, for prayer and giving of thanks. Yours may not be three times a day or at midnight like David did. We can make use of time that suits our own condition to thank and praise God.

Prayer

Lord, like these great men of old may I be intentional about praising You

Bible Reading Plan:
Isaiah 6 and 7, Proverbs 5, Zechariah 1

DAY 306 INTENT ON PRAISING HIM II: A RECORD OF GOD'S GOODNESS

Keeping records of the acts of God in our life is part of our intentional praise drive. God is very interested in records. The Bible says, **"Now Moses wrote down starting points of their journeys at the command of the LORD" (Numbers 33:2).** Numbers thirty-three is a detailed account of how God moved the children of Israel from point to point as they journeyed to the Promised Land. In the Psalms the word says, **"He has made His wonderful work to be remembered: The LORD is gracious and full of compassion" (Psalm 111:4).** To make sure we remember and not forget, recording is the answer. Israelites kept milestones as reminders of God's goodness and as way to communicate it to the next generation. Keep a record of God's goodness and wonders in your life. To record and think about them is not enough. You have to specifically thank the Lord for these acts of His goodness and kindness to you.

Prayer

 Lord, may I be deliberate in recording Your acts of goodness

Bible Reading Plan:
Isaiah 8 and 9, Proverbs 6, Zechariah 2

DAY 307 — INTENT ON PRAISING HIM III: THANK OFFERING

While giving of thanks was encouraged in word, song etc. Israelites were also encouraged to express gratitude by making an offering to God called a **"thank offering"**. This offering is a free will offering. The believer gives to God based on the level of expression of gratitude. The Bible says, **"When you sacrifice a thank offering to the LORD, sacrifice it in such a way that it will be accepted on your behalf"** (Leviticus 22:29 NIV). While it is a free will offering, it was not optional. It was a matter of when and not if. Would you consider all that the Lord has done for you and make it a subject of thanks offering?

Prayer

Lord, I pledge to give You a thank offering for Your goodness to me

Bible Reading Plan:
Isaiah 10 and 11, Proverbs 7, Zechariah 3

DAY 308 THE INCURABLE BARRENNESS

 *"Oh earth, earth, earth, hear the word of the LORD! Thus says the LORD: Write this man down as childless"* (Jeremiah 22:29-30).

Saul's daughter Michal is the only recorded woman in the Bible who was barren and never had child. If there was any woman who should be so grateful to God, that should be Michal. Her father was king and her husband too was king. She was royalty by birth and by marriage. She was princess slash queen. But according to her, royalty was too high to be brought low in praise and thanks to God. Her royalty produced disloyalty. Her ingratitude to God is exhibited by her despise for David's unreserved praise to God. The Bible says **"And the ark of the LORD came into the City of David, Michal, Saul's daughter, looked through the window and saw King David leaping and whirling before the LORD; and she despised him in her heart" (2 Samuel 6:16).** She played the observer and despised a man given to unreserved praise to God. She was barren all her life. Am I doing same in my local church? Playing spectator while criticizing those who are trying?

Prayer

 Lord, may I never tamper with Your praise or despise those who give themselves to praise You.

Bible Reading Plan:
Isaiah 12 and 13, Proverbs 8, Zechariah 4

DAY 309 CIRCUMSTANTIAL HUMILITY

"So Sarah said to Abram, see now the Lord has restrained me from bearing children. Please, go in to my maid; perhaps I shall obtain children by her. Abram heeded the voice of Sarai" (Genesis 16:2).

There are many whose loyalty and submission is a function of their neediness and estate in life. Beware of the humility of the needy. Such is the story of Hagar the Egyptian who was picked by Sarah in Egypt as house maid. All was ok until she was elevated by Sarah to bear a child for her husband; she had moved from maid to madam. But as soon as she had what Sarah did not have, she started to despise Sarah. The Bible says, **"Then Sarai said to Abram, my wrong be upon you! I gave my maid into your embrace; and when she saw that she had conceived, I became despised in her eyes. The Lord judge between you and me" (Genesis 16:5).** There are many who begin sober when they are in need and when their sense of need is taking care of, their attitude starts 'changing'. Is that the case with you?

Prayer

Lord, I pray for an attitude towards others that will not change because my sense of dependence on them has been removed.

Bible Reading Plan:
Isaiah 14 and 15, Proverbs 9, Zechariah 5

DAY 310 REGARD NO ONE ACCORDING TO THE FLESH

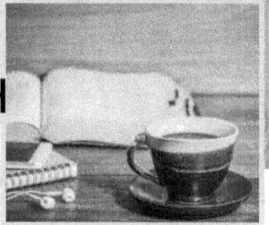

 *"Your people shall be my people and your God, my God"* (Ruth 1:16e)

Ruth is a Moabite woman. She had lost her husband who happened to be one of the sons of Naomi. It becomes obvious to Naomi that she has to return to her native Bethlehem: she had lost her husband and her two sons in the land of Moab. It was tragedy and a devastating moment for Naomi. It was a bitter experience. She was returning empty and bitter. She even asked that they call her Mara (meaning bitter) instead of Naomi (meaning pleasant) **(Ruth 1:20-21).** By all indications, Ruth had no prospects following this woman to Bethlehem. What did Ruth see in Naomi that Naomi didn't see in herself? Ruth saw beyond the natural. Herein lies the greatness of Ruth. She did not look at Naomi according to the flesh. If she had done so, she would have missed out on her prophetic destiny. Today, we read the story of Ruth in the genealogy of Jesus Christ. She saw beyond the flesh.

Prayer

 Lord, help me to see people and situations beyond the flesh

Bible Reading Plan:
Isaiah 16 and 17, Proverbs 10, Zechariah 6

DAY 311: REGARD NO ONE ACCORDING TO THE FLESH II

 *"Therefore, from now on, regard no one according to the flesh"* (2 Corinthians 5:16).

The Bible warns us not to regard anyone according to the flesh. This has several life applications. Many make marriage decisions based on what they see presently. They select a job based on the obvious package. A story is told of a lady who had set her standard for a husband: the man must have a car and settled in a good and well-paying job. It is said that a man walked up to her and wanted to know her better for a possibility of getting married to her. Her question to the man was, what do you do for a living? The man replied, I sell soft drinks. She was put off. She felt the man was a retailer of soft drinks. The man was marketing and sales director of the soft drink company in that country. That is how she missed out. Her greed didn't even allow her to ask any further questions like where is your shop, can I come and see and so on. Greed blinds.

Prayer

 Lord, may I see beyond the flesh. Amen

Bible Reading Plan:
Isaiah 18 and 19, Proverbs 11, Zechariah 7

DAY 312 A TALE OF LOYALTY

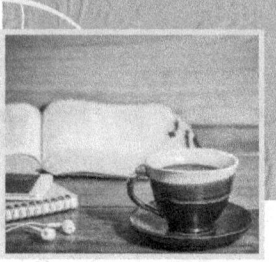

 *"Then they lifted up their voices and wept again; and Orpah kissed her mother-in-law, but Ruth clung to her"* (Ruth 1:14).

Ruth clings to Naomi and decides to follow her to Bethlehem. Why would she abandon her gods in the land of Moab and go after a God who turns a pleasant life into a bitter one. She saw beyond the tragedy. Did she succeed where Lot the father of her lineage failed? Could it be that God wanted Lot to be part of Abraham's prophetic destiny and Ruth was the restoration? Lot parted from Abraham when a crisis emerged but Ruth still clung to Naomi even in the face of a heart breaking tragedy and lack of prospects. Her test will come when she eventually gets married to Boaz and be the wife of possibly the richest man in the land. Will her attitude towards Naomi change? No. She sticks to Naomi till the end. The son of Ruth was named as a son born to Naomi. Naomi nursed the child as her own. This foreign woman entered the lineage of David the king and Jesus the King of kings (**Ruth 4:13-17).** Do I cherish loyalty? Can I stick with others right to the end? Loyalty is the path to royalty. Ruth entered the lineage of the Kings.

Prayer

 Lord, teach me loyalty; grant me a loyal heart

Bible Reading Plan:
Isaiah 20 and 21, Proverbs 12, Zechariah 8

DAY 313: THE RULE OF ABUNDANCE: CONTROL ON FAITH AND UTTERANCE

"Let the word of Christ dwell in you richly" (Colossians 3:16)

Our God is the God of abundance. Succeeding in the Christian life will require an understanding and application of the rule of abundance. How much we have of the word in us will influence a lot of things in a very natural and automatic way. The Bible says, **"For out of the abundance of the heart his mouth speaks" (Luke 6:45d).** Our speaking will flow from how much we have laid up. This is very crucial for ministers of the gospel. Many pray for utterance while making little investments in the word.

Also how much faith comes into our hearts will be determined by how much of the word we have. The Bible makes us know that faith comes by hearing and hearing by word of God **(Romans 10:17)**. This is in present continuous tense. One has to keep hearing over and over again. The more we hear the more faith.

Prayer

Lord, I pray that I will lay abundance of Your word in me so that I flow in faith and utterance

Bible Reading Plan:
Isaiah 22, 23 and 24, Proverbs 13, Zechariah 9

DAY 314: THE RULE OF ABUNDANCE II: CONTROL ON CLEANSING AND SPIRITUAL FIRE

The word also washes us and cleanses us (**Ephesians 5:26**). When we are cleaning, how much water we have matters. Imagine trying to wash the whole human body with a cup of water. In Leviticus, whenever a carcass fell anywhere, the place was declared unclean. The only places that were declared clean were fountains with plenty of water (**Leviticus 11:36**) (the word is water). A young man had asked a preacher how he could overcome lust, the preacher responded, read and store the word in you abundantly. The word washes. The more word the more water. Amen. The Bible says, **"You are already clean because of the word I have spoken to you"** (**John 15:3**).

The word is fire. Do you want more fire? Read and study more of the word. John Sung the great Chinese preacher was on fire for Christ. He read his Bible forty times in six months. That is once every four and half days. The Lord Jesus is an embodiment of volume. He Himself said, **"In the volume of the book it is written of Me"** (**Hebrews 10:7**). Lord I choose the way of volume and abundance in the spiritual life. I shun minimalism. Dear saint, go for volume. Go torrential. May the Lord bless you as you do. Amen

Prayer

Lord, I go for abundance; for more cleansing and fire of the word in me.

Bible Reading Plan:
Isaiah 25 and 26, Proverbs 14, Zechariah 10

DAY 315 HOLY DISSATISFACTION

 *"And the sons of the prophets said to Elisha, "See now, the place where we dwell with you is too small for us"* (2 Kings 6:1).

Progress is triggered when holy dissatisfaction is born. Thomas Edison the great inventor once said, **"Show me a thoroughly satisfied man I will show you a failure"**. There is a satisfaction that kills our drive and compels us to settle when God is expecting more from us or has given us more.

The sons of the prophet realized that where they dwelt was small. They were dissatisfied and that led to action. The good thing about dissatisfaction is that it leads to action. God has called us to stretch and expand. May we not settle for the small. The Bible says, **"Enlarge the place of your tent and let them stretch out the curtains of your dwellings; Do not spare; lengthen your cords and strengthen your pegs" (Isaiah 54:2).**

Our present level of progress may be excellent but time can render it irrelevant. We have to keep stretching and expanding.

Prayer

 Lord, I embrace expansion and enlargement. I renounce every satisfaction with smallness. All self-sparing and comfort-zoning, I let go in Jesus Name. Amen

Bible Reading Plan:
Isaiah 27 and 28, Proverbs 15, Zechariah 11

DAY 316 CONSCIENCE AND FAITH

 *"Having faith and a good conscience, which some having rejected concerning the faith have suffered shipwreck"* (1 Timothy 1:19).

Faith and a good conscience have mutual inclusiveness. As our conscience gets clearer so does our confidence in God increases. Condemnation in the conscience affects confidence toward God. The Bible says, **"Beloved, if our heart does not condemn us, we have confidence with God" (1 John 3:21).** Condemnation in the conscience affects our faith and certainty for answer to our prayer; we lose our sense of expectation or the ability to look up to God. We are bowed in shame because of our sin; **"My iniquities have overtaken me so that I am not able to look up" (Psalm 40:12b).** When the Blood of Jesus cleanses our conscience, we can stand before God in full assurance of faith. The word says, **"Let us draw near with a true heart in full assurance of faith, having our hearts sprinkled from an evil conscience, and our bodies washed with pure water" (Hebrews 10:22).** By the blood we can now enter into the Holy of Holies not on our own merits but on the merits of the blood of Jesus. Glory be to Jesus.

Prayer

 Lord, thank You for Your blood that cleanses me; so that I can pray with confidence before You

Bible Reading Plan:
Isaiah 29 and 30, Proverbs 16, Zechariah 12

DAY 317 EVER INCREASING STRENGTH

 *"As your days so shall your strength be"* (Deuteronomy 33:25)

Our strength should match or better still surpass our days. We do not know what tomorrow will bring. Growing from strength to strength is therefore crucial. As we move increasingly into the last days, things will get tougher. This is the truth. This is not about being dooms day preachers. We should therefore move from strength to strength. The Bible says, **"They go from strength to strength; Every one of them appears before God in Zion" (Psalm 84:7).** Our Scripture shows us how we can go from strength to strength: appearing before God in Zion. The word further says, **"May He send you help from the sanctuary, and strengthen you out of Zion" (Psalms 20:2).** Zion appears again and relating to strength. What then is Zion? Zion is the church; **"But you have come to Mount Zion and the city of the living God, the heavenly Jerusalem, to an innumerable company of angels, to the general assembly and church of the firstborn who are registered in heaven..." (Hebrews 12:22-23).**

This is time to stay in fellowship and be under the ministry of the local church. May we all return to the ministry of the local church; it is the place of strength. Many are weak spiritually and cannot understand why; they have minimal contact with the place of strength.

Prayer

 Lord, I return to Zion, to the church of the firstborn. Amen

Bible Reading Plan:
Isaiah 31 and 32, Proverbs 17, Zechariah 13

DAY 318 LITTLE THINGS MATTER

 *"And whoever gives one of these little ones only a cup of cold water in the name of a disciple, assuredly I say to you, he shall by no means lose his reward"* (Matthew 10:42).

Do you know that we do not need great faith to move big mountains? The Bible says, **"So Jesus said, to them, because of your unbelief; for assuredly, I say to you, if you have faith as a mustard seed, you will say to this mountain, move from here and there and it will move; and nothing will be impossible for you" (Matthew 17:20).** What is the size of a mustard seed? A mustard seed has the size of 2.5mm or 0.1 inch in diameter. That is how small it is but if my faith is just as small as that, I can move mountains and I will operate in the realm of possibilities; nothing will be impossible unto me.

Little things matter to God. God appreciates as little as a cup of cold water to reward on the last day. The Lord Jesus Christ gave thanks for seven loaves and two fishes, in the face of five thousand hungry people excluding women and children.

Prayer

 Lord, let me not neglect or minimize anything. Little things can make big changes. Amen

Bible Reading Plan:
Isaiah 33 and 34, Proverbs 18, Zechariah 14

DAY 319: THE DELIGHT TEST I: DELIGHT IN GOD AND HIS PRESENCE

 *"Delight yourself in the Lord and He will give you the desires of your heart"* (Psalm 37:4)

Delighting ourselves in God is to find great pleasure in God. In, fact, it tells of our enjoyment of God and in God. The reward for delight in God is granted desires. God can be enjoyed and should be enjoyed. For some, God and his presence is boring. According to A.W. Tozer, the greatest indicator of a person's readiness for heaven is whether the person enjoys God. Those for whom worship is boring, he doubts if they are ready for heaven. God is pleasurable and in His right hand there are pleasures forevermore; **"You will show me the path of life; in Your presence is the fullness of joy; At Your right hand there are pleasures forevermore" (Psalm 16:11).** In the presence of God there is joy; joy overflow. There are pleasures in his presence. The Bible says, **"They feast on the abundance of your house; you give them drink from the river of Your pleasures" (Psalm 36:8).** The Holy Spirit is that river of the pleasures of God. He is the river that makes glad the city of God. A person filled with the Holy Spirit will be communicated the delight in God; the work of the Holy Spirit in us is to impart spiritual delight. Do you enjoy God's presence?

Prayer

 Lord, I pray that I will cultivate your presence till my soul finds perfect delight in You

Bible Reading Plan:
Isaiah 35 and 36, Proverbs 19, Malachi 1

DAY 320 DELIGHT TEST II: DELIGHT IN GOD'S CHILDREN

 *"And to the saints who are on the earth, they are the excellent ones in whom all is my delight"* (Psalm 16:3).

As our delight in the Lord increases, so does our delight for His children and fellow believers will increase. A normal spiritual condition is revealed in the delight to be in the midst of God's children. When the desire for God fades, the desire for fellowship with God's people fades as well. David was glad to be in the house of the Lord; in fellowship with other believers. The house of the Lord connotes family of God's children and fellowship with others. The Bible says, **"I was glad when they said to me let us go into the house of the Lord" (Psalm 122:1).** The joy to be in the presence of God's children permeated the life of David. His love for God flowed to God's children. A normal spiritual conditions looks forward to the next meeting with God's people. The disciples in the Early Church also delighted in each other: **"Now all who believed were together and they had all things in common" (Acts 2:44).** This is the normal condition. All who believed were together. Do I long for the presence of God's people?

Prayer

 Lord, renew my love for You and the brethren.

Bible Reading Plan:
Isaiah 37 and 38, Proverbs 20, Malachi 2

DAY 321: DELIGHT TEST III: DELIGHT IN THE WORD

 *"But his delight is in the law of the LORD and on His law he meditates day and night"* (Psalm 1:2).

Delight in the Lord will also find expression in delight for the word of God. Men who love God also find deep pleasure and delight in His word. The delight will go beyond study or reading; there will be meditation day and night.

The Lord commands that we meditate on his word **(Joshua 1:8)**. Meditation has several meanings; in some cases, it means to mutter or speak the word to oneself and in other cases to think on the word deeply. The result of meditation is to obey God's word. What meditation does is to transform our thinking so that it aligns with God's word thus renewing our minds. Kenneth E. Hagin says **"What you are doing in renewing your mind is training your mind to think in line with God's word".** As God's word through meditation shapes our thinking and mind we begin to act accordingly. E.W. Kenyon said, **"The most deeply spiritual men and women I know are people who have given much time to meditation. You cannot develop spiritual wisdom without mediation".** Do I pass the test for delight in the word? Do I read and meditate on it daily? Do I obey the word?

Prayer

 Lord, fill my heart with delight for Your word. May I meditate on it day and night. Amen

Bible Reading Plan:
Isaiah 39 and 40, Proverbs 21, Malachi 3

DAY 322 NEVER ALONE: A TESTIMONY

 *"Be strong and of good courage, do not fear nor be afraid of them; for the LORD your God He is the One who goes with you. He will not leave you nor forsake you"* (Deuteronomy 31:6)

This verse in today's meditation is very particular to me. My elder sister who brought me to Lagos died and I was left to face life in a foreign country on my own. How was I going to fare henceforth? Should I just return to Cameroon? All these questions raced across my mind. But I decided to stay. As at then I had just an equivalent of an ND (National Diploma). One day on my way to school, around Festac Town area, someone gave me an inch-sized card with a Scripture on it. That scripture was the one at the top of this meditation: Deuteronomy 31:6. I took the card and read it and put in my pocket. I turned back to look at the person who gave me the card and I saw nobody. The boy could not be found any more. I held that Scripture as God's special word to me in the light of the circumstances I was going through. That Scripture became my favourite Scripture. Today, I hold two masters' degrees and countless other certificates and God is using what I went through to encourage another person out there: that God will not leave you nor forsake you. Take your eyes off what you are going through. Focus on Him.

Prayer

 Lord, thank You, for You will never leave me nor forsake me; I am not alone. You are with me

Bible Reading Plan:
Isaiah 41 and 42, Proverbs 22, Malachi 4

DAY 323 WAITING ON GOD ALONE

"My soul wait silently for God alone, for my expectation is from Him" (Psalm 62:5)

Waiting on God alone is the one of the proofs of real faith. Most often the prospect of waiting only on God looks risky. What if God fails or does not come through? In the process we also look up to men as safety nets. Whether we wait on God alone for our expectation or not depends on the degree to which our faith and trust in Him has been cultivated and that is a function of our knowledge of Him. Those who have cultivated their knowledge of God, reap the reward of the kind of faith that can stake all on God and God alone. God can be trusted. He is reliable and is worthy of our total trust and reliance: God is faithful and true. He is not a liar and none who have trusted in Him have been put shame. The Bible says, **"Behold, I lay in Zion a Chief cornerstone, elect, precious and he who believes on Him will by no means be put to shame" (1 Peter 2:6).** Some versions say, shall never be disappointed. God does not disappoint but men are sure to disappoint. To avoid bitterness, one should rely on God and God alone

Prayer

Lord, for the faith to rely on You and You alone; You can be trusted Lord.

Bible Reading Plan:
Isaiah 43 and 44, Proverbs 23

DAY 324 — THE LIFE OF GOD IN US I: IMPARTATION OF DIVINE NATURE

 *"I have come that they may have life and that they may have it more abundantly"* (John 10:10)

The Lord Jesus came that we might have life and that abundantly. This life can only be possessed however, by those who have made Jesus Christ their Lord and Saviour. Therefore, once one has received Jesus Christ, the Son of God, as Lord and Saviour, he or she has life: eternal life. The question then before us is: What is Life or Eternal Life? The word life has two connotations or meanings in the Bible: The first is the Greek word, psuche which represents human or physical life. The second and the one referred to in the Scriptures above, which we receive when Jesus comes into our hearts is called zoe: The God-kind of life. Therefore, those who have received the Son of God now possess the divine nature as indicated by the apostles Paul and Peter **(Acts 17:29, 2 Peter 1:4).** So, eternal life represents the communication and the impartation of God's very nature and kind of life in us and to us. We are born of God; thus we are like Him. Amen

Prayer

 Lord, thank You for Your divine nature imparted to me at new birth; a nature in holiness and the righteousness of God

Bible Reading Plan:
Isaiah 45 and 46, Proverbs 24

DAY 325 THE LIFE OF GOD IN US II: KNOWING GOD

Another key aspect of what is eternal life is revealed in the John 17: 3; **"Now this is eternal life: that they may know You, the only true God and Jesus Christ whom You have sent"(John17:3).** Thus eternal life is to know God. What does the word 'know' in our passage mean? In Genesis, the Bible says, **"Adam knew his wife again and she bore a son and named him Seth" (Genesis 4:25).** Mary also said, **"How can this be since I do not know a man?" (Luke 1:34**.) How do men know women? It's by intercourse.

Thus eternal life in this context represents spiritual intercourse: that is a vital, personal relationship with the Lord Jesus. It is our spirits being joined with God in a vital relationship with Him. The Bible says, **"But he who is joined to the Lord is one in Spirit with Him" (1 Corinthians 6:17).** Our spirit is now joined to the Lord and we are now one in Spirit with Him. There is no more separation between you and God due to sin. You now have access to God through the Holy Spirit. Hallelujah

Prayer

Lord, thank You for such a life. I pray that I will not neglect such a great salvation. Amen

Bible Reading Plan:
Isaiah 47 and 48, Proverbs 25

DAY 326 THE CAPACITY NOT TO SIN

 *"For sin shall no longer have dominion over you, for you are not under law but under grace"* (Romans 6:14)

> The normal Christian experience is to live without Sin
> **-Watchman Nee**

When the believer receives the life of God, the nature of God is imparted and since God is Holy, the Holiness of God becomes part of our nature and living in sin becomes an impossibility for the saved. The Bible says, **"Whoever has been born of God does not sin, for His seed remains in him; and he cannot sin, because he has been born of God" (1 John 3:9).** If we are living in a known sin, then we are certainly not His. The Bible says, **"He who sins is of the devil" (1 John 3:8).** Through the price that the Lord Jesus paid we can be free from dead works in order to serve the living God. The Bible says, **"How much more shall the blood of Christ, who through the eternal Spirit offered Himself without spot to God, purge your conscience from dead works to serve the living God?' (Hebrews 9:14).** If you have not truly made Him your Lord and Savior, you can do so by praying the following.

Prayer

 "Lord Jesus, I have sinned against You in thought, word and deed. Forgive me of all my sins and cleanse me. Receive me, Savior and transform me into a child of God. Come into my heart now and give me eternal life now. Amen"

Bible Reading Plan:
Isaiah 49 and 50, Proverbs 26

DAY 327 THE PRICE OF SUCCESS

 *"Keep this Book of the Law always on your lips; meditate on it day and night, so that you may be careful to do everything written in it. Then you will be prosperous and successful"* (Joshua 1:8 NIV).

The price of success is obedience to the Word. God told Joshua not to allow the Book to depart from his mouth. This means the Book will attempt to depart from his mouth and so he needed to exercise some personal discipline to ensure that it does not depart. Those who think that their attitude towards the word will always naturally favor their attention are in for a great shock. Almost everything around you will attempt to hinder you from giving the needed attention to God's Word. The Lord is pointing out that the price of lasting success and prosperity lies in constant meditation on the word. To meditate means to mutter, to speak silently to oneself, to declare what the word is saying to yourself. It also means to think on the word over and over in one's heart. As you meditate on the Word, your spirit is fortified and enabled to render wholehearted obedience to God.

Prayer

 Lord, I pray for the right priority concerning the discipline of meditation and grant me the power to obey, as I meditate on the word

Bible Reading Plan:
Isaiah 51 and 52, Proverbs 27

DAY 328 SURRENDER YOUR WEAKNESS

 *"Alas, Sovereign Lord," I said, "I do not know how to speak; I am too young"* (Jeremiah 1:6 NIV)

To live and serve effectively, one doesn't only have to be aware of his or her strengths but of his or her weaknesses too. When you acknowledge those weaknesses which can stand as barriers to effective living and service, do not let them become a limitation. Every unsurrendered weakness will hinder your availability to God and His kingdom and by consequence limit the extent to which you can be used of God. Do you feel inadequate for the task God has called you to? Do you have genuine excuses and authentic limitations you think will hinder God from using you? I want you to know that throughout Bible history, such limitations have always been welcomed by God, they have been opportunities for Him to demonstrate His infinite wisdom, power, and grace. Surrender that weakness to God and allow His sufficient grace work in your life.

Prayer

 Father, I lift my eyes above and beyond this weakness of mine unto You who is able to make me competent for Your service

Bible Reading Plan:
Isaiah 53 and 54, Proverbs 28

DAY 329: YOUR DEFICIENCY FOR HIS SUFFICIENCY

 *"But the Lord said to me, "Do not say, 'I am too young.' You must go to everyone I send you to and say whatever I command you. Do not be afraid of them, for I am with you and will rescue you," declares the Lord. Then the Lord reached out his hand and touched my mouth and said to me, "I have put my words in your mouth"* (Jeremiah 1:7-9 NIV).

When you concentrate on your weakness, it is not a sign of humility but a sign of pride. When you declare about yourself what God has not said about you it brings displeasure to God. The fact of the matter is, Jeremiah was indeed young at the time the Lord was sending him, but the truth is that his deficiency was an opportunity for him to experience the sufficiency of God. That's why the Lord rebuked him for declaring that about himself. It is written that, **"Let the weakling say**, **'I am strong!'" (Joel 3:10b NIV)** because what you declare of yourself is what you become. Remember the Lord said of the Israelites, **"So tell them, 'As surely as I live, declares the Lord, I will do to you the very thing I heard you say" (Numbers 14:28 NIV).**

Prayer

 Lord, help me to know what You say about me and to declare it, even when contrary to the facts.

Bible Reading Plan:
Isaiah 55 and 56, Proverbs 29

DAY 330 — EXPECTATION-YOUR TOOL FOR EXPANSION

"Jabez cried out to the God of Israel, "Oh! that you would bless me and enlarge my territory! Let Your hand be with me, and keep me from harm so that I will be free from pain." And God granted his request" (1 Chronicles 4:10 NIV).

Jabez expected an enlargement of his territory - the domain of his influence financially, socially, materially, and spiritually and his expectation was granted. He expected the hand of God to be with him, gracing all that he did and his request was granted. He expected a life free from pain and suffering he had so much experienced, and God met his expectations. God was so pleased with Jabez's expectations for expansion that he caused him to become the owner of a city **(See 1 Chronicles 3:55)**. Being the owner of the city meant an expansion in his financial domain. It meant an expansion socially, materially and otherwise. There is room for you too to expand and extend your sphere of influence whether spiritually, socially, financially, materially, intellectually or otherwise. All it takes is the right kind of expectations.

Prayer

Lord, I pray for a heart that seeks greater expansion like Jabez in all areas of my life; I refuse to settle for the small.

Bible Reading Plan:
Isaiah 57 and 58, Proverbs 30

DAY 331 EXPECTATION- YOUR KEY TO RESTORATION

 *"Lift up your eyes and look around; all your sons gather and come to you. As surely as I live," declares the LORD, "you will wear them all as ornaments; you will put them on, like a bride. Though you were ruined and made desolate and your land laid waste, now you will be too small for your people, and those who devoured you will be far away"* (Isaiah 49:18-19 NIV).

No matter the calamity which has befallen you, no matter the extent to which the storms of life have stripped you of your blessings and possessions, if you do not allow the storms of life to cut off your hope then a double restoration is your guaranteed portion when the storms are over. The capacity to see a bright future through the darkness of the storms is that which expectation births in a man. And when you hold on to this picture of a bright future, restoration is bound to come. Restoration is not automatic after the storms of life. Your degree of expectation will determine your degree of restoration of what has been lost in the storms. No matter the prison or dungeon in which you find yourself, if you have not lost hope, then a double restoration will come to you. The LORD is saying to you, **"Return to your fortress, O prisoners of hope; even now I announce that I will restore twice as much to you" (Zechariah 9:12 NIV).** Amen

Prayer

 Lord, I refuse to lose hope; I believe a restoration is coming

Bible Reading Plan:
Isaiah 59 and 60, Proverbs 31

DAY 332 THE SECRET TO VICTORY

"Moreover thou shalt say unto them, thus saith the Lord; shall they fall, and not arise? Shall he turn away, and not return? Why then is this people of Jerusalem slidden back by a perpetual backsliding? They hold fast deceit, they refuse to return" (Jeremiah 8:4-5 KJV).

The secret to victory lies in the ability to rise up quickly after a fall. It is acceptable when one falls and quickly rises again but unacceptable to fall and remain fallen. The prophet Micah said, **"Do not gloat over me, my enemy! Though I have fallen, I will rise (Micah 7:8a NIV).** Humility is what makes a man rise up when he falls. Pride is what keeps a man fallen instead of rising up after a fall. When you stay longer in a fallen position it gives the enemy the opportunity to gloat over you.

I don't know where you have fallen, or what has caused you to stumble. It is not time to wallow in the puddle you fell into, but time to rise up from the puddle, clean up yourself, and move on. The Lord Jesus Christ said, **"Remember therefore from whence thou art fallen, and repent..." (Revelation 2:5 KJV).** How do you rise up from a fall? Through repentance and returning to the things you abandoned.

Prayer

Lord, I repent; I return to the things I had abandoned.

Bible Reading Plan:
Isaiah 61 and 62 Ecclesiastes 1

DAY 333 A TOUCH FROM GOD

 *"Jesus reached out his hand and touched the man. "I am willing," he said. "be clean!" immediately he was cleansed of his leprosy"* (Matthew 8:3 NIV).

A touch from God is one thing most of us, children of God, desire, pray for, and seek as we walk with the Lord. I remember a song I loved that says, "Touch me one more time O Lord, touch me one more time O Lord, I need a touch from the Master, I need a touch from the Lord, touch me one more time O Lord". The good LORD longs to touch us at the point of our need more than we desire His touch. Jeremiah presented to the Lord his incapacity to speak publicly, and the Lord reached out and touched his mouth: **"Then the Lord reached out his hand and touched my mouth and said to me, "I have put my words in your mouth" (Jeremiah 1:9 NIV).** The touch of God empowered and equipped Jeremiah for the calling of God upon his life. Is there an area of your life needing God's touch? Why not call on the Lord?

Prayer

 Lord, for an empowering touch that makes my weaknesses become strengths for Your service.

Bible Reading Plan:
Isaiah 63 and 64 Ecclesiastes 2

DAY 334 CONTENDING FOR WHAT IS YOURS

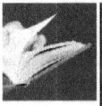 *"Beloved, when I gave all diligence to write unto you of the common salvation, it was needful for me to write unto you, and exhort you that ye should earnestly contend for the faith which was once delivered unto the saints "(Jude 1:3 KJV).*

Whatever God has entrusted to you can either decrease or increase, be lost or maintained by you. You are the guarantor of what God has entrusted to you. Jude exhorted the saints to contend for the faith that was once entrusted to them. To contend, in this verse, means to do battle, to fight for, to wage war, to wrestle. Jude doesn't just ask you and I to contend, but to earnestly contend. It means you have to fight with all seriousness. Every territory you will ever gain in this fight of faith is by contending for it. What God has ordained for you is to be contended for. There's nothing you will receive on a silver platter. Breaking into new grounds will require contention. Remember that you are exhorted to **"fight the good fight of faith" (1 Timothy 6:12a NIV).**

Prayer

 Lord, help me to earnestly contend to maintain, and increase that which You have entrusted to me.

Bible Reading Plan:
Isaiah 65 and 66 Ecclesiastes 3

DAY 335 DISCRETION PROTECTS

"And the Lord said unto Samuel, how long wilt thou mourn for Saul, seeing I have rejected him from reigning over Israel? fill thine horn with oil, and go, I will send thee to Jesse the Bethlehemite: for I have provided me a king among his sons. And Samuel said, how can I go? if Saul hear it, he will kill me. And the Lord said, Take an heifer with thee, and say, I am come to sacrifice to the Lord. And call Jesse to the sacrifice, and I will shew thee what thou shalt do: and thou shalt anoint unto me him whom I name unto thee" (1 Samuel 16:1-3 KJV).

God was sending Samuel to anoint a king, as the principal item on his agenda, but he counselled him to say he was going there to sacrifice to the Lord. In other words, the LORD asked Samuel to hide behind sacrificing to the Lord in order to go anoint a king. This was to make sure God's plan was not aborted by the rejected king Saul. As long as there was a sacrifice that Samuel offered, there was no falsehood. You do not owe everybody every detail of what, when, how, and why, and when you are doing a particular thing God has asked you to do. Not everyone is entitled to certain information, especially those who may cause unnecessary trouble. Things done in a low profile are usually more effective and durable. We all need wisdom from God on how to go about His business without attracting enemy's attack unnecessarily. May you not be attached to fanfare and the spirit of exhibition.

Prayer

Pray for discretion to keep a low profile on those things the Lord is doing through you.

Bible Reading Plan:
Jeremiah 1 and 2 Ecclesiastes 4

DAY 336 AVOID USELESS BATTLES

"After this, Jesus went around in Galilee. He did not want to go about in Judea because the Jewish leaders there were looking for a way to kill him" (John 7:1 NIV).

"The prudent see danger and take refuge, but the simple keep going and pay the penalty" (Proverbs 22:3 NIV)

On this road to Destiny land, God has ordained for us to contend for all that He has ordained for us. The Christian life is a life of warfare from beginning to end, with varying intensities. Although God has called us to be soldiers of the cross, we must choose our battles wisely. It is not every danger we must confront and not every battle we must fight. It is said that, there was time the Lord Jesus avoided Judea because of a plot on His life. Remember, He had said no one could take His life from Him, except that He laid it down on His own accord. Why then did He avoid going to Judea? We believe he stayed in Galilee to avoid fighting unnecessary battles in Judea at the time. He was not afraid of the Jews, but avoided useless confrontation. May we not engage in unnecessary battles and confrontations. If the Lord could avoid Judea, who are we to act otherwise.

Prayer

Lord, grant me the wisdom to distinguish between faith and presumption so as to know when to face a danger and when to flee from it, in Jesus' Name.

Bible Reading Plan:
Jeremiah 3 and 4 Ecclesiastes 5

DAY 337 EXHAUSTING POSSIBILITIES AND EMPLOYING ALTERNATIVES

"But, brothers and sisters, when we were orphaned by being separated from you for a short time (in person, not in thought), out of our intense longing we made every effort to see you. For we wanted to come to you—certainly I, Paul, did, again and again—but Satan blocked our way" (1 Thessalonians 2:17-18 NIV).

Paul's desire to visit the church in Thessalonica had grown into an intense longing so much so that he tried over and over to visit them to no avail. He said, he had made every effort but was stopped by Satan. In what things have you made every effort to do for the Kingdom of God? Are you one who easily gives up and abandons after one or two trials?

To make every effort means to employ all of one's knowledge, skills, resources etc. to see something come to pass. Whatever it is you are trying to do, may you be able to say you have made every effort. Although Satan was able to stop Paul's visit to the Thessalonians, he was unable to stop his epistles from reaching them. There is always an alternative way to accomplish that which the enemy is hindering in your life. The letters of Paul to the Thessalonians, I believe, have had more impact across the generations than his physical visits could.

Prayer

Lord, help me to be open, flexible to explore alternatives in my service for You

Bible Reading Plan:
Jeremiah 5 and 6 Ecclesiastes 6

DAY 338 FROM BEHIND

"Now these were the kings who reigned in the land of Edom before any king reigned over the children of Israel" (Genesis 36:31).

God clearly states that he loved Jacob and hated Esau **(Romans 9:13).** We learn from the Scriptures that Esau is Edom **(Genesis 36:8).** Therefore, the Edomites are the descendants of Esau. We see in Scriptures that the Edomites made progress than the Israelites initially: The Edomites had seven kings before Israel had a king. While Israel was still wandering in the wilderness, the Edomites were already settled. Israel even asked for permission from the Edomites to pass through their land on their way to the promised land **(Judges 11:17).**

Today, the Edomites don't make a country of their own; they form part of a country called Jordan. The GDP of Jordan as a whole is 43.80 billion dollars. Israel is a nation today with a GDP of $410 billion dollars. Israel is about ten times richer than the whole of Jordan. About 50% of the billionaires in the US are of Jewish origin. The greatest number of Nobel Prize winners are Jews. Today, Israel has overtaken the Edomites and has far exceeded their progress. Don't envy the wicked when they seem to be 'ahead'. You are destined to be the head.

Prayer

Lord, I trust in You even when nothing seems to be happening in my life; my time will come

Bible Reading Plan:
Jeremiah 7 and 8 Ecclesiastes 7

DAY 339 FROM BEHIND II: JUDAH AND THE LINEAGE OF OVERTAKERS

Judah was not destined to have the inheritance for rulership. The inheritance was first that of Reuben, then it later went to Joseph. But Judah came from behind. The Bible says, **"Yet Judah prevailed over his brothers and from him came a ruler, although the birthright was Joseph's (1 Chronicles 5:2).**

The next in line, in the genealogy of Judah also came from behind. Judah had two sons; Perez and Zerah. When there were born, Zerah was in front apparently and the midwife had even tied his hand with a thread to say this one came first from the womb. But Perez overtook his brother from the womb and they had to name him Perez; meaning breakthrough. There is a prophetic word in that passage from the midwife, **"Then it happened as he drew back his hand that his brother came out unexpectedly; and she said, how did you breakthrough? This breach be upon you. Therefore, his name was called Perez" (Genesis 38:29)** which means to break forth or breakthrough, and the midwife was saying this breach or capacity to come from behind and overtake be upon you. You too have the grace and anointing to overtake. We see you coming from behind and overtaking. Amen

Prayer

Lord, I activate the over taker's anointing in my life; to catch up and overtake for I am the head and not the tail.

Bible Reading Plan:
Jeremiah 9 and 10, Ecclesiastes 8

DAY 340: FROM BEHIND III: DAVID AND THE LINEAGE OF OVERTAKERS

What of David who is the next major character in this lineage. He too came from behind. The king was supposed to come from the tribe of Judah but it went to Saul, who is a Benjamite (Joseph's lineage). The tribe of Judah prevailed again and the kingship returned to them. Remember David came from behind? When Samuel came to anoint a king David was not first considered, it was his brother, Eliab. David was the last born (the seventh in the house of Jesse) who became the first; far behind. Amen

Lastly the Lord Jesus; the Lion of the Tribe of Judah. Our Lord also came from behind. He came second; He is called the Second Adam but has now become the first; the Firstborn of all Creation. Hallelujah. The Anti-Christ will even arrive before Jesus Christ. He will come second but will overtake and destroy the man of lawlessness with the breath of his mouth. Dear saint, may be you feel you are behind today, but rest assured that your plugging into Jesus Christ who is the Lion of the Tribe of Judah, you are part of a lineage of overtakers and prevailers. From behind you are taking your rightful position. Amen

Prayer

Lord, I activate the anointing to prevail and overtake in the name of Jesus Christ.

Bible Reading Plan:
Jeremiah 11 and 12, Ecclesiastes 9

DAY 341 SURE COMPLETION

"Being confident of this very thing, that He who has begun a good work in you will complete it until the day of Jesus Christ" (Philippians 1:6).

You may have started a project and as at now, you cannot boast of all the resources to guarantee the completion of the project and you are wondering whether you will be able to complete your project. We want to assure you dear child of God, that He who has begun this work with you will surely take it to completion. The apostle Paul says He is confident of the fact. Why was he so confident? God is the Beginning and the End, the Alpha and the Omega. When He starts with you, you are dealing with Him as the beginning. Since the same God is the End, it means that your project will also see completion. God cannot be the Beginning and not be the End. Starting something is the best sign that you will see it through. The Bible says, **"The hands of Zerubabbel have laid the foundation of this temple: his hands shall finish it" (Zechariah 4:9).** Laying the foundation is starting and it is a prophecy that it will be finished. You have started, you will finish.

Prayer

Dear, Father thank You for assuring me of completion of that which You have started in my life.

Bible Reading Plan:
Jeremiah 13 and 14 Ecclesiastes 10

DAY 342 SURE COMPLETION II

God does not take His glory lightly. His glory is the very essence of His being. The opposite of glory is shame. The Bible says, **"How long O you sons of men will you turn my glory to shame?" (Psalm 4:2)**

God is never associated with shame. God takes the glory when a task or a project or a work is completed. The Lord Jesus said, **"I have glorified You on earth. I have finished the work which you have given Me to do" (John 17:4).** So the Lord brought glory to God by finishing the work that God gave Him. The Father will also take glory because all that which concerns you will be completed. Amen

Shame will not be your portion. God is the glory and lifter of your head **(Psalm 3:3).** Your head will not be bowed down in shame. The project before you will be completed. God is committed to make sure that you are never put to shame when you trust Him. The Bible says, **"Whoever believes on Him will not be put to shame" (Romans 10:13).**

Prayer

 Lord, I thank You for Your promise not to allow me be put to shame. I commit the projects before me into Your hands. I believe You to bring all to pass. Amen

Bible Reading Plan:
Jeremiah 15 and 16 Ecclesiastes 11

DAY 343 NO PRECIPITATION

"He that believeth shall not make haste"
(Isaiah 28:16 KJV)

There is no glaring mark of unbelief as haste or acting hastily. The haste is born from the fear that if we don't act fast things will go out of control and we may lose. Our haste is lack of inner certitude and rest.

True faith on the contrary is not agitated and driven by the internal rush that is characteristic of lack of faith. Internal calm is the hall mark of faith. When we believe God and have called upon His name about a given situation, we have to trust His own timing in resolving whatever we have asked of Him. We tend to think that if God does not come at a particular time, then it will be too late for us to get a solution to our problem. He is never late and at the appointed time He will answer you. Internal stillness is a key to experiencing God; **"Be still and know that I am God" (Psalm 46:10).** Don't lose what God has for you through internal disturbance and precipitation. The Bible says**, "Because he knows no quietness in his heart he will not save anything he desires" (Job 20:20).**

Prayer

Lord, I embrace Your calm. I renounce all the internal rush stemming from unbelief. I decide to trust You and Your timing. Amen

Bible Reading Plan:
Jeremiah 17 and 18, Ecclesiastes 12

DAY 344 HE IS ABLE TO DO

"Now to Him who is able to do exceedingly abundantly above all that we can ask or think, according to the power that works in us" (Ephesians 3:20).

God is able and His ability is immeasurable. There is nothing He cannot do. In three different verses in the Bible, God has had to ask or say to doubting man, **"Is there anything too hard for Me?" (Genesis 18:14, Jeremiah 32:17, 27).** How we respond to this question will determine the demands we place on God and on life. There is no request that can exceed God's ability and power. Maybe you are in deep need of provision. God is able dear saint. One area where God manifests His ability is in meeting our needs: making sure we have all we need for all sufficiency and for every good work. The Bible says, **"And God is able to make all grace abound toward you, always having all sufficiency in all things, have abundance for every good work" (2 Corinthians 9:8).**

What God can do is limitless. What limits Him is our faith in His ability and this in turn limits what we are willing to engage or attempt. There is no need He cannot meet. He is able

Prayer

Lord, let believe in Your ability be born in me, so that I will begin to see the immeasurable dimension in my life. Amen

Bible Reading Plan:
Jeremiah 19 and 20, Songs of Solomon 1

DAY 345 THE REALM OF CERTAINTY

 *"His testimonies are very sure"* (Psalm 93:5)

God operates is the realm of certainty. All that is of God exudes certainty and surety. The atmosphere of God is an atmosphere of certainty. The essence and being of God is rooted in certainty. There is no variableness or change with Him. When God speaks, he communicates certainty and from a standpoint of certainty. Most times when the Lord speaks, He started with, most assuredly or verily verily or I tell you the truth.

Doubts are of the enemy **(Genesis 3:1).** In fact, all what casts a shadow of doubt and uncertainty is of the devil **(Matthew 5:37)** and doubts hinder the expression of our faith. The realm of certainty is the realm of miracles and mountain moving experiences. The Lord always chided people saying, "**Why did you doubt?**". Doubts are a result of satanic interaction with the mind of man. Doubts in the life of a child of God in a sustainable way is an abnormal spiritual condition. Lord, I arise with a renewed capacity to operate in the realm of certainty for all about You is sure. No doubts anymore about the future and Your promises.

Prayer

 I commit myself to spend a lot of time in Your presence and Your word so that I will be rooted in certainty. Amen.

Bible Reading Plan:
Jeremiah 21 and 22, Songs of Solomon 2

DAY 346 SPEAK

 *"For with the heart one believes to righteousness and with the mouth confession is made unto salvation"* (Romans 10:10).

When we believe, we will speak. The two great elements involve in salvation are believing and speaking or confession. Those who close their mouths have as well decided to remain in bondage or close their destinies. Professor Zacharias T. Fomum said**, "I confess the, it is written of God. You read it, you meditate upon it and then you confess it".** I have a file: **The Great Confessions of my Life** where I write **Scriptures that I confess like:**

By His stripes I was healed

By that one offering, I have been sanctified

I have been sanctified and am sanctified

I had been perfected and I am made perfect

The Bible says **"Open wide your mouth and God will fill it" (Psalm 81:10).** He will do the very things he hears us say **(Numbers 14:28)**.

Prayer

 Lord, I commit myself to speak Your word. Amen

Bible Reading Plan:
Jeremiah 23 and 24, Songs of Solomon 3

DAY 347 REJOICE ALWAYS

"Rejoice in the Lord always: and again I say, Rejoice" (Philippians 4:4)

Church records hold that this Epistle of Paul was written while he was in prison. Paul knew the real joy of the Lord. From a prison cell, he was writing to those out of prison not only to be joyful but to be joyful always. This is God's standard. We have to be joyful always irrespective of the situation. It is abnormal to remain in mood devoid of joy as a Christian. A. W. Tozer said, **"Why Christians should be sad is beyond me. We should be the most joyful people on God's green earth".** Joy is a fruit of the Spirit and its manifestation is an overflow of the work of the Holy Spirit in the life of believer. Joy is cardinal component of life in the kingdom. The Bible says, **"For the kingdom of God is not food and drink but of righteousness, peace land joy in the Holy Spirit" (Romans 14:17).** Am I joyful always? The Lord's standard is to rejoice always. May we rejoice always.

Prayer

Lord, let Your Holy Spirit work joy in me; joy that is not determined by circumstances

Bible Reading Plan:
Jeremiah 25 and 26, Songs of Solomon 4

DAY 348 REJOICE ALWAYS II: DEALING WITH SPIRITUAL DRYNESS

Joy is very important in the spiritual life. It irrigates and showers our spiritual life and efforts. Where a lot is done without joy there will be no fruit. The Bible says, **"Therefore with joy you will draw water out of the wells of salvation" (Isaiah 12:3).** No water, dryness follows. Joy is the fetcher in God's wells of salvation. Joylessness is spiritual desertification. Things dry up. The Bible says, **"The Vine has dried up and the fig three has withered; the pomegranate tree, the palm tree also and the apple tree-All the trees in the field are withered; Surely joy has withered away from the sons of men" (Joel 1:12).**

The Bible says, **"God loves a cheerful giver" (2 Corinthians 9:7).** God was angry with the Israelites not because they did not serve Him but because they did not serve Him with gladness; **"Because you did not serve the LORD your God with joy and gladness of heart, for the abundance of everything, therefore you shall serve thine enemies which the LORD shall send against thee, in hunger and in thirst and in nakedness and in want of all things..." (Deuteronomy 28:47-48).** Are your serving Him with joy and gladness?

Prayer

Lord, open my eyes to see the place of joy in Your kingdom. Lord, I commit myself to rejoice always. Amen

Bible Reading Plan:
Jeremiah 27 and 28, Songs of Solomon 5

DAY 349   FIG TREE DOES NOT BLOSSOM

 *"Though the fig tree may not blossom, nor fruit be on the vines; though the labour of olive may fail, and the fields yield no food; though the flock be cut off from the fold, and there be no herd in the stalls-yet I will rejoice in the LORD, I will joy in the God of my salvation"* (Habakkuk 3:17-18).

Habakkuk shows us that it is possible to be joyful even in difficult days and gives us the basis of the joy:

God Himself. This kind of joy is rooted in a life that has come to love God for who God is and not what God gives or will give. This is enduring joy. John Wesley, in his deathbed said, **"The best of all is, God is with us".**

God's salvation. To think that above all things we have been saved from eternal damnation with promise to live with God forever, should be a source of eternal joy. A Church in worldliness and sin loses its joy of God's salvation. In David's famous confession for his adultery with Bathsheba, he prayed, **"Restore to me the joy of Your salvation" (Psalm 51:12).** Is my joy solely dependent on circumstances?

Prayer

 Lord, I pray for the maturity to manifest joy even in the worst of times.

Bible Reading Plan:
Jeremiah 29 and 30, Songs of Solomon 6, Ezekiel 1

DAY 350 BELIEVING: THE FOUNDATION FOR JOY

 *"Yet believing, you rejoice with joy inexpressible and full of glory"* (1 Peter 1:8)

God has communicated hope and good things to his children through his word. There is no one who will believe God's word and be sad. The promises of God are great and precious. The Bible says, **"By which have been given to us exceedingly great and precious promises…" (2 Peter 1:4).** The promises are not only great; they are exceedingly great. They are also precious.

God's promises are not only great and precious, they are sure and true. We can rely on them. The Bible says, **"For all the promises of God in Him are Yes and in Him Amen, to the glory of God through us" (2 Corinthians 1:20).** All the promises of God in Christ are Yes and Amen. In Christ, all that God has promised us shall be so; meaning it shall be Amen.

This should be the source of great joy to the believer. Why should I be sad when God has so much in store for me. Are you in unbelief dear saint? Is joy absent in your life?

Prayer

 Lord, I pray for believe that will produce joy unspeakable in my life. Amen

Bible Reading Plan:
Jeremiah 31 and 32, Songs of Solomon 7, Ezekiel 2

DAY 351 SEEING HIM AS HE IS

 *"I will praise the Lord with a song and I will magnify Him with thanksgiving"* (Psalm 69:30).

God wants us to see Him as He really is. It is dangerous to see Him less. Remember a Don Moen song that starts, **"I have made You too small in my eyes, oh Lord forgive me; I have believed in a lie; that You were unable to help me"**. It's possible to make God look small in our eyes and when that happens we will tend to think we are helpless in the face of our need. If there is one thing worship and praise bequeaths to the soul is the majesty of God; imprinting on the human spirit the magnitude of God for lack of a better expression. Thanksgiving and praise are deep thoughtful expressions of the majesty and grandeur of God. As we engage in this thoughtful and deliberate process of thanking, praising and worshiping of our God, it inspires in our minds and hearts the grandeur and majesty of our great God. This logically impacts our faith and attitude in the face of trial. The devil is no match for the man or woman with the right perception and conception of God. Magnify Him with thanksgiving dear saint. See Him as He really is. It is key to a victorious mindset.

Prayer

 May I learn worship and praise. I want to see You as You really are, Lord; in Your grandeur and majesty.

Bible Reading Plan:
Jeremiah 33 and 34, Songs of Solomon 8, Ezekiel 3

DAY 352 SPECTATOR OR SPECTACLE?

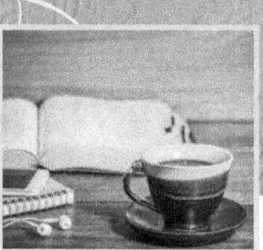

 *"And the ark of the LORD came into the City of David, Michal, Saul's daughter, looked through the window and saw King David leaping and whirling before the LORD; and she despised him in her heart"* (2 Samuel 6:16).

Michal looked through the window. She was not part of the worship and dance unto the Lord. There are many who are watchers today in the house of God. We must beware of Satan's massive campaign to turn the world into a bunch of spectators. The multiplication of games of sport and entertainment is all geared to raise watchers and spectators; a generation that is entertained. This has followed many into the church. We must insist on being spectacles and not spectators in life and ministry. We cannot be on the sidelines and make headlines.

Many forget that there are angels assigned to measure out our attitude in the house of God. The Bible says, **"Then I was given a reed like a measuring rod. And the angel stood saying, rise and measure the temple of God, the altar and those who worship there" (Revelation 11:1).**

God weighs our actions. May we be amongst those who worship Him in spirit and in truth.

Prayer

 Lord, I pray that I will not be a spectator in Your house. Lord, I will not look while others worship and praise You. Amen

Bible Reading Plan:
Jeremiah 35 and 36 lamentations 1, Ezekiel 4

DAY 353 THE KEY TO SPIRITUAL KNOWLEDGE

 *"If any of you really determines to do God's will, then you will certainly know whether my teaching is from God or is merely my own."* (John 7:17 The Living Bible)

The key to growth is revelation knowledge, when the spirit receives and conveys to the natural man, insight from the Holy Spirit. At such a time, a man knows that he knows a thing. Spiritual knowledge enhances growth and maturity in the Christian life. If the key to growth is spiritual knowledge, then what is the key to spiritual knowledge? Obedience is the key! Obedience to God's word is a matter of choice. The NIV renders John 7:17 as, "If a man chooses to do God's will…" If you have to obey God, you must choose to do so, you must make up your mind i.e. be determined to. This is the key to revelations or spiritual knowledge. God reveals the mysteries and gives the keys of the kingdom to those who are disposed to obey.

Prayer

 Lord, help me to radically obey You in all things

Bible Reading Plan:
Jeremiah 37 and 38, Lamentations 2, Ezekiel 5 and 6

DAY 354 — TRUSTWORTHINESS, A KEY TO PROMOTION

 *"Like a snow-cooled drink at harvest time is a trustworthy messenger to the one who sends him; he refreshes the spirit of his master"* (Proverbs 25:13 NIV).

"Well done, my good servant!' his master replied. Because you have been trustworthy in a very small matter, take charge of ten cities" (Luke 19:17 NIV).

An element of trustworthiness is diligence. You can trust a diligent person to put in his all in the execution of an assignment. A trustworthy messenger who is sent will also execute his assignment well and this brings joy to the heart of the one who sends him. In fact, he will refresh the spirit of those who send him. After you have sent such a messenger you relax and are sure that he is going to do exactly what he was asked to, when he was asked to do it and how he was asked to do it. There are people to whom you give a responsibility and you are sure that come what may they will carry it to the end. Others, you may have to check often to see if at all they are doing the job. Such ones are not trustworthy because they are not diligent. They are eye servants. Am I a trustworthy servant? Are your masters at rest when they send you? Am I jeopardizing my promotion because of untrustworthy service?

Prayer

 Father, help me to be a diligent and trustworthy servant; refreshing those who send me.

Bible Reading Plan:
Jeremiah 39 and 40, lamentations 3, Ezekiel 7 and 8

DAY 355 COINCIDENCE OR DESTINY

 *"Now the donkeys belonging to Saul's father Kish were lost, and Kish said to his son Saul, "Take one of the servants with you and go and look for the donkeys. Now the day before Saul came, the Lord had revealed this to Samuel: "About this time tomorrow I will send you a man from the land of Benjamin. Anoint him ruler over my people Israel; he will deliver them from the hand of the Philistines. I have looked on my people, for their cry has reached me." When Samuel caught sight of Saul, the Lord said to him, "This is the man I spoke to you about; he will govern my people""* (1 Samuel 9:3, 15-17 NIV).

To the Kish family the loss of the donkeys was just another family misfortune. To Saul, it was just another opportunity for his father to send him on another mundane assignment, another routine, looking for lost donkeys. From God's perspective it was an appointment with destiny. The straying of the donkey was divinely orchestrated. The disappointments and frustrations in trying to locate the donkeys were divinely planned. Everything was planned by God to lead Saul to his encounter with prophet Samuel. Unknown to Saul, in searching for his father's donkeys he was on his way to honor an appointment with destiny. As a child of God, you must understand that your steps, stops, and bends are ordained and directed by God. A surrendered life is one lived in holiness and love, with the assurance that God is coordinating everything in accordance with His plan for your life. Nothing happens to you but by divine providence when you are walking in love and living by faith

Prayer

 Lord, thank You because nothing in my life is a coincidence; all is well arranged and planned

Bible Reading Plan:
Jeremiah 41 and 42, Lamentations 4, Ezekiel 9 and 10

DAY 356 UNLIKELY DESTINY HELPERS

 "When they reached the district of Zuph, Saul said to the servant who was with him, "Come, let's go back, or my father will stop thinking about the donkeys and start worrying about us". But the servant replied, "Look, in this town there is a man of God; he is highly respected, and everything he says comes true. Let's go there now. Perhaps he will tell us what way to take". Saul said to his servant, "If we go, what can we give the man? The food in our sacks is gone. We have no gift to take to the man of God. What do we have?" The servant answered him again. "Look," he said, "I have a quarter of a shekel of silver. I will give it to the man of God so that he will tell us what way to take... "Good," Saul said to his servant. "Come, let's go." So they set out for the town where the man of God was" (1 Samuel 9:5-10 NIV).

Usually when people talk of destiny helpers, they are referring to the strong and mighty, those who matter in society, friends in high places, or gatekeepers to circles of influence. Saul came to a point of exhaustion in his search of the donkeys. He was out of steam, out of options, and out of resources and was about giving up on his assignment. Then came the counsel from his servant about the presence of prophet Samuel and the need to seek his counsel.

Sometimes people get stuck in life because they are waiting for help only from those they think matter in life. It was a servant boy who suggested that Saul visit the prophet. It was still the same servant boy who made his resources available to Saul. There are unlikely destiny helpers God has placed on your road to destiny. Do not despise them.

Prayer

 Lord, let me not despise anyone; for You can use any one to achieve your purpose

Bible Reading Plan
Jeremiah 43 and 44, Lamentations 5, Ezekiel 11 and 12

DAY 357: BEWARE OF FOCUSING ON THE EXTERNAL

 *"Saul approached Samuel in the gateway and asked, 'Would you please tell me where the seer's house is?'"* (1 Samuel 9:18 NIV).

Saul mistook Samuel for the gateman since he met him at the gateway. May God open your eyes to see beyond the surface, and may He restrain you when you are about to make consequential errors because of focus on the external.

Remember when God asked Samuel to go to the house of Jesse to anoint a new king. The Bible says, **"When they arrived, Samuel saw Eliab and thought, "Surely the Lord's anointed stands here before the Lord." But the Lord said to Samuel, "Do not consider his appearance or his height, for I have rejected him. The Lord does not look at the things people look at. People look at the outward appearance, but the Lord looks at the heart"** (1 Samuel 16:6-8 NIV).

Of the Lord Jesus, it was prophesied that **"He will not judge by what he sees with his eyes, or decide by what he hears with his ears" (Isaiah 11:3b NIV).** He reprimanded the Jews to **"Stop judging by mere appearances, but instead judge correctly" (John 7:24 NIV).**

Prayer

 Lord, help me not to make judgments because of what I see with my eyes and hear with my ears, but by Your Spirit.

Bible Reading Plan:
Jeremiah 45 and 46, Ezekiel 13 and 14

DAY 358 BEWARE OF EASY ACCESS

 *"Now Saul's son had two men who were leaders of raiding bands. One was named Baanah and the other Rekab; they were sons of Rimmon the Beerothite from the tribe of Benjamin…Now Rekab and Baanah, the sons of Rimmon the Beerothite, set out for the house of Ish-Bosheth, and they arrived there in the heat of the day while he was taking his noonday rest. They went into the inner part of the house as if to get some wheat, and they stabbed him in the stomach. Then Rekab and his brother Baanah slipped away. They had gone into the house while he was lying on the bed in his bedroom. After they stabbed and killed him, they cut off his head. Taking it with them, they traveled all night by way of the Arabah"* (2 Samuel 4:2, 5-7 NIV).

King Ish-Boseth was so dependent on Abner for everything, even his own protection and access to his immediate presence so much so that when Abner died there was a great void. It appears there was no bodyguard for the king and any "leader" had direct access any time to the king even at his very vulnerable moments. Think about your life for a moment. Who are those with direct access to you? What checks and balances have you put in place for your own safety? Can you so easily be slain by renegades like Ish-Boseth was? Again, I ask you, what are the security checks around you? Who grants others access to your presence?

Prayer

 Lord, help me to erect security checks around my life, such that not everyone has easy access to my life

Bible Reading Plan:
Jeremiah 47 and 48, Ezekiel 15 and 16

DAY 359 TWO THINGS TO NEVER REWARD

 *"And David answered Rechab and Baanah his brother, the sons of Rimmon the Beerothite, and said unto them, As the Lord liveth, who hath redeemed my soul out of all adversity, When one told me, saying, Behold, Saul is dead, thinking to have brought good tidings, I took hold of him, and slew him in Ziklag, who thought that I would have given him a reward for his tidings: How much more, when wicked men have slain a righteous person in his own house upon his bed? shall I not therefore now require his blood of your hand, and take you away from the earth? And David commanded his young men, and they slew them, and cut off their hands and their feet, and hanged them up over the pool in Hebron"* (2 Samuel 4:9-12a NIV).

There are two things, like David, one should never reward in life: first, never reward raising one's hand against ordained leadership. This means you refuse to include in your inner circle or anywhere near your entourage anyone who has raised his or her hand against another leader even when branded as loyalty to you. Anyone who hurts another person on your behalf will one day hurt you on another's behalf. Second, never reward anyone rejoicing at or seeking promotion at the fall of another leader even when branded as loyalty to you. Be the kind of person, like David, who defends and protects the reputation of other leaders, even after their death, from traitors. Are there people in your inner circle who have the blood of others reputation, honor, or position in their hands?

Prayer

 Lord, help me not to reward disloyalty and betrayal of the trust of others even when branded as loyalty to me.

Bible Reading Plan:
Jeremiah 49 and 50, Ezekiel 17 and 18

DAY 360 PAY ATTENTION EVEN TO THE COUNSEL OF THE POOR AND WEAK

"Naaman's servants went to him and said, "My father, if the prophet had told you to do some great thing, would you not have done it? How much more, then, when he tells you, 'Wash and be cleansed'!" So he went down and dipped himself in the Jordan seven times, as the man of God had told him, and his flesh was restored and became clean like that of a young boy" (2 Kings 5:13-14 NIV).

In one of our previous meditations, we talk of Saul's servant boy, whose counsel set Saul on his path to encountering prophet Samuel, an encounter that closed one chapter of the life of Saul and opened a new glorious chapter. Here too, we see Naaman set on a journey to Israel in search of a solution, at the counsel of a servant girl. Sometimes, the people who are poor, weak, and uneducated have access to information that the rich, erudite and powerful do not. In life you must be open and flexible to learn new things and receive counsel even from those you may consider the underprivileged in society. Those whom society considers uncivilized usually hold keys to useful knowledge that even university education cannot bring. Naaman came out of his predicament of leprosy because he took counsel from the weak and poor.

Prayer

Lord, grant to me an open heart, mind, and ear to the counsel of those around me irrespective of their status in life. May I never shut my ears to counsel because of one's status

Bible Reading Plan:
Jeremiah 51 and 52, Ezekiel 19

DAY 361 LIFE-CHANGING ENCOUNTERS

 *"And the angel of the Lord appeared unto him, and said unto him, The Lord is with thee, thou mighty man of valour"* (Judges 6:12 KJV).

There are encounters we all need in life. Such encounters close the door to one of life's chapters and opens the door to the new; they bring healing to the past and usher in the future. Such encounters are of two categories: encounter with divinity and encounters with humanity.

Gideon's encounter with the angel at the threshing floor closed the chapter of the coward boy oppressed by the Midianites and opened the chapter of the warrior and ruler of a liberated people. Mary's encounter with Angel Gabriel closed the chapter of humanity' bondage to sin and opened the chapter of Salvation in Christ Jesus for all of humanity.

As example an of encounter with humanity, Saul's encounter with Samuel closed the donkey-searching chapter of his life and opened the reigning king chapter. Had he missed this encounter with Samuel, he would have stayed longer running behind donkeys.

Prayer

 Heavenly Father, please position me for my encounter with divinity and with humanity that will change my life

Bible Reading Plan:
Ezekiel 20, 21 and 22

DAY 362 MINISTRY OF LIFE

"For the life of the flesh is in the blood"
(Leviticus 17:11)

The Lord Jesus came that we might have life and have it more abundantly. That life was in his blood. The Bible says, **"Then Jesus said to them, Most assuredly, I say to you, unless you eat the flesh of the Son of Man and drink His blood, you have no life" (John 6:53).**

The blood was shed by the agony and painful death on the cross. That blood imparts life to us today. Ministry is life. Ministry flows from what we have gone through. God's minsters are forged from bleeding circumstances. Tim Dilena, the Pastor of Times Square Church, founded by David Wilkerson in New York says, **"God has to bruise You before He can use you"**. May be you are deeply wounded inside; and you are bleeding due to a betrayal or any other painful incident. Dear saint your pain is not in vain. You are in God's school for ministry based on life: not stories. God has others in mind who will be helped by your pain. The comfort and the ministry that you are receiving now as a result of what you are going through is what God will use to minister to others **(2 Corinthians 1:3-4).**

Prayer

Lord, let me not waste this bruising and bleeding moments. Amen.

Bible Reading Plan:
Ezekiel 23, 24 and 25

DAY 363 — WHAT DO YOU WANT

"What do you want me to do for you?"
(Mark 10:51)

One of the keys to successful praying is specificity. Prayer should be based on something very specific. There is no gain in being vain and vague in prayer. The Bible says, **"Therefore I say to you whatever things you ask…" (Mark 11:24).** Prayer has to be based on a thing; it must be tangible and well defined. The story of blind Bartimaeus in Jericho is a clear example of the effectiveness of specificity in prayer. When Jesus and His disciples came to Jericho, blind Bartimaeus sat by the road side begging. And when he heard that Jesus was passing, he cried twice: "Son of David have mercy upon me". When by his insistence Jesus ordered that blind Bartimaeus be called, the Lord said, **"What do you want me to do for you?".** The Lord wanted blind Bartimaeus to be specific like He wants us His children to be specific in prayer also. This time Bartimaeus gets the message and does not cry anymore saying, "Son of David, have mercy on me" but rather specifies his need saying, **"Rabboni, that I may receive my sight" (Mark 10:51).** The specificity of Bartimaeus unlocks his miracle of healing from blindness. Jesus said to him, **"Go your way; your faith has made you well" (Mark 10:52).**

Prayer

Lord, I pray that I will be clear and specific in my prayers; stating clearly what I want. Amen

Bible Reading Plan:
Ezekiel 26, 27 and 28

DAY 364 IF YOU SAY TO THIS MOUNTAIN

 *"Assuredly I say to you, if you have faith and do not doubt, you will not only do what was done to the fig tree, but also if you say to this mountain, 'Be removed and be cast into the sea, it will be done"* (Matthew 21:21).

The mountains in our life can be moved. There are two ifs in the passage above; meaning there are conditions that must be in place for us to be able to move our mountains;

We must have faith and not doubt. Faith and doubt cannot co-exist. Where there is doubt then there is no faith and without faith it is impossible to please the Lord **(Hebrews 11:6).** We have to speak to the mountain. Faith speaks. Our God also speaks and addresses situations. In the context in which this Bible text is based, the Lord had just said to the fig tree, "Let no fruit grow on you ever again" and the fig tree withered immediately. We too have to speak what we want to see and remove what we don't want to see with our saying. Finally, we have to give specific instructions to our mountain. Our saying to our mountain has to carry specific orders. This is the way to moving mountains.

Prayer

 Lord, forgive for closing mouth when there are many mountains before me. Today, I rise up in faith and begin using my mouth to speak and address situations. Amen

Bible Reading Plan:
Ezekiel 29 and 30

DAY 365 — THE RECIPE FOR GREAT THINGS: THE PLACE OF THINKING

 *"O Lord, how great are your works. Your thoughts are very deep"* (Psalm 92:5)

"You plan and do great things" (Jeremiah 32:19 NCV)

Intimate ties subsist between thought and all production
-Emerson

The recipe for great things as shown in our passages above is to plan or think and then do great things. Our God thinks and his thoughts are deep. His great and wonderful works as we see in nature flow from His depth of thinking. Many believers are very afraid to be involved in deep thinking as this is considered to be practices from Easter Religions. This is another lie of the enemy. Oswald Chambers says, **"We owe it to God that we refuse to have rusty brains…. we can never become God's people by thinking but we must think as God's people"**. A.W. Tozer said, **"We need sanctified thinkers"**. God thinks and His great acts came from His thinking. We too have to be thinkers.

Prayer

 Lord, I choose to love You with my mind; to become a thinker, for You are a thinking God and I decide today that I will begin to think through things. Amen

Bible Reading Plan:
Ezekiel 31, 32 and 33

DAY 366 THE RECIPE FOR GREAT THINGS: THE PLACE OF THINKING II

In the illustration of a man who wants to build a tower, the Lord says, **"For which one of you when he wants to build a tower does not first sit down and calculate the cost, to see if he has enough to complete it..." (Luke 14:28 NASB).** The Lord compares following Him to a man wanting to build a tower; sitting down first to consider the cost. This is thinking things through. A successful spiritual life will require deep thinking just as a great work of building a tower.

The Lord expects people to think and asked what they thought about Him. The Bible says, **"Saying, what do you think about the Christ?" (Matthew 22:42).** This is very crucial. Any wrong thinking about the Christ jeopardizes eternity.

In the last days, thinking and use of mind is called for; **"Here is wisdom. Let the person who has insight calculate the number of the beast, for is the number of a man. His number is 666" (Revelation 13:18).** To calculate involves thinking. May we recapture thinking in our lives and in the church.

Prayer

Lord, I pray that the church of God will recover and restore thinking as part of the spiritual life

Bible Reading Plan:
Ezekiel 34, 35 and 36

DAY 367 WATCHING OVER THOSE UNDER YOU

 *"The LORD God took the man and placed him in the garden to work it and watch over it"* (Genesis 2:15, Christian Standard Bible).

Adam was commanded not only to work the garden but also to watch over it. Work without warfare is a waste. Nehemiah understood this principle. With one hand they built and with another they held a weapon. The Bible says, **"Those who built the wall and those who carried burdens, loaded themselves so that with one hand they worked at construction and with the other held a weapon" (Nehemiah 4:17).** Most men or family heads have abandoned their homes spiritually and the devil has access to their children, wife and all that concerns them. Job had a hedge around his family. Satan had tried to penetrate his family and household but he noticed that Job had a hedge of protection over his life and household. Job had not abdicated his spiritual role. In fact, we learn that he used to offer sacrifices on behalf of his children in case they had sinned against God **(Job 1:5).** The Bible even says, thus did Job continually. He was spiritually consistent in watching over his household and because he did, God also blessed him materially and protected his household. He could only be attacked after God allowed the devil to do so. We have to watch over those under us. Am I watching?

Prayer

 Lord, I pray that I will watch over those You have placed under me. As I work, I will also war.

Bible Reading Plan:
Ezekiel 37, 38 and 39

DAY 368 DEVELOP SPIRITUAL ROOTS

 *"But he who received the seed on stony places, this is he who hears the word and immediately receives it with joy; yet he has no root in himself, but endures only for a while. For when tribulation or persecution arises because of the word, immediately he stumbles"* (Matthew 13:20-21)

Without deep spiritual roots, falling away or stumbling is the result when persecution or tribulation arises.

God's will is that, we receive Jesus, walk with Him, built up and rooted in our faith in Christ **(Colossians 2:6-7).** Thus, it doesn't end at believing. I have to develop spiritual roots and be established in faith. If we do not want to be blown away by the winds of persecution and all the false teachings today, we have to invest in the word, building our foundation on the rock. The Bible says, **"And the prophets have become wind, for the word is not in them" (Jeremiah 5:13).** The word in us gives us weight. Am I a spiritual light weight or heavy weight? Is the word abounding in me?

Prayer

 May I be rooted in the word and be able to stand all that can come against me and my faith in Jesus Name. Amen

Bible Reading Plan:
Ezekiel 40, 41 and 42

DAY 369 DILIGENCE

 *"Seest thou a man diligent in his business? He shall stand before kings; he shall not stand before mean men (Proverbs 22:29 KJV).*

Obscurity is a choice. Prominence is not a gift. It takes work and work to stand before men of renown. Hesiod, the Greek philosopher, said, **"Before the gates of excellence the high gods have placed sweat; long is the road thereto and rough and steep at first; but when the heights are reached, then there is ease, though grievously hard in winning"**. Of Napoleon, the French emperor in his student days, it is said, **"He was already learning to get by with minimum sleep; he rose at 4.0 am, took just one meal a day to save money and went to bed at 10 pm, after eighteen hours of study"**. From a minority region of the Island of Corsica (which even wanted to secede from France) he rose to be emperor of France.

Prayer

 Lord, I pray that I will be diligent in my work

Bible Reading Plan:
Ezekiel 43, 44, and 45

DAY 370 DILIGENCE II

In the spiritual life, diligence is the rule that delivers divine rewards. The Bible says, **"But without faith it is impossible to please Him, for he who comes to God must believe that He is and that He is a rewarder of them that diligently seek Him" (Hebrews 11:6).** Of A. W. Tozer, it is said, **"He educated himself by years of diligent study and a constant prayerful seeking of the mind of God…. when he felt he needed an understanding of the great English works of Shakespeare, he read them through on his knees, asking God to help him understand their meaning. This procedure was typical of his method of self-education. With no teacher but the Holy Spirit and good books, A. W. Tozer became a theologian, a scholar and a master craftsman in the use of English language".**

Prayer

Lord, I embrace diligence. Every lazy habit of the past I lay it aside. I wake up to work in Jesus Name. amen

Bible Reading Plan:
Ezekiel 46, 47 and 48

THE DAILY DYNAMIC ENCOUNTER

The need to remain on fire for God is all the more critical as we head into the last days. The icy hands of Satan, sin and the pleasures of this life will freeze the love of many. The Lord will come for a church and believers whose lamps are burning and are on fire for God. The Bible says "Let your waists be girded and your lamps burning and you yourselves be like men who wait for their master, when he returns from the wedding, that when he comes and knocks they may open to him immediately" (Luke 12:35). To be like men or women who wait for the return of their master; we have to gird our waists and our lamps have to be burning.

Our call to be priests is a call to keep a constant spiritual temperature: keep the fire burning. The Bible says, "And the fire on the altar shall be kept burning on it; it shall not be put out and the priest shall burn wood on it every morning...." (Leviticus 6:12). The minimum requirement of the Lord for us as priests is that the altar of our hearts should burn perpetually with fire. This requires personal spiritual responsibility, discipline and routine; the priest had to put wood every morning.